Terrorism and Political Violence
Motives and Motivations

Terrorism and Political Violence
Motives and Motivations

Rakesh Bhambri

MD Publications Pvt Ltd
New Delhi
www.mdppl.com

Published by :

MD Publications Pvt Ltd
"MD House", 11, Darya Ganj,
New Delhi - 110 002
Phone : +91-11-41563325 (Customer Service)
+91-11-41562846 (Editorial)
E-mail (orders): order@mdppl.com
Website: www.mdppl.com

ISBN: 978-81-7533-193-8

Published and Printed by Mr. Pranav Gupta on behalf of **MD Publications Pvt Ltd** at Times Press, New Delhi.

PREFACE

Political violence is one of the most disturbing problems the world is facing now. The twentieth century has in particular witnessed more violence than hitherto known to mankind. It is found in almost all parts of the world, be it industrialized-capitalist societies, or the developing countries of Asia and Africa.

Violence is a common means used by people and governments around the world to achieve political goals. Many groups and individuals believe that their political systems will never respond to their political demands. As a result they believe that violence is not only justified but also necessary in order to achieve their political objectives. By the same token, many governments around the world believe they need to use violence in order to intimidate their populace into acquiescence. At other times, governments use force in order to defend their country from outside invasion or other threats of force. When social tension and group interests find violent expression directed against the state power, they acquire a political colour then such violence is called a political violence.

Some form of political violence is prevalent world over. However, the nature and cause of violence may differ from place to place and culture to culture. It depends among others on the nature of political institutions and the level of economic development and major theories for its occurrence are: frustration-aggression complex, relative deprivation theory, modernisation process and conflict as an inherent process of social change.

It aims to give academic rigour to a field which hitherto has lacked it, and encourages comparative studies. In addition to focusing on the political meaning of terrorist activity, it also reflects on various related forms of violence by rebels and by states, on the links between political violence and organized crime, protest, rebellion, revolution, and human rights. Political Violence perils are highly unpredictable and can have a catastrophic impact upon a corporation's people, assets and ability to continue trading. Traditional property and liability insurers have proven reluctant to adequately cover the full consequences of political violence.

I am very grateful to Mr. Pranav Gupta, Director of MD Publications Pvt Ltd, New Delhi, for his cooperation and support for this book.

Rakesh Bhambri

Contents

1

Introduction

Following the tragedy of 9/11, history's most deadly terrorist attacks, the U.S. declared War on Terror. As a result, terrorism has become a source of pervasive fear and loathing across America. On September 12th the nation awakened to a reality already known throughout much of the world and the first question Americans asked was, "Why do they hate us?" But few waited to hear the answers. Perhaps some thought it was a rhetorical question, while others waited for the government and media to provide answers. The first rule of war is to know your enemy. Terrorists are not a simple enemy to know. They have a myriad of complex motivations as individuals and as groups. In fact, few people can even agree on a definition of terrorism. Many people agree that terrorism is a despicable crime, but others argue that one person's terrorist is another's freedom fighter.

This series of Issue Briefings attempts to present some alternative viewpoints, not to justify or condone terrorism (mandatory disclaimer), but to shed some light on what motivates people to kill and die for a political purpose and to suggest some different perspectives and ways to approach the problem of political violence. In 2001, the U.S. State Department had officially designated 22 foreign terrorist organizations. By 2003 the list had grown to 36 organizations with dozens more groups listed as unofficial terrorist organizations. Either terrorism is a tremendous growth industry, or the definition of terrorism has become increasingly liberal in its designations. Terrorism is not a mysterious phenomena; it's simply a form of political violence. It's a tactic, not a movement. Terrorism represents the final escalation in the process of political violence. Arguably, terrorism or less deadly forms of political violence would not exist if other non-violent methods of reform and conflict resolution were available to the dissidents.

Virtually every book on terrorism begins with a discussion of the problem in agreeing on a definition and no single definition has universal acceptance. For the purposes of this report, however, we have chosen the definition of terrorism used by the U.S. State Department, contained in Title 22 of the United States Code, Section 2656f (d). That statute contains the following definitions:

"The term 'terrorism' means premeditated, politically motivated violence perpetrated against noncombatant targets by sub national groups or clandestine agents, usually intended to influence an audience.

The term 'international terrorism' means terrorism involving citizens or the territory of more than one country. The term "terrorist group" means any group practicing, or that has significant subgroups that practice, international terrorism."

Non-combatant is interpreted to include civilians and military personnel who at the time of the incident are unarmed and/or not on duty (a point of dispute). Attacks on military installations or on armed military personnel, when a state of military hostilities such as bombings against US bases in the Persian Gulf, Europe, or elsewhere, are also considered terrorism. The U.S. also recognizes that, "terrorist acts are part of a larger phenomenon of politically inspired violence, and at times the line between the two can become difficult to draw." This definition, like most others, raises more questions than it answers. Is airline hijacking, or kidnapping violence? Is a government building a non-combatant? If innocent civilians are casualties of violence directed against a legitimate target (collateral damage) is the act terrorism, or a tragic mistake? If violence against non-combatants is perpetrated by a state, is that not terrorism? If not what it? And, why does it matter?

Applying the "terrorist" label to an organization immediately demonizes that group, invalidates their objectives and disqualifies its followers from any voice in the political process. Ironically, such consequences reinforce the situation that motivated the group to resort to violence in the first place. Many states assert that they will make no deals with, or concessions to terrorists. It is standard practice to also deny dissidents access to the public media and airwaves to explain or advance their causes. Governments that refuse to talk to, or negotiate with terrorists foreclose opportunities for early resolution. Meanwhile some countries have been considerably more willing to negotiate, often paying ransoms, arranging prisoner releases, or agreeing to other demands.

The current interest in terrorism focuses on the violence perpetrated by Islamic Fundamentalists (Islamists) Terrorism has been used as a tactic for centuries but has become more pervasive since the 1960s. After World War I and II, colonial powers redrew the maps in many parts of the world and gradually reduced their colonies. This led to a rise in nationalist movements seeking self-determination, or seeking to replace rulers that had been imposed by the colonists. Many of the resulting conflicts have involved revolutionary warfare strategy and guerrilla tactics. However, traditional guerrilla warfare is often inappropriate in urbanized countries. For instance, rebels cannot gain and hold control over land when opposed by superior forces and cannot employ overt hit-and-run attacks effectively, without large losses. What emerged was a new doctrine of urban guerrilla warfare, which has evolved to include terrorist tactics.

Until recently, terrorism has been most closely associated by ethnic and minority group struggles for independence and self-determination. The primary area of conflict could usually be defined, as could the adversaries and their various aspirations. During the 1990s a new form of international terrorism emerged that appears less rational, less focused, more international and more deadly – Islamist Terrorism.

In fact, many of the causes and motivations remain strikingly similar to what could be called traditional modern terrorism. What is different is the religious ideological foundation, the broad definition of adversaries, the evolution in terrorist tactics and the desire and potential for devastating levels of destruction. Islamist extremists appear willing to ignore taboos against killing innocents and able to rationalize their actions by distorting Islamic teachings. The potential to use chemical, biological, nuclear and radiological weapons of mass destruction has created a new level of terror that demands effective solutions.

Unfortunately, states have had relatively poor results deterring, containing or eliminating political violence. Those that have been successful have used extreme, repressive measures that have threatened the rule of law, personal freedoms and human rights. There must be a better answer. Terrorism doesn't just happen. Terrorism is an advanced stage of a failed political process that begins with inequities and injustice, and moves from frustrated attempts at reform that breed fear and anger, to political confrontation that erupts in violence, which can be exploited to rationalize the use of any form of violence against any target. It seems that solutions to terrorism could be found at any stage of the evolving, or deteriorating political process. This suggests that we must start by understanding the historical context for today's conflicts.

Since the end of the Cold War, world conflicts have changed. Today's conflicts tend to be internal or intra-state conflicts, rather the conflicts between states. Many states were created by the former colonial powers after World War I and again after World War II. Westerners, the former colonial powers, drew the boundaries of these new states with little regard for ethnic and religious demographics that had existed for centuries.

The Kurds, for example, were promised a state of Kurdistan after WWI, but when the lines were drawn, the Kurdish people had no state and were divided among Turkey, Iraq and Iran. Iraq was overlaid on a region inhabited by Kurds and Arabs, with the Arabs further divided between Sunni and Shia' Muslims, even though the Shia' more closely identified with people of Iran. Palestine was partitioned to create a Jewish state - Israel. Ireland was partitioned with the South becoming Ireland, while the North was retained as part of the United Kingdom. Elsewhere, national groups were absorbed into a larger, multi-dimensional state. The Basques of the northern Iberian Peninsula were absorbed into Spain. A wide array of ethnic groups merged to become Turkey, Yugoslavia and the USSR. The Tamil people were absorbed into Sri Lanka and so forth.

Few people are willing to abandon their ethnicity, culture, language, religion or traditions to pledge allegiance to a new, artificial and unproven state. Yet to survive states had to compel people to accept their authority. Their challenge was to create a nationalist identity where there was none. Rulers often resorted to oppressive tactics: imposing a state religion or language, banning certain cultural traditions and imposing limitations on public gatherings, organizations, expression, or participation in the political process.

After World War II, America becomes the world's powerful economic powerhouse. Europe was rebuilt and re-established its economic strength as the world economy developed. Meanwhile many of the new states floundered, while some with natural resources, like oil, prospered - but those that prospered rarely shared the wealth. Only the ruling classes enjoyed the economic benefits. In some cases the ruling class was the majority, in others the rulers were a privileged minority group that had been favored by the former colonial administrators and retained their grip on power. As members of disadvantaged classes became better educated and aware of the relative deprivation suffered by their people, demands for reform were heard, but rarely heeded, driving people to organize in resistance to their unjust state. The stage was set for violent confrontation. Dissidents quickly learned the lessons from China, Brazil and Cuba and acted to provoke the state regimes to repressive over-reaction that would serve to drive people to rebellion and rebels would emerge as freedom fighters.

Every cause needs a theme and for people who are economically disadvantaged the clarion call is invariably redistribution of wealth – power to the people. Throughout Latin America, for instance, peasants demanded land reform so they could own their land instead of working as servants to the rich landowners. The landowners had close ties to ruling regime and the customers for their products. In many cases the landowner was the United Fruit Company, an American corporation. It could, as easily be an oil company or mining firm.

When revolt broke out, America would predictably side with the regime to protect and preserve its "national interest." The rebels would be demonized as communists, or Marxists bent on spreading their anti-American ideology. America would be condemned as "Imperialist." The Castro revolution in Cuba was anathema to America because it set a precedent that might inspire others.

The Cold War ideological struggle between communism and democracy continually resulted in

America taking sides with repressive, elitist regimes that exploited the poor and working classes. This historical pattern continues today to influence dissidents and insurgents to dismiss the U.S. as an imperialist power bent on maintaining the status quo. It also leads to criticism that America promotes democracy, justice and human rights in words only, and only for Americans.

If Cuba was the inspiration for the era of Latin American revolutions, the 1979 Islamic Revolution in Iran has been the catalyst for the current era of Mid-East turmoil. America again demonstrated that it would take sides with the Kings, Sheiks, and Shahs that controlled the precious resources at the expense of the common people. The Palestinians became the symbol for America's self-serving foreign policy.

In its efforts to protect Israel, the US subverted the fledgling pan-Arab movement. With US support, Israel developed into a major military and nuclear powerhouse. Presumably to balance Israel's military strength, America supplied military aid and training to nearby Arab states. Eventually it became evident that there was no Arab-Israeli parity – the only plausible use for Arab military hardware would be between Arab states, or against a state's own citizens. There are no democratic states in the Middle East. The oil-rich regimes have done little to benefit their citizens, creating anger and discontent. Countries like Jordan and Syria that have no oil are even more prone to upheaval, and in all cases it is the US that is seen as the key obstacle to change.

It's not surprising to see the emergence of al-Qaeda, an organization that points the fingers of blame at America, at repressive regimes and at a nuclear-armed Israel. It's also not surprising to see the Saudis supporting madarasas (Islamic religious schools) that teach a curriculum of fear and hate – it's no more illogical than America arming its future adversaries. What is curious is that the U.S. and other western democracies appear capable of repeating its previous foreign policy errors, denouncing reformers, while supporting oppressors.

Terrorism Today

Some of the reactions to terrorism play into the hands of the perpetrators and help further their goals and objectives. For example: A fundamental goal of any opposition movement is publicity, denying access to media, or censoring news can force extremists to blast their way into the news. Before reacting to political violence, it's important to identify the dissident's goals and objectives. The following list identifies a number of possible objectives, not all of which may apply to any specific group.

Terrorist objectives may include:

1. Attract public attention to the group's grievances
2. Encourage empathy for their unfair/unjust situation and sympathy for the cause
3. Demonstrate the inability of the state to provide security
4. Demonstrate the illegitimacy of the state's institutions
5. Polarize the public to simplify the debates and arguments
6. Coerce the public into pressuring the state into compromise solutions
7. Force the state into repressive reactions that discredit the government
8. Force the state into repressive reactions that serve to recruit new members and supporters
9. Demonstrate the economic consequences of continued violence
10. Highlight the potential political consequences of continued conflict
11. Attract international attention and encourage intervention

12. Provoke widespread civil uprising to change the government, or form a separate state

Publicity has traditionally been a major dissident objective, as Brian Jenkins of the Rand Corp. has commented that, "terrorist don't want a lot of people dead; they want a lot of people watching." Jenkins has also described terrorism as a form of political theater. This may be true of national liberation movements, but today's Islamist extremists now want a lot of people dead.

Terrorism has been described, correctly, as a tactic of the weak. It's adopted by groups of dissenters who lack the resources to attack the state and its forces. Clearly a rebel force that had the capacity to attack and defeat the government's forces would do so to achieve their goals as quickly as possible. Such opportunities rarely, if ever, exist in strong states. The alternative is to wage a war of attrition, gradually wearing down the state's and public's resolve. Terrorists seek to instill a climate of fear that erodes the public psyche, and to impose escalating economic costs, draining the state's financial resources and the collective will.

Many of these objectives could be pursued without resorting to terrorism against innocent civilians. However, States recognize that their forces and facilities are the primary targets of political violence and they adopt security and force protection measures that deny insurgents the ability to strike at these priority targets. By hardening priority targets, states all but force insurgents to attack softer targets in the civil sector. When the insurgents comply, the inevitable consequence is civilian casualties, whether intentional, or accidental. Insurgents have now become terrorists for perpetrating violence against non-combatant targets. In fact, the "targets" may not have been non-combatants, but such distinctions are rarely considered.

Once dissidents have crossed the threshold to terrorism

the rules change the costs and risks escalate and the challenge to maintain and build public support increases. For dissidents terrorism is the tactic of last resort, when all else has failed. One can argue that for weak regimes, lacking broad public support and legitimacy state terrorism is also a tactic of the weak, but the tactic of first resort.

The international community has often demonstrated a willingness to tolerate political violence against civilians perpetrated by states – state terrorism. Repressive states have been responsible for far greater terrorism than any so-called terrorist organization, yet they are allowed to continue their participation in the world's political and economic community. Only in the most enduring and grievous cases does the international community sanction, or exclude a repressive state. In addition, countries and arms merchants sell arms, provide military training and economic support to repressive, even terrorist regimes, seemingly oblivious to the fact that state repression breeds international terrorism and that terrorists will target those who lend support to their adversaries. It's little wonder that terrorism has emerged as a major threat to world security and peace.

One aspect of political violence and terrorism that's rarely discussed in depth is the economic impacts, both negative and positive. The direct costs incurred to defend against and counter terrorism is enormous, worse still are the incalculable social and human costs. But terrorism has its upside too, creating an economic boom for defense-related industries and private contractors. Repairing and rebuilding cities like Beirut, or London's financial district and Lower Manhattan are a windfall for those who profit from the efforts. Constructing forts and security installations, or erecting Berlin-style peace walls and security fences through Belfast, or around Israel's Occupied Territories, shift limited state funds from more socially useful services, but create business opportunity and profits. The unspoken issue is that these expenditures create a new constituency that benefits from continued violence. The beneficiaries can become influential, if conflicted, advocates of hard line policies that suit their business objectives.

Motivations for Political Violence

Karl von Clausewitz described "war as politics by other means." One might describe terrorism in the same way, or as "war by other means." There are two types of terrorism: rational and irrational. Rational terrorism has a political goal and a purpose. Irrational terror might be described as mindless violence that serves some dark psychological imbalance and is as difficult to understand as the motives of serial killers. As such this is the realm of psychologists and psychiatrists, not political scientists, politicians, statesmen, and security specialists. This briefing deals only with "rational terrorism."

Rational terrorism is an outgrowth of public dissatisfaction and political dissent and a form of revolt against the established order, or regime. Few, if any, dissident movements willingly adopt terror as a conscious tactic, namely because such tactics provoke public revulsion and condemnation. Dissident movements will usually begin as reform movements that fail to achieve their demands and proceed through stages of escalating fear, frustration, anger and hardening attitudes:

- Identifying inequities
- Frustrated Attempts at Reform
- Organized Dissent
- Civil Disobedience
- Reactionary Counter Attack
- Political Violence
- Terrorism

Violent political conflict can be categorized in terms of the motivation and aspirations of the combatants.

Political – In some cases the dissidents have what may best described as political motivations. It's said that war is diplomacy by other means; violent political conflict could be described as politics by other means. The motivation may be to affect a political reform, or overthrow a regime perceived as illegitimate or lacking public trust and support. Terrorism may be used as to demonstrate the weakness and vulnerability of the regime, to reveal its inability to provide security, to provoke government repression to help recruit followers, and ultimately to force leaders from power. This motivation has been most common in Latin America, and would be typical where there is an oppressed majority population that is denied political influence.

Cultural – This motivation is most common in situations where an ethnic or religious group fears extermination, or loss of their common identity, language or culture. It may also be combined with political motives, where the rulers discriminate against the ethnic group in terms of jobs, economic opportunity or access to the political process. In the case of oppressed minorities, opposed by a strong, entrenched regime, terrorism may be seen as the only available option. This is especially true where demands for political reform are ignored, where there are few, if any, external allies, and where the regime resorts to collective punishment for what are seen as reasonable and justified demands.

Psychological – A surprising number of pro-government analysts favor this explanation, which asserts that some terrorists are unbalanced, violent individuals suffering some form of psychosis. Others may be egomaniacs driven to achieve recognition through violence, and who attract a following of other dysfunctional individuals. This characterization may be accurate in cases where terrorist appear to have no logical goal, or motivation, or a purpose that makes little sense to normal people. This can include cases where the goal is the psychological benefit achieved by vengeance (Timothy McVeigh and the

Oklahoma City bombing). Psychologically motivated terrorism is simply a criminal act, like serial killing, and doesn't qualify for analysis as political violence.

Cultural motivations can be further classified into three broad, but non-exclusive categories.

Separatism – (let's separate) in situation where the ruling group is seen to be unfair and unjust in its government administration, dissident groups fight to form a separate state. Example would include the aspirations of Tamils in Sri Lanka, or Basques in Spain to establish a separate state for their people.

Irredentism – (let's get back together) the objective is to re-unite an ethno-political group that has been divided and separated by an arbitrary state border. An example is the conflict in Northern Ireland where Irish Republicans (typically Catholics) aspire to unify the 6 northern counties with the Republic of Ireland.

Nationalism – (let's organize ourselves) the aspiration of a national group (people related by ethnicity, religion, language or culture) to create a formal state for their nation. An example is the aspiration to establish Kurdistan as a homeland for the Kurdish people. This entails elements of both separatism and irredentism of Kurds living in Turkey, Iraq and Iran.

In today's world there are any number of intractable conflicts, some active, others dormant but unresolved. Some of the most enduring are the divisions in Ireland, Korea and Cyprus, each one dividing people by artificial borders. Many are described in Flashpoints Country Briefings. Most of these can be classified as traditional forms of political violence, including terrorism.

Many analysts and scholars draw distinctions between traditional terrorism and the new international terrorism, represented by al-Qaeda and the militant Islamist movement. But is this really new, or just a different manifestation of political unrest, with a violent twist and more deadly potential? Up until 2001, the number of terrorist incidents had been declining, but the attacks were becoming more deadly, culminating with 9/11. Since invading Afghanistan and Iraq that trend has clearly been reversed. Day in and day out, the news reports attacks against occupying coalition forces (as insurgency) and escalating attacks against civilian targets to deter collaborators.

Some Conventional Wisdom

Much of the conventional wisdom is highly politicized and may be better characterized as propaganda. One current theme is that terrorism is not the result of poverty and economic deprivation. Research shows that terrorists are never poor and uneducated. "While some on the left urge policymakers to address the root causes of terrorism, Laqueur says that such an approach won't yield the desired results, since the commonly identified wellsprings of terrorism — poverty and political oppression — fail to account for the terrorism that most threatens the United States. According to Laqueur:

Almost no terrorism occurs in the world's poorest 49 countries, and of course the Sept. 11 terrorists all came from middle- and upper-middle-class families.

Similarly, the 20th century's most repressive regimes (Stalin's Soviet Union and Hitler's Germany) were free of terrorism, while in South America in the 1970s terrorism first broke out not in the harshest dictatorships, but in Uruguay, the most democratic state.

Contrary to the conventional wisdom, then, terrorism flourishes in countries "democratic in character, or alternatively, in a wholly inefficient dictatorship," Lacquer writes." Source: The Roots of Terrorism, Daily Policy Digest, 17 June 2003

Lacqueur's tortured logic implies that harsh repressive measures, such as those used by Russia and Germany will eliminate terrorism. Between them Stalin and Hitler are responsible for killing as many as 30 million people. The obvious counter argument is that with state terror at such a level, there's little opportunity for dissent and citizen's terrorism. It begs two questions; would people resisting such regimes have been labeled as terrorists or freedom fighters? And, is extreme state repression the kind of solution appropriate for modern Western democracies?

If terrorists are not poor, the unspoken idea is that their grievances are unfounded and they don't deserve consideration. Hence their mindless violence justifies the harshest responses.

Although it seems obvious that the "might is right" approach is ethically wrong, impractical and counterproductive, many security analysts and policy makers advocate this approach. Arguably, the strongest advocates are hard line Israelis, like Netanyahu and Sharon. Their strategy is simply to crush terrorists in any way possible. Since 9/11, this strategy has found new advocates in the U.S. Richard Pearl, a member of the Bush administration's Defense Policy Board co-authored a new book suggesting the "kill 'em all, and let God sort it out" strategy. When asked about the use of a carrot and a stick, Pearl responded that, "the carrot is that we won't use the stick."

"Other analysts take a different view. According to Alan Krueger, "No other factor besides a lack of civil liberties — including the literacy rate, infant mortality rate, terrain, ethnic divisions and religious fractionalization — could predict whether people from that country were more or less likely to take part in international terrorism. Thus economically well off countries that lack civil liberties have spawned relatively many terrorists. Poor countries with a tradition of protecting civil liberties are unlikely to spawn terrorists."

Another common theme is that terrorist organizations are Marxist in ideology. This view is more a remnant of the cold war perspective than a reality. Virtually every dissident group seeks to define an ideological foundation for their cause. Since most repressed and disadvantaged people seek to share in their countries wealth, the inevitable call is for redistribution of that wealth through land reform, private ownership or expropriation of foreign-owned business. To their adversaries this sounds like, and can be condemned as communism. History shows that few, if any, revolutionary movements result in communist governments. Today, with communism discredited, it's even less realistic to fear the onset of Marxist, or communist states.

Different Perspectives

It's doubtful that terrorism is any sane person's first choice. Most disgruntled people would start with a petition stating their grievances and setting forth their demands for reform. If denied, they might organize to demonstrate, or protest and might engage in civil disobedience – all design to attract public attention and broaden their support. If denied again, they might attempt legal action, if such avenues are open to them and if they fail, what then? And what if the denial involves being attacked and beaten by authorities, or being arrested and imprisoned? The reactions of the state government can directly influence the course of future events.

Oftentimes, counter-demonstrators who fear that the government will give in to dissident's demands confront demonstrators. These clashes can lead to violence and destroy hope for resolution of the problems. A classic example comes from Northern Ireland.

Northern Ireland

In 1969, disadvantaged Irish Catholics demanding reforms in housing, employment, civil rights staged a protest march. Counter demonstrators attacked them, while the police first stood by, and then joined in the attack.

Later, the government appeared willing to address the Catholic grievances, so Protestants mobs attacked Catholic homes with firebombs, forcing terrorized residents to flee as entire streets were burned, while police failed to protect the Catholic communities and/or joined in the attacks and thus emerged the Irish Republican Army to protect catholic communities under attack.

The Catholic communities were unarmed and unprotected by the police, yet Protestant attacks continued and escalated, including a series of bombings, until Catholics were killed. The purpose of these "loyalist" attacks was to convince the government to ignore catholic demands. Unable to quell the inter-community violence the government brought in British troops. This was a temporary improvement until the soldiers also took sides against Catholics.

The IRA was weak, essentially unarmed and out-gunned by the police and British army, while the citizens remained under threat from loyalist bombs, firebombs and personal attacks. But Ireland is an agricultural country with plenty of fertilizer and diesel fuel and the IRA soon developed skills at bomb making and soon surpassed the skills of their loyalist adversaries. Although the IRA's initial targets were the security forces, it wasn't long before plans went awry and civilians were killed – once that happened the terrorist label was applied, never to be removed. And once a person is condemned and vilified as a terrorist, the response becomes "I might as well be hung for a sheep as a lamb," and violence escalates.

Israel & Palestine

The conflict between Israel and the Palestinians had a very different beginning. The U.N. voted to create the state of Israel on the land where the Palestinians lived, under British authority, but without self-government. The Jews attacked immediately to claim their land. As the British exited, neighboring Arab states also claimed the land. The fledgling UN never did intervene to establish two governments as decreed in the UN resolution. Palestinians lost out, but never accepted defeat. Once Egypt and Jordan renounced their claims to Palestine, the Palestinians opted to fight for their own future. By this time Israel was a substantial military power with American warplanes, attack helicopters, tanks and their dreaded bulldozers, used to demolish Palestinian homes and orchards.

The out-gunned PLO had two choices, ignore the injustice and surrender their aspirations, or continue the struggle by whatever means possible. They chose the later and defined a new form of high-profile international terrorism: high jacking airliners, kidnappings, bombings and hostage taking. Their goal was to shock the world, attract attention to their cause and encourage international intervention.

Perhaps, as a result of their high-visibility terrorism, states, namely U.S. presidents, accepted the need to negotiate a solution to the Middle East conflict. From the Palestinian perspective, however, the result has been to isolate Palestine, subverting their Arab allies and providing little action to address the most enduring grievances.

An essential part of Israel's grand nation-building plan is to encourage immigration of Jews from other countries to Israel. As millions of Jews move to Israel, the state must provide jobs and housing settlements. With over 300,000 settlers now living in the Occupied Territories, claimed by Palestine, it's difficult to accept that Israel will ever withdraw. But Palestinian extremists have a plan.

The current rash of terrorist suicide bombings are intended to exacerbate the climate of fear and increase security costs for a nation that is financially vulnerable. The terrorist's goals are to discourage Jewish immigration, motivates others to leave Israel, and thereby force the government to ultimately agree to Palestinian demands. The violence may be unconscionable, but it is not mindless. Surely, there are also extreme factions that somehow envision the destruction of Israel, but the radical fringe exists in every conflict and it is counter-productive to act as if the extremists speak for all the people, or to allow them to scuttle solutions.

Fundamentalist Islam

It's important to note that Islam is a worldwide religion, not just an Arab religion. The foundations of Islam lie in Saudi Arabia and Iraq, but Muslims number in the hundreds of millions around the globe. Polls indicate that only 15 percent of Indonesians, 7 percent of Saudis and 15 percent of Turks have a favorable image of America. The fact that the governments of these states have friendly relations with Washington suggests the different perspectives of those who benefit and those who suffer from US policy. It is those who continue to languish without prosperity and hope that are the targets of the Islamist dissidents.

Like secular revolutionaries, Islamic Fundamentalists (Islamists) seek to establish an ideological foundation for their struggles. To do so, they distort the teachings of Islam to define a common enemy. That enemy is the Western culture of democracy (scorned as un-Islamic by ideologues of Islamic terrorism), capitalism (decried as Imperialist exploitation), and individualism (opposed by Islamists who believe in a new Caliphate to lead the community of Muslims worldwide.

Again, there are conflicting viewpoints. Michael Radu writes, "We are told, the Islamic states are poor and undemocratic, which justifies rebellion against their tyrannical rulers. Why is that so, and what can be done about it by Muslims and others? Perhaps most Muslim countries are undemocratic because they are Muslim.

When given an electoral choice in 1992 in the first and last democratic elections in the Arab world, most Algerians preferred the Islamic Salvation Front (FIS) over the secular (and corrupt) ruling socialist party — although perfectly aware that FIS's ideology meant not just "one man, one vote" but "one man, one vote, one time." Which raises a very uncomfortable question for both conservatives in the U.S., who routinely blast the lack of democracy in the Arab world, and the human rights fundamentalists such as Amnesty International on the left, who support absolute democracy and at the same time condemn the Islamist disregard of all freedoms, as in Iran.

This line of thought suggests that Islam is inherently defective and leads to the clash of civilizations viewpoint that is then twisted to argue for holy war against Islam. In his report "Islam and Democracy" published by the U.S. Institute of Peace, David Smock writes that, "The explanation of why so many Muslim countries are not democratic has more to do with historical, political, cultural and economic factors than with religious ones."

There is much to support this view. Democracy is a Western concept, barely 200 years old. It has been slow to take root not only in the Muslim world, but also in Latin America, Asia, and Africa. Each of these regions is home to ancient civilizations, cultures and traditions. Like Islam that embraces shura, or "consultative decision-making," other religions and cultures have accepted methods of governance. Is democracy the answer?

Democracy is inherently unfair; it provides for majority rule. If the majority is unfair and unjust, the minority will eventually rebel, as they so often do. Throughout the colonial era, democratic Western powers often granted power to rule to minorities, as a means to divide and conquer large masses of people. Given the inconsistencies associated with Western democratic principles and the way they've been applied, it's not surprising that democracy is not always seen as the solution to life's political problems.

As Western powers continue attempts to establish democracies in Muslim countries, or in states like Haiti, Cuba, North Korea or Rwanda and Angola, one predictable consequence will be a continuation of political violence and terrorism.

2

The Emergence of Insurgencies and Terrorism

It is important to note at the outset that the Russian Academy of Sciences-National Academies Project on Conflict and Reconstruction in Multiethnic Societies was initiated in early 2000, preceding the terrorist attacks of September 11, 2001, in the United States. Hence it originally had the substantially broader focus that its title suggests than the general subject of this meeting. The scope of activities as it was then anticipated is largely reflected in the publication of the proceedings of a U.S.-Russian workshop, *Conflict and Reconstruction in Multiethnic Societies*. This concern for relatively diffuse and heterogeneous sources of violence has been somewhat but not completely overtaken by the impacts of rapidly developing international networks of a generally Islamist, more specifically terrorist, character. By design, the binational group was composed of scholars seeking to establish broad patterns with a comparative approach, and not with individuals having the real-time concerns of national policy makers and those charged with the active suppression of terrorist acts.

In fact, this experience leads me to believe that terrorist activity can be better explained by placing it in a fairly wide array of insurgent movements, rather than by focusing on a wholly committed terrorist group. Engagement in degrees of arguably terrorist activity extends across an irregular continuum, from occasional, part-time, and even one-time participation to full-time involvement. By far the larger numbers of those falling to some degree under this heading are in the less committed category, and most of their behaviour and ideas blend into those of much larger groups of which they remain members.

Core groups of fully committed terrorists have exhibited serious, sophisticated concern for their own security. The conspicuous lack of success that U.S. and Iraqi national forces have had in capturing members of the al-Zarqawi leadership is evidence of that. On the other hand, emphasis on a tight-knit cellular structure amplifies such groups' prevailing difficulties and slowness in communication with its dispersed members. This has the effect of loosening central control and encouraging independence of action. Moreover, in a context of widespread support for insurgency and publicly perceived terrorist effectiveness against seemingly overpowering military forces, new cells quickly form and take action on their own while typically exhibiting less and less concern for unity of program and action. Again, this is being repeatedly demonstrated not only in Iraq but also in Western Europe. Hence there are multiplying targets for antiterrorist intelligence and action, presenting widely differing degrees of difficulty of access. It cannot be an acceptable strategy for counterterrorist policy makers to narrow their focus to what they, but not necessarily the subject population at large, perceive as the original, innermost circles at the heart of the challenges they face.

More spontaneous and marginal participants have not infrequently proved to be approachable by journalists and unofficial informants. While some insights into the dynamics of these groupings can be gained in this way, as well as from comparative and historical data, specific, time-sensitive, action-oriented, information is prevailingly beyond reach. Valery Tishkov's early warning networks are a useful innovation that relies on the reporting by trained local observers of depersonalized, essentially contextual criteria to identify impending conditions of threat or tension, but they, too, have limits. Typically extended and intense, fully candid networks of communication tend to shrivel up as tensions rise, so that when we most need them they become progressively more circumscribed and fragile.

Great states that are victimized by terrorism may resist accepting this, but rigid definitions of what is terrorism are elusive and contentious. Targeting civilian noncombatants is a common shorthand description, but it has obvious limitations in situations of asymmetrical warfare. Are there genuine noncombatants when much of a region's population is either actively up-in-arms or at least passively in support of those who are? Insurgents have to make use of the crude, low-tech, not very selective weapons they can readily seize or have at hand. Organized military forces, on the other hand, make use of much more powerful and destructive weapons, particularly air and heavy artillery bombardment, and then too frequently dismiss attendant civilian casualties as mere collateral damage.

The affected population, of course, may view this differently. Certain egregious acts clearly qualify as terrorism, and certain organized groups like al Qaeda clearly see themselves as systematically engaged in exploiting precisely such egregious acts to enhance their reputation for fearful conduct. I am personally uneasy when the uniform characterization of terrorist is used without qualification along its wide and heterogeneous borderlands. Terrorism in varying forms has appeared in other, earlier times and settings. We should not forget the current or recent examples of the Red Brigades, the Irish Republican Army (IRA), the Euskadi Ta Askatasuna (ETA), and the Tamil Tigers, among others. Modern occurrences, most generally, are in contexts that blur the line—certainly in the perceptions of contending participants—between terrorism per se and some other types of insurgent (for example, religious, ethnic, or nationalist) violence. Typically the contexts involve what is locally perceived as longstanding, repressive discrimination in access to land, employment, education, and other resources, or military occupation that forecloses other, less violent types of civic protest or even involvement.

This clearly does not provide an acceptable rationale for what committed terrorists are trying to do, but it drastically loosens all existing restraints on the wider communities in which they move. Intersecting networks of large and small grievances are formed, for which no orderly remedies are in sight. Leaving aside full committed terrorist cadres, individuals living in an insurgency thus often find themselves confronting multiple pressures calling for allegiance with or opposition to other organized groupings in their immediate surroundings. Dominant personal selections among these alternative identifications naturally are at first fluid, unstable, rarely well articulated or perhaps even understood. Peer pressure is obviously a factor in recruitment, but so are older attachments and rivalries, and even events that may range in scale from major to microscopic. Urgently we would like to obtain some general insights about relations between terrorists and the societies that sustain them (not completely unwillingly, or the terrorist cores could not operate and survive).

In trying to find a constructive path through this conundrum there is an approach that deserves serious consideration. What can be learned from manifestations of civic violence involving the emergence of insurgent formations to which the term terrorist applies only questionably or not at all? Here our focus is on better understanding the dynamics of group formation under conditions of widely prevailing violence, if that permits us to learn from examples that are relatively more open to serious investigation. While one cannot take for granted that any such examples are similar in their essentials to the challenges of terrorism confronting us today, they may at least guide us to a better understanding of some important aspects of the problem, for example, on how insurgencies

- recruit their members, and then sustain themselves in the face of withering losses to better armed adversaries
- relate to the relatively more passive population around them from which they themselves are drawn
- establish and communicate the goals for which they are ready to fight and make sacrifices
- generally have to settle for at best very partial successes

An outstanding example of a study of this kind deserves brief description, emphasizing once again that it is insight into processes of insurgent group formation, coherence, and effective action amid sacrifices we are looking for, not rules that apply with any closeness of fit to the subject of countermeasures to terrorism that brings us together. I refer to a very recent monograph by Elisabeth Wood, *Insurgent Collective Action and Civil War in El Salvador*. On the basis of sensitive, long-continuing fieldwork, she traces evolving forms of militant peasant collective action in a series of representative Salvadoran case-study areas.

Collective violence first occurred there in connection with a mass social movement in the mid-1970s. By the early 1980s a loosely knit insurgent army had come into being, with scattered but vital covert support. Around this there emerged a vibrant civil society, capable of holding its own in what became a military stalemate. Wood conducted extended interviews over many years with hundreds of insurgents, landlords, nonparticipants, and commanders of military and guerilla forces. By repeated, extended, ultimately interlocking cross-checking of individuals' own accounts of their motives and actions with those of other participants, she was able to establish a high, although she is careful to insist never absolute, level of veracity. The prevailing form of collective action was the seizure of lands from great haciendas and its distribution among militant cooperatives.

A very heavy price was paid for this, the result of long-continuing, low-intensity warfare with regular military forces and vigilante death squads, assassinations, and unaccounted-for disappearances. From an annual high of around 20,000 war-related deaths in 1980, it tapered off to 2,000 or so in 1984 and stabilized there until peace was negotiated after 1990. El Salvador today faces other problems in maintaining a course of economic development and dealing with massive emigration, but the insurgent cooperatives have largely secured their place in a new, relatively stable social order. Still, as one rebel activist noted with apparent puzzlement some years later, "We shed blood all these years [just] in order to buy land at market prices?"

Wood was at pains to probe the question of motivation. Personal gain she found she had to exclude: At great personal risk and loss, the insurgents shared what was won completely with nonparticipants. Similarly, she could not identify a pattern of preexisting community loyalty and well-established social networks. Two-thirds of the residents in the areas studied lent no active support to the insurgents. Instead, Wood finds that the backgrounds and motivations of the insurgents were highly diverse, from personal grievances and perceived injustices to liberation theology. Her important conclusion is that, once joining the insurgency, individuals all "took pride, indeed pleasure, in the successful assertion of their interests and identity"—in what she terms the "pleasure of agency." In short, insurgents "were motivated in no small part by the value they put on taking part in the making of history."

A unifying set of themes was characteristic of those campesino-insurgents who engaged in and actively supported the insurgency—resentment at the social conditions before the war, aspirations for a different, hopefully more just social and economic order, moral outrage at earlier repression, and pride in what the insurgency achieved. All these themes were muted or absent in interviews with those who did not support the insurgency. This strongly suggests that a new political culture emerged during the civil war among those who supported and joined the insurgency. From diverse beginnings, their political identities were transformed through the struggles of the years of civil war. A new, more explicitly political culture emerged as the insurgent formations constituted themselves and took action, at the same time shaping those involved into new identities as militant activists. "[I]t was participation, rather than other factors," Wood concludes, "that accounts for insurgent political ... culture."

Insurgency is an emergent phenomenon, in other words. Its shape and dynamic follow no general laws of cause and effect but instead are outcomes of highly complex processes of feedback and interaction. Does the same apply to terrorism as a subset of insurgencies, and in particular to the radical Islamist variety of it that the world now confronts? I am very skeptical of any overall pattern of congruence, as noted earlier, but at the level of a newly emergent organizational structure that generates its own identities and loyalty, this at least deserves serious consideration. Efforts to deal with indigenous practices or occasions of terrorism may need to have the same flexibility of structure, goals, and tactics and a readiness both for sudden, resolute advance and strategic compromise or withdrawal, as was characteristic of other insurgencies like the well-reported one in El Salvador.

In contrast, foreign, internationally moving and communicating networks of fully committed terrorists are an essentially different question. Rootless in a given country of operations, they are relatively unrestrained by gradations and qualifications of support from the population of the host country. Moreover the psychological and socioeconomic impacts they seek are international, with little regard for the interests of the host country. As a result, their growing influence and (perhaps exaggerated reputation for) effectiveness is perhaps the most dynamic and dangerous challenge the world now faces. Experience gained in this project, however, and in the comparative material, with which it provided some familiarity, unfortunately provides little or no information that is helpful in dealing with them.

Methods of Terrorism and its Immediate Results

Two years before the April 1995 bombing of the Alfred P. Murrah Federal Building in Oklahoma City, the February 1993 World Trade Center bombing had already marked a watershed in America's perceived vulnerability to terrorism1 on its own soil. Prior to the World Trade Center bombing, modern terrorism was generally regarded as something that happened elsewhere: a problem of the unsettled Middle East and Latin America, which on occasion spilled over into the streets of London or other major cities. While Americans have often been targeted by terrorists abroad, this attack demonstrated that they can no longer believe themselves immune to terrorist violence within their own borders. The Oklahoma City bombing showed that the United States continues to be vulnerable to terrorist attacks.

Three bombings in July 1994 also underscored the attractiveness and vulnerability of civilian buildings as terrorist targets. On July 18, 1994, a massive car bomb destroyed the Jewish Community Center in Buenos Aires. One week later, another car bomb exploded outside a London apartment adjacent to the heavily guarded Israeli

Embassy. Less than 12 hours later, a London building housing a number of Jewish community organizations was the target of still another car bomb.

This chapter presents a background on the motives, methods, and immediate results of terrorist activities, including such topics as statistical patterns of recent terrorist acts and the types of damage to structures and critical building systems, and of injuries that can be expected after a bomb detonates.

The State Department defines "terrorism" as premeditated, politically motivated violence perpetrated against noncombatant targets by sub national groups or clandestine agents, usually intended to influence an audience.

Motives for Terrorist Attacks

Terrorists' specific motives for attacking buildings are diverse, but they might be grouped into the following categories:

- To obtain publicity for the terrorist group and its cause,
- To exert political pressure or make a symbolic statement,
- To destroy some asset within or part of the building,
- To achieve financial gain through ransom or extortion,
- To advance a religious imperative,
- To kill or injure occupants, and/or
- To seek vengeance or revenge.

Publicity appears to be the most common objective, although any particular terrorist attack often combines several of the above-listed motives. While the actual intent of the World Trade Center bombers remains unclear, a major motive was no doubt publicity, together with a protest of U.S. support for conservative Arab governments and Israel, as the bombers explained in a letter they later sent to the *New York Times* claiming credit for the bombing.

In addition to a quest for publicity, a major motive for a terrorist attack is to exert political pressure or to make a symbolic statement. For this reason, buildings are often the objects of terrorist attacks because of their specific occupants. Targeted tenants in the U.S. and worldwide have included governmental agencies, such as in the Oklahoma City bombing, storefront military recruiting stations, diplomatic and consular facilities, post offices, defense contractors, banks, corporate offices, and commercial establishments.

Terrorists rarely appear to target a building simply to destroy the building itself or to damage some asset inside. While there is some indication that the World Trade Center bombers actually intended to bring down one of the twin towers, and the suicide bombers who attacked the U.S. facilities in West and East Beirut in the early 1980s sought—among other objectives—to destroy those structures, the damage sought in these and similar cases generally appears to have been a secondary goal, the primary goal being publicity and the exercise of political pressure. Perhaps the first well-publicized incident in which terrorists sought to destroy some specific asset inside a building was the 1946 bombing of Jerusalem's King David Hotel in what was then British-ruled Palestine.

Jewish terrorists targeted the hotel, where the headquarters of the British administration and military command for Palestine was located, to destroy vital Jewish documents that had been seized by the British Army a month earlier and were believed to be stored on two floors of the west wing. Terrorists as well as nonpolitically motivated individuals have also targeted commercial buildings purely for economic gain. Terrorist organizations and criminal gangs in Latin America and Northern Ireland, for example, regularly extort protection money from building contractors, owners, and tenants.

In some cases, the extortion amounts demanded, and the damage caused to the property of those who refused to comply, have been extraordinarily high. In August 1980, for instance, after a Nevada casino did not respond to extortion demands, a homemade bomb caused more than $12 million in damages to the casino. In many bombing incidents, it is often difficult to single out a specific motive for the attack. Although terrorist attacks on civilian buildings do not generally appear to have the sole intention of killing or injuring the occupants, in several instances, such as the bombings of the Alfred P. Murrah Federal Building in Oklahoma City and the Jewish Community Center in Buenos Aires that was certainly a result. Similarly, attacks with apparent religious or vengeance overtones such as the World Trade Center bombing may have other motives as well.

For example, suspicions have been raised that the World Trade Center bombing was masterminded by politically motivated agents who have little in common with the religious movement to which the convicted bombers belonged. Should this be the case, it would suggest that one organization with a particular agenda may manipulate another group with different objectives and motivations to carry out the act.

Patterns of Terrorist Attacks

Bombing has long been the most common terrorist tactic. Bombings account for nearly half (46 percent) of all international terrorist attacks carried out since 1968, a proportion that has rarely fallen below 40 percent or exceeded 50 percent in any year. Terrorists' reliance on bombing is not surprising, given that bombs provide a dramatic, yet fairly easy and often relatively risk-free (to the perpetrator) means of drawing attention to the terrorist cause. Few skills are required to manufacture a crude bomb, surreptitiously plant it, and then be miles away when it explodes. Terrorist attacks typically involve only one or two persons and, in general, do not require the same organizational expertise, logistics, and knowledge required of more complicated or sophisticated operations such as kidnapping, barricade and hostage situations, assassination, or assaults against defended targets.

Armed attacks on buildings (including assaults with automatic weapons as well as hand grenades, bazookas, and rocket-propelled grenades, drive-by shootings, arson, vandalism, and sabotage other than bombing) represent a distant second to bombing, accounting for 22 percent of all terrorist operations since 1968.

Forty-four percent of all terrorist attacks between 1968 and 1969 involved bombings, 53 percent involved bombings in the 1970s, 49 percent in the 1980s, and 39.5 percent between 1990 and 1993. Not surprisingly, the frequency of various types of terrorist attacks tends to decrease in proportion to the complexity or sophistication they entail. Hijackings are the third most common tactic, accounting for 12 percent of terrorist attacks, 4 followed by assassination (6 percent), and 5 kidnapping (1 percent).

The Sarin gas attack in Tokyo in 1995 represents a new method of attack, but it is too early to assess the likelihood of an increase in that mode of terrorism. The choice of bombing as the preferred terrorist tactic in the United States is evidenced by Federal Bureau of Investigation statistics. Between 1982 and 1992, bombings accounted for 77.5 percent of all terrorist incidents in this country. Most of the targets were commercial establishments (36 percent of all incidents), followed by military personnel and facilities (20 percent), federal and state government office buildings and property (19 percent), private residences (11 percent), diplomatic establishments (10 percent), and educational establishments (4 percent).

These figures augment the FBI statistics by including bombing attempts in addition to actual bombings (explosive and incendiary) by both terrorist and non terrorist perpetrators for the period 1989–1993. 8 Bombings of commercial buildings figure prominently in these statistics. Ease of access, entry, and escape figure prominently in terrorists' selection of sites and methods of attack. In choosing a target, terrorists assess buildings' physical layouts and locations, more specifically, the patterns of public vehicular and foot traffic into and out of a building, physical security measures and visitors' entrance procedures, and the existence of multiple entry and exit points. The lightly guarded public parking lot beneath the World Trade Center was very likely a factor that made this structure—in contrast to the considerably older Empire State or Chrysler buildings, which lack such facilities—operationally attractive to the terrorists who bombed it. Similarly, the unrestricted public access in front of the Murrah Building in Oklahoma City and its relatively short setback distance from the street may have influenced the choice of that target.

A building's physical location may similarly be a critical factor in target selection. Terrorists may be unable to gain access to their primary target site and therefore must settle for detonating a bomb inside or outside an adjacent building. A block of apartments in London's exclusive Kensington Palace area was bombed in July 1994 apparently because of its location adjacent to the well-protected Israeli Embassy. Several facts suggest that the terrorist threat to buildings will remain significant. First, there is the relative ease with which access can be gained to commercial establishments.

Such structures are necessarily open to the public, are subject to heavy daily pedestrian and vehicular traffic, and generally have few formidable access barriers. In contrast, other attractive terrorist targets—such as embassies, consulates, and military facilities—are often better protected and guarded, and sometimes physically and structurally reinforced. The latter are deliberately formidable targets, but an unintended effect of their "hardening" may be to displace the terrorist threat onto more vulnerable structures, such as commercial buildings. Another reason the terrorist threat to buildings will likely persist, as the Oklahoma City, the World Trade Center, and other numerous recent major bombings demonstrate, is that attacks on buildings (especially by bombing) are a proven means for terrorists to attract attention to themselves and their causes.

It is interesting to note that simple homemade devices fabricated by amateurs have proven just as destructive and lethal as more sophisticated terrorist weapons. The explosive device used at the World Trade Center, for example, was made out of ordinary, commercially available materials—including lawn fertilizer (urea nitrate) and diesel fuel—and cost less than $400 to make. The device used in the Oklahoma City bombing was likely of similar construction.

The World Trade Center bomb was composed of some 1,200 lbs of common sulfuric and nitric acids used in dozens of household products and urea used to fertilize lawns. The detonating device was a more complex and extremely volatile mixture of nitroglycerine enhanced by tanks of compressed hydrogen gases that were designed to increase the force of the explosion. Similarly, in April 1988 a Japanese Red Army terrorist was arrested while en route to New York City on a bombing mission. Found in his possession were gunpowder, hollowed-out fire extinguishers in which to place the explosive materials and roofing nails as crude anti-personnel weapons.

The sophistication of terrorist weapons, then, especially bombs and explosive devices, may well be in their simplicity. Unlike military ordnance, such as plastic explosives for example, the materials used in homemade bombs are readily commercially available; they are thus perfectly legal to possess until actually concocted or assembled into a bomb. These ordinary materials are also far more difficult for authorities to trace or for experts to obtain a "signature" from. For foreign governments seeking to commission terrorist attacks, such homemade bombs also help enable the state sponsor to avoid identification and any possible military retaliation or international sanction.

Furthermore, terrorists can improve their methods readily. As the World Trade Center bombers included a chemical engineer in their operations, future terrorists targeting a building may, for example, include a structural engineer in their plans to help ensure the collapse of the building. Terrorists study the "lessons" of comrades and other terrorist groups, and are often more sophisticated in their operations and know more about security-force tactics and countermeasures than their predecessors. Finally, again, the increase in internal security at many buildings in the wake of recent bombings may not eliminate the terrorist threat to buildings, but rather displace it to more accessible buildings.

Bomb Damage to Buildings and Occupants

A bomb explosion within or immediately nearby a building can have catastrophic effects, destroying or severely damaging portions of the building's external and internal structural framework, collapsing walls, blowing out large expanses of windows, and shutting down critical fire- and life-safety systems, such as fire detection and suppression, ventilation, light, water, sewage, and power. Loss of life and injuries to occupants can result from many causes, including direct blast-effects, debris impact, fire, and smoke. The indirect effects can combine to inhibit or prevent timely evacuation, thereby contributing to additional casualties.

The following sections describe examples of these damaging effects. Bomb damage to buildings depends, of course, on the type of building and the nature of the explosive device and its location relative to the building. Other factors determining damage relate to the specifics of the building's design and the immediate surroundings and the location and disposition of its occupants. The first section below describes the structural damage to a building from the direct effect of an explosion. Collateral damage to building subsystems is discussed, and the final section describes how injuries are sustained by people within the building.

Structural Damage

Recent terrorist attacks against commercial buildings dramatically illustrate the influence of bomb placement and building design on the nature and extent of direct structural damage. The devastating car bomb attack against the Jewish Community Center in Buenos Aires illustrates the damage potential of an external explosion against a multistory building of masonry load-bearing construction. A similar attack against a multistory office building of more modern concrete column and slab construction at St. Mary Axe in London, inflicted a different type and level of damage. In marked contrast, a much larger car bomb detonated in an underground garage of the World Trade Center, a modern steel and concrete skyscraper did substantially less structural damage than was probably intended. The structural consequences of these terrorist attacks and bombings in Staples Corner, London, and Oklahoma City are briefly reviewed here.

Jewish Community Center, Buenos Aires

On July 18, 1994, a van loaded with about 275 kg of high explosive was detonated in front of the Jewish Community Center located in a densely constructed area of Buenos Aires. The explosive is thought to have been arranged to focus the blast on the building, 3 to 5 meters away. The exterior walls of this five-story building were of brick masonry construction, which supported the floor slabs. The air blast from the bomb totally destroyed the exposed load-bearing walls which, in turn, led to progressive failure of the floor slabs and virtually total collapse of the building. Such wall-bearing buildings are notable for their tendency to be brought down in this manner by localized damage.

Staples Corner, North London

On April 11, 1992, an explosion occurred at Staples Corner. The building's nearest corner was 17 m from the explosion and its farthest corner 95 m away. The building was clad with light-profiled steel sheeting on light purloins in the walls and roof and is a good example of frangible construction, that is, where the resistance of the cladding is much less than that of the supporting framework. Severe damage occurred to the cladding, sheeting, purloins, block work lining wall, and finishes and fittings in areas nearest the blast. However, the main steel frame sustained only minor damage. The stripped sheeting generally rebounded outward toward the bomb.

World Trade Center, New York City

The terrorist attack against the 110-story World Trade Center on February 26, 1993, involved a much larger car bomb than the London or Buenos Aires attacks. While damage and injuries in the World Trade Center bombing were extensive, they differed substantially from those in the other cases because of differences in bomb placement and building structure. The bomb, estimated to be about 900 kg of high explosive, was detonated against the south wall of the north tower in an underground garage two levels below grade. The most severe structural damage occurred to the sub grade levels, with the bomb crater measuring 24 m to 36 m across on some of the levels. Two levels of reinforced concrete slabs, about 280 mm thick, were blown out and the debris completely covered refrigeration equipment on the fifth sub grade level, rendering it inoperable. A shock wave propagated throughout the sub grade structure, causing the parking-level slabs to fail at column capitals and other "hard points."

Steel columns that supported both the adjacent Vista Hotel and parts of the World Trade Center Plaza and concourse area that before the explosion were braced by the closely spaced parking levels stood naked as high as 21 m without definable lateral support. At the crater's edge, the slabs had sheared free of their supporting columns, settling several feet to form "ski jumps" into the crater. Elsewhere, multi-ton portions of concrete were literally dangling from reinforcing steel.

The photograph was taken at the south end of the parking garage; the explosion occurred at the north end. Segments of the masonry wall along the south wall of the north tower were blown into the building; masonry work surrounding elevator shafts was blown into those shafts, causing the air locks to be breached, particularly for the north tower. With the loss of the air locks, smoke and dust-laden air was drawn into and upward through the towers by stack action. Breaching of the air locks accounted for the majority of personnel injuries, as discussed later in this chapter.

While the intent of the terrorists may have been to bring down the tower, its structural integrity was never threatened. This achievement undoubtedly can be attributed to the ductility of the structural steel shell and the conservative requirements used in its design: to withstand a 240-kph wind storm, the loss of perimeter columns by sabotage, and the impact of a fully fueled 707 aircraft anywhere along the tower height. A more immediate reason the tower did not collapse is because the lateral (horizontal) blast pressure was not large enough to cause the column to fail in shear or combined axial load and bending. The adjacent column bracing and floor framing did fail due to the blast pressure. The adjacent Vista Hotel, less massively constructed, did sustain extensive damage, which threatened its structural integrity.

The bombing of the Federal Building in Oklahoma City on April 19, 1995, was the largest such terrorist attack in the United States to date. A car bomb, estimated to contain about 1,800 kg of high explosive and located 3–5 m from the north face of the building and about 12–15 m from the east end, caused 168 fatalities, numerous injuries, and an estimated $50 million in damage to about 75 buildings in the area. The Murrah Building was a nine-story tower of reinforced concrete slab and column construction measuring 61.5 m × 21.5 m. The frame had 10.7 m × 6.2 m typical bays, created by a column line along each face and one down the center. Four of the north-face columns, spaced at 12.3 m and unsupported for two stories, formed an atrium at street level. A 61.5-m-long third-floor spandrel beam transferred loads from the columns on floors above to the 8-m-tall exposed columns.

The explosion destroyed three of the four front columns and a centerline column. With four columns shattered, the upper floors toppled northward as the 200-mm-thick slabs separated from centerline columns. As a consequence, 8 of the 10 bays along the northern half of the building collapsed into a heap. In the southern half of the building, two bays collapsed on either side of the failed center column. Inside the south entrance, slabs collapsed in adjacent bays on two floors.

Damage to Building Subsystems

Certain building subsystems, if lost, render the building unable to protect the occupants or assist in their survival and otherwise make the building uninhabitable or unusable. Typical of these subsystems are fire-detection and suppression systems; water and sewer service, including sanitation; means of egress, including corridors, stairs, lobbies, and exit doors; elevators; primary and emergency electrical systems; and rescue operation systems, including voice and data communications, ventilation, and smoke control.

A bomb detonation inside a building's parking garage probably would cause the most serious damage to building subsystems simply because several critical subsystems originate there, along with much of the control and distribution equipment. A garage-level detonation has a significant potential for fire and smoke production because the parked vehicles contain large amounts of combustible materials. Also, the fire-suppression system would likely be made inoperable, since it is exposed and very fragile.

The World Trade Center bombing, unfortunately, was a very good example of these observations: extensive damage occurred to communications, life-safety, electrical, and mechanical systems; the emergency generator plant shut down because of loss of cooling water; the elevator and stair shafts were breached; smoke from burning automobiles on the parking levels was forced up the shafts of both towers; and the underground tower's operations control center was put out of commission, leaving building occupants without important information.

Street-level explosions can also cause serious damage to critical building subsystems. Most urban office buildings have extensive street-level fenestration consisting of glass panes, some as large as 2 m × 4 m set in narrow aluminum extrusions. This assembly typically has little or no blast resistance, and a blast wave can enter the street-level lobby area virtually unattenuated. Consequently, extensive damage can occur to the fire control room usually located near the lobby, to elevators, to egress stairways, and to the service risers that pass through the street-level floor. Service risers generally are concentrated in one of a few vertical shafts or "chases" that rise up through the core of the building, usually contiguous with the elevator shaft(s).

Typically they contain the heating and cooling hydraulic lines, domestic and sanitary systems, electrical distribution and communications lines, fire standpipes, and supply/return ducting and condenser water lines. Building codes require that these chases be fire-rated, but they are generally constructed of relatively light materials. Their blast resistance typically is poor and at least some of the service risers would likely be severed. The lateral distribution of services on the upper floors is accomplished by equipment and conduits above the ceilings of occupied spaces—systems that can be damaged by a street-level depending on the location of the service risers relative to the point of detonation. The ceilings are commonly constructed of loose fiber tiles laid in a lightweight grid work and offer little to no protection.

Blast damage to the elevators from either a garage- or street-level detonation is usually extensive and most disruptive to occupancy in mid- to high-rise buildings. Elevator doors may collapse into the hoist way, and there will be damage to hoist way components directly from the explosion and from flying structural debris. Elevator cabs that are at rest on the floor where the explosion occurs will be damaged, perhaps beyond repair. In multi-elevator banks, damage to only one cab or hoist way may cause the electrical and mechanical safeties to shut down the entire system, thereby preventing the surviving cabs from being operated manually or on fire service.

Stairways used to evacuate the building in the event of a fire or explosions are similar in construction and vulnerability to the elevator shafts and would experience similar damage from a street-level blast. Collapse of the stairway shaft walls may make the stairway impassable, impeding or even preventing evacuation, and the situation is made still more serious because the main lobby level is often one means of egress from the building.

Hazards to People

Personnel injuries and loss of life can result directly from the bomb's explosion; blast pressure, impact of high-speed glass fragments or other structural debris, collapse of structural members, fire and smoke inhalation, or a variety of other causes associated with the general confusion that may follow an explosion and a possibly prolonged evacuation period. If the explosion is sufficiently close to a wall or floor, there can be gross disintegration, with either spalled pieces on the back side or the wall materials themselves being propelled as missiles. These missiles can injure people and damage property, and if structural support is sufficiently disrupted, the building may collapse. Except when people are trapped in collapsed building spaces, most injuries occur from missile penetration or from smoke inhalation.

Breaching of elevator and stairwell doors (more likely for street-level explosions) allows smoke to migrate upwards into the building, carried by the building's stack effect during winter months. Elevators are likely to be occupied throughout the day, and persons may be trapped within them, either as a result of damage to the elevator shaft or hoists, or as a result of loss of power or controls. In the World Trade Center bombing, the north tower air locks were destroyed and smoke and dust-laden air was forced to the upper floors, accounting for most of the over 1,000 personnel injuries.

3

Knowledge for Blast-Effects Mitigation and Protective Designs

This chapter contains an assessment of the state of the art in blast-effects mitigation and protective design technologies and highlights blast-hardening capabilities developed by the military that are applicable to the civilian sector. The introductory section outlines the historical development of the existing knowledge base, the nature of explosions, and the induced physical behaviour of materials. This is followed by a section on experimental and simple analytical approaches to blast-effects mitigation and structural design. The far-ranging needs of military organizations to protect key assets from enemy attack, together with the large cost and practical limitations of field testing, has led to a strong emphasis on developing analytical methods and advanced computer models for simulation of blast-effects on building structures. The third and fourth sections summarize applicable military design manuals and computational approaches, respectively, to predicting blast loads and the responses of structural systems.

Although the majority of military design guidance is based on semi-empirical relationships, much of the existing knowledge of blast environments and the effects of high-intensity, short-duration loadings on the behaviour of structures, systems, and components is embodied in sophisticated "first-principle" computer programs as well as in simplified, design oriented and semi-empirical software. Accordingly, the fifth section discusses specific computer programs, followed by a section on code validation which looks at comparisons of computational calculations of the response to an explosion to the actual experimental results. The final section of the chapter reviews the applications of the computational methods to terrorist threats.

Although not directly related to the subject of this study, two previous National Research Council (NRC) studies have dealt with terrorism and bombing: The first is The Embassy of the Future (NRC, 1986), which reviews the measures that could be applied to new foreign service buildings for all categories of threats, including bombs. The Department of State has since developed a large body of data and design guidelines related to countering terrorism through design. The second study is Protection of Federal Office Buildings Against Terrorism (NRC, 1988) which addresses the protection of existing domestic federal buildings from various threats, including bombs. Historical Background Explosive devices have been used for hundreds of years, yet comprehensive treatment of blast-effects and their mitigation appeared in the Western Hemisphere only during and after World War II. Following the war, the Office of Scientific Research and Development (National Defense Research Committee, 1946) produced the seminal, unclassified document on weapons and penetration capabilities.

This report remains of value today. While the document is difficult to locate, some of the information it contains has been republished. Of special interest in the latter publication is information that permits estimates to be made of the penetration resistance of structural elements of various materials to projectiles of many forms. World War II was the first international conflict that resulted in massive destruction of cities, mostly with high explosives, which also inflicted enormous casualties. In the latter stages of that war, the use of two nuclear weapons demonstrated the destructive capability of such weapons. The accelerated arms race during the Cold War, from 1945 through 1990, led to research and development of modern nuclear weapons during this time period, and a major research program on protective structures and systems was established, largely sponsored by the Armed Forces Special Weapons Project, later renamed the Defense Atomic Support Agency, and thereafter the Defense Nuclear Agency (DNA).

Throughout this period, DNA, in cooperation with the U.S. Air Force, the U.S. Navy, and the U.S. Army, conducted major test programs in laboratories and field test facilities. In addition, theoretical and experimental work sponsored by these agencies was carried out in various companies and universities. In the United States a comprehensive program of research over the past half century was undertaken to increase the blast resistance of military structures such as weapons storage facilities and command, control, and communication facilities. Much of this research was in response to deployment of ballistic and guided missile systems. In addressing both the nuclear threat and the threat of conventional weapons, a number of widely used manuals on protective structures were developed. These manuals reflect the improvements in engineering practice that occurred over the years.

This progression of manuals concentrated on techniques for estimating the loadings from nuclear weapons explosions, attenuation of pressure effects in the air and ground, simple analytical techniques for design and proportioning of structural elements, guidelines for designing and analyzing equipment, and many other related topics. Although nuclear weapons effects were the primary focus of protective design through the 1970s, related work was ongoing to develop quantitative procedures for the design of structures subject to accidental explosion. Extensive research and development programs, including numerous full- and small-scale structural response and explosive effects tests, form the empirical basis for Structures to Resist the Effects of Accidental Explosions.

Several other manuals dealing with blast effects and the design of protective structures have also been developed for use by the military services. Although none of these manuals is dedicated solely to the subject of this report, taken together, they provide a range of structural data and design procedures for protective structures useful to designers and which have applicability to the design of more explosion-resistant buildings. Increased terrorist activity throughout the world and in the United States has also led to a number of specialized studies in recent years. These studies and a variety of design manuals are discussed later in this chapter. Nature of Explosions, Explosive materials are designed to release large amounts of energy in a short time.

The explosion arises through the reaction of solid or liquid chemicals or vapor to form more stable products, primarily gases. A high explosive is one in which the speed of reaction (typically 5,000–8,000 m/s) is faster than the speed of sound in the explosive. High explosives produce a shock wave along with gas, and the characteristic duration of a high-explosive detonation is measured in microseconds (10-6 s). Explosives come in various forms, commonly called by names such as TNT, PETN, RDX, and other trade names (U.S. Department of the Army, 1986; McGraw-Hill Encyclopedia of Science & Technology, 1987). A common explosive employed in rack blasting, called ANFO, is composed of ammonium nitrate and diesel fuel oil—products that are readily available. Dynamite, of which there are many kinds, is also readily available, and theft and misdirection in shipping occur occasionally. The lethality of high explosives has been increasing since the nineteenth century.

For someone bent on destruction, high explosives are relatively easy to make or acquire, and detonation, though technically more complicated, is not difficult for someone with even modest training in explosives. The effects of explosions on structures are directly related to stress-wave propagation as well as impact and missile penetration. In all close-in explosions, where shock waves must travel through the surrounding medium to cause damage to a facility, a realistic description of the wave-propagation phenomena is needed. The literature on these subjects can be divided into two groups: one group addresses the classical issue of wave propagation, with emphasis on linear-type problems, and the second group is more focused on nonlinear problems.

The effects of an explosion are varied. For explosions close to the targeted object, the pressure-driven effects occur quickly, on the order of microseconds to a few milliseconds. The air-blast loads are commonly subdivided into (1) loading due to the impinging shock front, its reflections, and the greatly increased hydrostatic pressure behind the front, all commonly denoted as overpressure; and (2) the dynamic pressures due to the particle velocity, or mass transfer, of the air. It is customary to characterize the pressure loadings in terms of scaled range, as given by Z = R/W1/3, in which Z is the scaled range, R is the radial distance between the explosion center and the target, and W is the explosive weight (normally expressed as an equivalent TNT weight). Units for charge weight and distance should be either pounds and feet or kilograms and meters. In the scaled-range concept, as long as the value of Z remains the same, the same parameters for the explosive effects (i.e., peak pressure, positive duration, etc.) should be obtained. If an explosion is confined by a chamber or room, the gas pressure increases rapidly to a sustained level and then decays by venting out.

Under these conditions shock reflections occur and the overall effect can be greater than that of the incident shock. The effects of internal explosions can be devastating to buildings and their occupants, which supports evaluation of the possibility of mitigating blast-effects by controlled venting. There is a considerable body of knowledge available concerning blast-effects mitigating techniques for buildings subject to accidental explosion, which may have applicability to the design of civilian office structures. There are three additional explosion-related phenomena relevant to this study, namely impact of objects propelled by the explosion environment, penetration of such objects, and ground-transmitted shock.

Induced Physical Behaviour. If the explosion originates at a sufficiently great scaled range (i.e., a small charge or a large distance from a structure), then the structure will be loaded in a manner that leads to global deformation, meaning that all the elements provide some degree of resistance to the loading. The definition of the expected loading, and the provision of resisting elements to accommodate the loading, is the essence of dynamic design, analysis, and construction; these issues are addressed in the previously cited design manuals and by the computer codes discussed later in this chapter. If the explosion is sufficiently close to a wall or floor (that is, with a small scaled range), there can be gross disintegration, with either spalled fragments coming off the front and back sides or wall fragments themselves being propelled as missiles. These fragments can injure people, damage property, and, if structural support is sufficiently disrupted, cause the building to collapse.

At intermediate scaled ranges, both global and localized response, including severe cracking, with near-face disintegration and spalling on the rear face, can be expected. When an explosion impinges on a structural element, a shock wave is transmitted internally at high speed; for example, dilatational waves (tension or compression) propagate at speeds of 2,700–3,400 m/s in typical concrete and 4,900–5,800 m/s in steel. At these speeds, reflections and refractions quickly occur within the material (within milliseconds), and, depending on the material properties, high-rate straining and major disintegration effects can occur. For example, under extremely high shock pressures, concrete, a relatively brittle material, tends to undergo multiple fractures which can lead to fragmentation. In steel, under similar conditions, depending on the material properties and geometry, yielding and fracture can be expected, especially if fabrication flaws are present, with fragmentation occurring in some cases.

Primary, fragments are produced when a detonating explosive is in contact with a material such as concrete or steel. The initial velocity of the primary fragments depends in part on the detonation pressure. Secondary fragments are produced by the effect of the blast wave on materials not in contact with the explosive. Openings such as doors and windows require special design considerations if intrusion of the explosive shock wave is to be averted, or damage mitigated. Where high levels of blast-effects mitigation are sought, labyrinth (and) entrances, possibly with blast doors, as well as ventilation blast valves, can be used. As described earlier, explosions in a partially or fully confined space, as a room or garage, can be even more devastating, with higher pressures than would occur in free air and a longer duration of loading. In such situations significant damage can be expected.

Other explosion-generated effects are also produced, such as fire (including smoldering fires), smoke, pressure damage to ears and other organs, and violent motion of the structure and its contents. Such shock-related motion can result in personal injury and equipment damage and cause the loss of lifelines such as utilities and communications cables. Experimental and Simple Analytical Approaches Theory and experiments are essential for predicting the blast effects of an explosion. Experimental data may be combined with certain aspects of explosion theory to properly characterize material behaviour at high strain rates, which in turn can be employed in developing computational approaches for estimating structural and equipment reaction to an explosion. It is important to validate such computational approaches by experiment whenever possible.

Some military testing programs have concentrated on the effects of nuclear weapons, frequently employing specially designed high-explosive devices to simulate either close-in or far-field effects of nuclear blast waves. The large-scale ANFO testing program using full-scale structures conducted by the military is one example of data collection specifically addressed to the issue of analytic verification. In these tests, approximately 450 metric tons of ANFO charges were used to produce overpressure loadings below approximately 0.69 megapascals (100 psi) corresponding to a 1 kt nuclear weapon; other high-explosive techniques were employed occasionally to obtain higher pressures. The most common method used in this type of testing has been to load reduced-scale structures with either weapons or special high-explosive devices. In many cases, testing conditions permit only one structural scale and charge per study rather than a range of scaled sizes and charge weights, and, for a variety of reasons, comprehensive post-test studies often have not been conducted. Although the voluminous data available from weapons-systems test procedures and related military experiments may require extensive analysis and interpretation before the results can be fully incorporated into the knowledge base, this data provides a rich source of information not readily available elsewhere.

The Accident Data Base of the Department of Defense Explosives Safety Board (DDESB) is another valuable source of empirical data on explosive events. The DDESB accident reports analyze damage sustained by structures in accidental explosions and can provide considerable insight into the performance of structural elements following an explosion. The majority of tests were conducted to determine the survivability of existing or proposed blast-hardened U.S. facilities: other tests were conducted to determine the vulnerability of possible enemy facilities, hardened or otherwise. From a survivability perspective, test objectives dealt with determining margins of strength of fully described facilities, whereas from a vulnerability perspective, the objectives concerned failure modes of facilities whose characteristics were known only approximately. Thus, what was conservative in one type of test, tended to be unconservative in the other, and extreme care must be taken in evaluating specific results for application in civilian practice.

The ability to design and construct safe buildings depends on an understanding of how such buildings behave under severe loads (i.e., cause-and-effect relationships). Unfortunately, past experiments, performed mainly by the military, have shown that supposedly identical high-explosive devices frequently produce significantly different loading environments. Consequently, progress in designing structures subject to explosive loading has been difficult to attain. A program of precision testing and code simulations in which loads are well defined and the outcome is well documented and assessed is clearly a prerequisite to further progress in designing blast-resistant buildings. The results of full-scale tests for strengthening existing civilian structures against terrorist attack were recently reported at an international symposium.

Results were obtained for windows, doors, and light ceilings and roofs, and appear to be limited to failure pressures; no computational analyses of these tests have been reported. The suitability of these results for computer program validation is questionable because of limited data. Two companion papers report on measures to increase the blast resistance of walls and ceilings and windows and doors. There has also been an extensive test program on windows in the United States and the United Kingdom. Over the years, as a result of research coupled with test programs, computational approaches have been developed for estimating the responses and behaviour of simple structures subjected to blast loading. In turn, based on experimental data, field-test observations and analytical procedures, a number of technical design manuals were developed, as described in the next section.

Technical Design Manuals Structures to Resist the Effects of Accidental Explosions, TM 5-130. This manual appears to be the most widely used publication by both military and civilian organizations for designing structures to prevent the propagation of explosion and to provide protection for personnel and valuable equipment. It includes step-by-step analysis and design procedures, including information on such items as (1) blast, fragment, and shock-loading; (2) principles of dynamic analysis; (3) reinforced and structural steel design; and (4) a number of special design considerations, including information on tolerances and fragility, as well as shock isolation. Illustrative computations are also included in many cases. Guidance is provided for selection and design of security windows, doors, utility openings, and other components that must resist blast and forced-entry effects. The manual contains a valuable listing of relatively current references. Distribution is unlimited.

This manual provides guidance to the designers of facilities subject to accidental explosions and aids in the assessment of the explosion-resistant capabilities of existing buildings. It includes chapters on air blast; catering and ground shock; fragment ballistics, including a thorough description of secondary debris hazards, secondary explosions, and the dynamic properties of materials. It is intended to be used in conjunction with other structural design manuals and provides a comprehensive listing of references. Distribution is unlimited. This manual provides procedures for the analysis and design of protective structures exposed to the effects of conventional (non-nuclear) weapons and is intended for use by engineers with basic knowledge of weapons effects, structural dynamics, and hardened protective structures. Chapters cover topics such as uncertainties in protective design, air-blast effects, fragment protection, loads on structures, resistance of structural elements, and dynamic responses of structures. Distribution is limited.

This manual provides procedures for the design and analysis of protective structures subjected to the effects of conventional weapons. It is intended for use by engineers involved in designing hardened facilities. It includes chapters on air-blast effects, fire, incendiary and chemical agents, loads on structures, and auxiliary systems (piping, air ducting, and electrical cable). Distribution is unlimited.

Design of Structures to Resist Nuclear Weapons Effects, Manual 42 (ASCE, 1985). This manual was prepared for civilian use, and has been widely distributed throughout the world. It contains information on weapon detonation characteristics, radiation shielding, blast and shock-loadings, applicable limit-load theory, simplified dynamic analysis procedures, and design procedures for structures as well as equipment. Even though the procedures emphasized are perhaps oversimplified, the manual has a broad audience. Distribution is unlimited.

The Design and Analysis of Hardened Structures to Conventional Weapons Effects (DAHS CWE) (DNA, 1995). This new Joint Services manual, written by a team of more than 200 experts in conventional weapons and protective structures engineering, supersedes U.S. Department of the

Army TM 5-855-1, Fundamentals of Protective Design for Conventional Weapons (1986), and Air Force Engineering and Services Center ESL-TR-87-57, Protective Construction Design Manual (1989). The manual is based on state-of-the-art design information and methods for protective structures and includes new, recently analyzed and validated test data from the DNA test programs on conventional weapons effects, as well as design examples. Selected sections of the manual have unlimited distribution, but the manual as a whole has limited distribution. In parallel with this effort, a DAHS CWE hypertext system based on the DAHS CWE hardcopy manual is being developed. This electronic hypertext version is intended to transform the manual into an interactive computer product complete with text, figures, graphs, tables, equations, and a number of stand-alone computer codes such as BLASTX and FOIL. All DAHS CWE system software and codes will be produced and distributed on CD-ROM and will eventually operate on both DOS- and Unix-based platforms. The hypertext system is expected to be completed in the fall of 1995, Security Engineering, TM 5-853. The Department of Defense has recently shown an increased interest in applying systems engineering approaches to the design of military facilities for increased physical security against a range of threats, including terrorist attack. A three-volume security engineering manual has been developed that is intended for new construction and provides designers with guidance for protecting assets within facilities against a range of criminal, protester, terrorist, and subversive threats. Distribution is limited.

Terrorist Vehicle Bomb Survivability Manual (Naval Civil Engineering Laboratory, 1988). This manual contains information on vehicle barriers and blast survivability for buildings. It provides information to aid owners in protecting their property, assets, and personnel against terrorist vehicle bombs. This manual includes information on access control, vehicle barrier systems and testing, and sample blast vulnerability analyses. Distribution is limited. Structural Design for Physical Security—State of the Practice Report (ASCE, 1995). This report is intended to be a comprehensive guide for civilian designers and planners who wish to incorporate physical security considerations into their designs or building retrofit efforts. Individual chapters are devoted to threat determination, load definition, structural systems behaviour and design philosophy, structural components behaviour and design, security window design, door design, utility opening design, and retrofitting existing structures. Publication is expected in 1995. Balanced Survivability Assessment DNA has developed and uses a method of survivability assessment that also appears applicable to architectural design, particularly for retrofitting existing buildings. This method incorporates a comprehensive systems approach to survivability assessment. Its elements include consideration of a full-threat spectrum analysis, assessment of the capabilities of all the physical systems of the facility to meet the threat (system wide and single-point assessment), with assessment identification of the likelihood of failure and consequences on mission readiness and capability. It appears to the committee that this approach could be adapted to civilian application with relative ease. Computational Techniques During the past 25 years, powerful computer programs have been developed for predicting blast loads and the resulting structural response. This section discusses the methods used in and the validation of these programs. To provide the non expert reader with some background on the need for validation, the classifications of semi-empirical and first-principle programs and linear and nonlinear problems are introduced. The purpose of this discussion is to support the theme that since blast evolution and response problems are highly nonlinear, validation of the computer programs by experiments is a necessity.

The section also notes that a considerable degree of expertise is needed to use these programs effectively. DNA and other military organizations have conducted numerous tests and experiments for validating these computer programs over the years, and the need for validation is discussed later in this chapter. However, the structures in these validation tests and experiments were generally representative of military applications. It is not clear how relevant these previous tests are to civilian structures which are typically lighter in construction yet at the same time more structurally complex than the military structures tested. First-Principle and Semi-Empirical Methods Computer programs for the prediction of blast-effects can be subdivided in two groups: first-principle and semi-empirical. In first-principle programs, mathematical equations are solved that describe the basic laws of physics governing a particular problem. These principles are conservation of matter, momentum, and energy. In addition, mathematical relationships called constitutive equations, which describe the physical behaviour of materials, are needed. If these equations are solved accurately with suitable mathematical models, they should predict the blast loads and structural response. However, there are several barriers to accurate prediction of the effects of an explosion through the use of first-principle programs.

Among them are the following:

- In the calculation of blast due to explosions in air, the response of the air often involves complicated phenomena, such as dust-air mixtures, boundary effects, and turbulence. Turbulent flow, for example, cannot be calculated without the addition of models governed by empirical parameters.
- Calculation of the pressures imparted by a detonating explosive on the structure involves multiscale phenomena that are very difficult to deal with; such phenomena also occur in the structure during failure.

- In the calculation of structural failure, the behaviour of the materials is neither well understood nor readily characterized; in other words, accurate constitutive equations are not available for the materials, particularly in fracture or fragmentation.

While these deficiencies in first-principle codes are often compensated for by the use of engineering judgment, the main objective of first-principle techniques is to provide predictions in new domains where the experience that makes engineering judgment possible is not available. Semi-empirical computational methods are based on simplified models of physical phenomena, which are developed through analysis of test results and application of engineering judgment. These methods rely on extensive data and case studies. They involve fewer equations and require far less computer time, which makes them more practical than first-principle codes for design purposes. The computer programs applied in the evaluation of explosive effects cover two physical disciplines:

- Computational fluid dynamics (CFD), which is used for the prediction of the air blast caused by the explosion and the pressures applied to surfaces exposed to the propagating air blast; and
- Computational solid mechanics (CSM), which deals with the prediction of the response of structures to loads.

The pressures and the response of the structure are interrelated, and in many cases "coupled" analyses of the fluid and structure (where the fluid solution is obtained interactively with the structural solution) are needed. Coupled CSM-CFD solutions entail the use of much larger computer programs and are more costly, but they can provide more accurate predictions. Linear and Nonlinear Problems Computer models and programs have become indispensable in engineering design and development. The complexity and dependability of the models varies dramatically. To provide a perspective for blast programs, this section introduces several classifications. An important classification of computer simulation models and analyses is whether the governing equations and response are linear or nonlinear. Linear analysis is applicable when the displacements of a structure or medium are small and the stresses can be related to the deformation by linear relationships. Examples of linear analyses include acoustic-wave propagation and stress analyses of structures and machines under normal operating loads.

- Many parameters need to be input, including artificial viscosities and choices among methodologies, and their selection requires considerable experience.
- The development of inputs requires construction of detailed finite-element or finite-difference models, which entails selection of the features of the physical sites that are important and have knowledge of how to model them.
- Considerable skill is required to evaluate the output, both as to its correctness and its appropriateness to the situation modeled; without such judgment, it is possible through a combination of modeling errors and poor interpretation to obtain erroneous or meaningless results.
- Conversely, the generality of these programs and the relative ease with which details of a physical system can be incorporated in the simulation model, even by those without the requisite expertise, can lead to unwarranted confidence in the validity of specific results.

Therefore, successful computational modeling of specific scenarios by engineers unfamiliar with these programs is difficult, if not impossible. Current research is seeking ways to make these and other sophisticated computer programs more intuitive and user-friendly. The committee learned of one such effort to develop a powerful methodology which facilitates simulation-based design by providing the user with an expert system to assist in the development of the model and specification of the parameters required for a computational simulation. Such tools would make the programs developed for blast-effects simulation more accessible to engineers who are not experts in the programs themselves. Another impediment to the use of these programs is the magnitude of computational resources required. Some of the simulations take 20–100 hours on the most powerful supercomputers, such as the Cray C-90.

Small-scale, two-dimensional calculations can often be made on workstations in a matter of minutes or hours, but the time required grows rapidly as the model increases in detail. Other Applications of Numerical Simulation Techniques Computational methods are proven techniques that are used extensively in commercial engineering design and evaluation. For example, in the automotive industry, crashworthiness design is based on computer simulations which can predict passenger acceleration levels, and hence whether the crash can be survived without serious injury. CFD programs, similar to those used for blast prediction, are used to design the air flow for cooling the engine compartment and for drag reduction. The use of computer models in the automotive industry has reduced the numbers of prototypes that must be built during the design cycle and thus shortened the time required from inception of design to production. The automotive industry is able to amortize the cost of computer modeling over the large number of units produced.

Nonlinear computational mechanics is finding increasing application in design manufacturing processes, such as sheet-metal forming, extrusion, forging, and casting, and to simulate prototype tests, such as drop tests for electronic products and durability tests of safety-critical components. The methods used for prediction of blast effects and structural damage are identical to those used in manufacturing and some of the same computer programs are used in both areas. Computer Programs for Blast and Shock Effects Computational methods in the area of blast-effects mitigation are generally divided into those used for prediction of blast loads on the structure and those for calculation of structural response to the loads. Computational programs for blast prediction and structural response use both first-principle and semi-empirical methods. The governing equations of physics include conservation of momentum, conservation of energy, measures of stress and strain, and laws governing the relation between stress and strain, which depend on the physical properties of materials involved.

To some extent, prediction in solids is simplified as compared to fluids, since there is no counterpart to turbulence; however, the dynamic behaviour of solid materials generally is far more complicated than fluids, particularly when the structure fractures or fragments. Most explosion-induced structural response calculations are made in an uncoupled manner. This involves calculating blast loads as if the structure (and its components) were rigid and then applying these loads to a responding model of the structure. The shortcoming of this procedure is that when the blast field is obtained with a rigid model of the structure, the loads on the structure are often over predicted, particularly if significant motion or failure of the structure occurs during the loading period. An example of this was the over prediction of pressures in a numerical simulation using the FEFLO program after the World Trade Center bombing.

A current, active area of research is addressing the need for coupled calculations. In coupled calculations, the CFD model for blast-load prediction is solved simultaneously with the CSM model for structural response; that is, for a coupled calculation, the blast prediction program is linked with a structural response program. By accounting for the motion of the structure while the blast calculation proceeds, the pressures that arise due to motion and failure of the structure can be predicted more accurately. Several efforts in this direction are now under way. Under DNA sponsorship, FEFLO has been coupled to DYNA3D and its adaptivity features added to DYNA3D. This change allows FEFLO to be used for the blast calculation and DYNA3D for the structural response calculation.

Representative Computer Programs Used to Simulate Blast Effects and Structural Response Summary of Computational Codes Name Purpose Type Corporate Author Reference BLASTX Blast prediction Semi-empirical SAIC Britt and Lumsden, 1994 CTH Blast prediction First-principle Sandia National Laboratories McGlaun et al., 1990 FEFLO Blast prediction First-principle SAIC Baum et al., 1994 FOIL Blast prediction First-principle Applied Research Associates, Waterways Experiment Station Windham et al., 1993 HULL Blast prediction First-principle Orlando Technology, Inc. Gunger, 1992 SHARC Blast prediction First-principle Applied Research Associates, Inc. Hikida et al., 1988 DYNA3D Structural response First-principle Lawrence Livermore National Laboratory Whirley and Engelmann, 1993 EPSA-II Structural response First-principle Weidlinger Associates Atkatsh et al., 1994 FLEX Structural response Firm-principle Weidlinger Associates U.S. Department of Energy, 1992 ALEGRA Coupled analysis First-principle Sandia National Laboratories Budge and Peery, 1993 ALE3D Coupled analysis First-principle Lawrence Livermore National Laboratory American Society of Mechanical Engineers, 1993 DYNA3D/FEFLO Coupled analysis First-principle Lawrence Livermore National Laboratory/SAIC Löhner et al., 1995 FUSE Coupled analysis First-principle Weidlinger Associates Sandler and Rubin, 1990 MAZe Coupled analysis First-principle TRT Corporation Schlamp el al., 1995.

Code validation has occurred in all cases, with the rigor of a particular validation depending on such factors as code maturity, urgency of application, availability of funding, etc. Software availability to the private sector varies, with some codes being currently available for sale (e.g., FLEX), others classified as "export-controlled" (CTH), and some having limited availability due to national security classification. Corporate authors can provide availability information for particular codes. Except for a few cases where the code can be run on a personal computer (e.g., FLEX), these codes are generally of sufficient complexity to require workstation or mainframe hardware. Code Validation Prediction of the blast-induced pressure field on a structure and its response involves highly nonlinear behaviour. Computational methods for blast-response prediction must therefore be validated by comparing calculations to experiments. It is important to note, however, that experimental validation applies only to the class of events (or domain of applicability) encompassed by the experiments.

For example, an experiment involving explosive loading of an unreinforced concrete wall subject to a blast pulse of 20.67 megapascals (3,000 psi) peak pressure and with duration of 10 ms could be used only to validate a computer program for predictions for structures with similar characteristics and stiffness loaded over a similar pressure pulse. During the past 30 years, many experiments and tests have been conducted by the Department of Defense for the purpose of code validation. At the beginning of this period, CFD and CSM developments were in their infancy, and few experiments were designed specifically to validate individual codes; tests mainly focused on determining response modes and failure mechanisms of representative military structures. The response of this class of structures may be significantly different from conventional civilian structures for the reasons mentioned earlier. DNA recently conducted a series of experiments to evaluate the effects of penetrating weapons on hardened, reinforced concrete structures and to validate first-principle blast and structural response programs.

The test structure had reinforced concrete walls and horizontal slabs 45–60 cm thick and consisted of a series of rooms interconnected by corridors and door like openings. Tests were carried out at full scale and at one-third and one-sixth scale; in each experiment a high-explosive charge (representing the penetrated weapon) was detonated in one room, and blast pressures and response measurements were obtained in adjacent rooms. For this series of tests, the first-principle codes FEFLO, HULL, and SHARC were used for both blast propagation and structural response analyses. Initially, all calculations were two dimensional in that only the plane of the test structure was modeled. The results of the computations exhibited subtle differences, which were slight in the source chamber but showed substantial pressure differences in adjoining chambers.

This result was attributed to the large effect of turbulence on the transmitted pressures triggered at the doorways. Subsequently, full three-dimensional calculations were made with both first-order (HULL) and second-order (FEFLO) programs. The former, without adaptivity, under predicted the pressures in the adjoining chambers, but did exhibit the delay in the pressure spikes observed in the experiments; the FEFLO calculation compared quite well with the measurements. The response of the structures was determined in an uncoupled manner with FLEX, DYNA3D, and TRT computer programs, using computed pressures as a loading on the structures. The predictions of failure did not match the experiment in any of the analyses.

The discrepancy was ascribed to the difficulties in modeling the tensile failure of the concrete, an area of modeling that is still not well in hand. Recent tests performed by DNA on shallow-buried structures to validate an application of the DYNA3D and FLEX programs provide an example of the accuracy with which the deformation of a structure can be predicted when the structure remains homogeneous (i.e., does not encounter any tearing, fracture, or fragmentation). The tests were intended to study the interaction between the structure and the surrounding soil for different types of soil. A cylindrical structure was tested in both clay and sand. The cylinder and the surrounding soil were modeled in detail, and the pressures measured on the surface of the soil during the experiment were applied to the top surface of the model. The computations were made prior to the release of experimental response data, so there was no opportunity to "tune" the analysis.

The deformation can be seen to depend markedly on the surrounding medium; the deformations in clay are much larger and exhibit a different pattern of deformation. The computation accurately predicted the difference in the response in soil and clay and the magnitude of the deformation, illustrating the predictive capabilities of first-principle programs in certain instances. Some programs, under certain conditions, have produced results in excellent agreement with observations. In other cases, the differences between observed and predicted results have been great. These points to the need not only for ongoing testing but also for care in the selection of an appropriate model and input parameters and equal care in the interpretation of the results. Once a model has been validated over an experimental range, its real value lies in the richness of the predictive domain thus established. For example, the effects of attributes such as various window shapes, geometrical configurations, percentage of reinforcement, Adaptivity refers to the ability of a simulation model to initiate modifications to the analytic procedure(s) during program execution based on the model's "sensing" the results of the ongoing analysis.

The designers of civilian structures can make use of these validated results in the quest for improved building performance. Applications of Computational Methods to Terrorist Threats Several of the programs described above have already been applied to the evaluation of terrorist threats and events. The FEFLO code was used to analyze the explosion in the World Trade Center. This computation required 10,000,000 equations and approximately 150 hours on the Cray C-90. The model of the geometry of the area affected by the explosion was extremely detailed; even the cars in the parking lot were modeled. Nonetheless, in the later stages of the calculation, after the shock passes and turbulence develops, even this detailed a mesh was found to be inadequate for resolving the turbulent flow field. This calculation overestimated the blast loading because it did not account for the failure of the floors, the modeling of which would require coupling the program with a structural response program.

Several other analyses of the World Trade Center bombing were done with different suites of codes. One analysis using the CTH, BLASTX, and FLEX programs focused on interpreting explosive effects on the floor and roof slabs and failure patterns of the floor slabs. The analyses coupled the blast prediction with the floor response and showed that the principal mechanisms that limited the damage were due to the decrease in pressure and impulse that resulted from the progressive venting of the gas pressure and the large displacement of the slabs. Good correlations were obtained between computed and observed damage patterns in floor and ceiling slabs. Another analysis used BLASTX and some simple computer models of the floor slabs, but BLASTX proved inadequate for this class of problems because the long span wise dimensions of the parking floors led to significant over predictions of the impulse. The CTH, BLASTX, and FLEX suite of codes was also used to develop guidelines for the protection of U.S. embassies against explosions from terrorist attacks.

Tests were conducted with a one-third scale model to validate the computational results. Both internal and external explosions were considered. The predicted peak displacements of the exterior wall were within 15 percent of the measured values, but the final displacements differed by almost a factor of two. Nonetheless, the analyses were used to develop guidelines for structural design, including layout and anchorage of beams and slabs, and recommendations for mitigating progressive collapse due to detonation of explosives hand-carried into the building. The CTH and FLEX codes were also used by Weidlinger Associates to perform a vulnerability study of a hotel due to a car bomb explosion in the JFK Airport east parking garage, and to develop protection schemes for the Rockefeller Center control room against the threat of briefcase bombs.

The FLEX and FUSE codes were used to develop procedures for blast-hardening areas of a federal court building to explosions from package bombs; a similar study was made for the World Trade Center control center prior to the bombing. Summary Observations Over the past 50 years, design procedures have been developed for structures subjected to explosive blast loads. These procedures are based largely on synthesis of test data and simplified computational models and apply for the most part to the type of hardened structures found in military construction. These design procedures are codified in a variety of manuals and computer programs. While this body of knowledge can serve as a foundation for designing civilian buildings to be more blast-resistant, substantial effort will be required to make the methods more directly applicable and useful for civilian design professionals.

The available computer programs for prediction of blast-effects and structural response have been described and classified in several ways. From the viewpoint of a user, the most important classification is whether the programs are semi-empirical or first-principle in nature. First-principle codes are more generally applicable, but they require the user to be well versed in structural dynamics and explosive behaviour. For both classes of computer programs, validation by tests is imperative. To date, very little test data have been obtained for structures representative of civilian building design and construction practice. Application of these programs to blast-resistant design strategies in civilian buildings is of limited usefulness without appropriate experimental validation. Extending this technology to civilian design and construction practice affords a valuable opportunity to both solidify and advance the state of knowledge in this field. There are difficulties in understanding and mathematically modeling structural behaviour in transition regions of response from predominately flexural behaviour into domains dominated by boundary or punching shear, and ultimately to material disintegration. Also, material constitutive relationships are less well understood in these transition regions.

Nevertheless, computations can give valuable information about the magnitude and type of damage. The pressures resulting from complex, non-spherical explosive charges (e.g., car bombs) are not well understood and carefully controlled experiments are vital for a better understanding and validation of computer programs. Wherever possible, tests of civilian buildings and component types should be conducted at sufficiently large scale to allow the use of actual design details, materials, and construction practice. Despite some success in re-creating the observed effects of actual bombings and the cited examples where numerical codes were applied to specific design problems, it is not clear that the routine application of these programs to civilian buildings will become widespread.

The cost and complexity of the analysis, coupled with uncertainty regarding threat levels and the low probability that a specific building will actually become a target, all suggest that they will not. However, where these programs could prove very valuable is in testing a wide range of building types and structural details over a broad range of hypothetical explosion events. The knowledge gained from such testing, verified by experimentation, could transfer directly to civilian practice through manuals and other design aids, and ultimately into building codes, in much the same way as the application of seismic design principles has become routine.

Blast-Effects Mitigation Potential for Commercial Buildings

This chapter explores opportunities to apply blast-effects mitigation techniques to commercial buildings. Such opportunities may occur in several areas: in the architectural planning process, specifically, for example, in site selection or physical space planning; and in the design and placement of critical building systems, such as electrical and communications systems. Also special considerations are discussed for blast-effects mitigation in commercial buildings, such as below-grade vulnerabilities and the stack effect in high-rise buildings (two areas of vulnerability shown dramatically in the World Trade Center bombing). Where issues applicable to civilian buildings are addressed by military technical literature, these are pointed out as potential transfer opportunities.

Assessing Threats to Civilian Buildings In the aftermath of attacks on civilian buildings in the United States, many building owners must now consider the following questions when deciding whether their property might potentially be a target of terrorism:

- Who or what is the threat?

- Is a bomb a possible choice of weapon?
- What are the most likely scenarios or tactics for introducing a bomb into or near the building?

If an owner decides that there is reason to believe the property could be a target for a terrorist bomb, then the consequences of taking action should be considered:

- What resources, including technologies, are available to respond to the threat?
- What are the costs of applying those technologies?
- What the building tenants and occupants will tolerate the inconveniences or added expense for security measures?

U.S. Department of the Army (1993) Technical Manual TM 5-853 (Security Engineering) provides a systematic methodology to analyze "aggressor threats and tactics," including a system for rating potential risks and developing appropriate responses. The Defense Nuclear Agency (DNA) has developed an integrated systems approach, the balanced survivability assessment method, to evaluate the survivability of facilities against a wide spectrum of threats. Both of these techniques are directed primarily at military needs, though they could be used effectively for civilian applications. Answers resulting from these analyses would need to be weighed in the context of the functional and financial goals of the building owner.

Architectural Planning Process Having decided that a proposed or existing building requires protection from attack, the owner must assess what can be done to mitigate the effects of an explosion should one occur. Blast-hardening refers to all measures to reduce or eliminate the effects of an explosion. These included techniques such as physical space planning that deliberately use architectural location and organization of spaces and other nonstructural features to minimize the effects of an explosion on people and property. These options are discussed in U.S. Army

Technical Manual TM 5-853 to a limited degree, though the planning techniques in this manual are strongest in the area of supporting access control to the facility. All such options can be applied in the normal design of a building, just as designers now routinely incorporate seismic, wind, and fire protection features and systems in buildings.

The architectural planning process itself involves less technology than awareness and design skill, although technology may be needed to validate or revise empirical planning and design assumptions. In considering opportunities for technology transfer, it is useful to discuss here these planning techniques and consider how they might supplement or be supported by the technologies of hardening. Improving the performance of conventionally designed civilian buildings following an explosion begins with site selection and the architectural planning process. One of the first steps in protective planning for a new facility is to select a building site that allows access to the facility to be easily controlled so as to make delivery or placing of an explosive as difficult as possible. Locations to avoid, for example, include congested urban areas where it is difficult and costly to secure distance between the building and uncontrolled public rights-of-way.

Preferably, the site, its entrances, and the building itself should all be placed out of alignment with potential high-speed approaches by vehicles, such as would be the case of an entrance drive opposite a street. Distance between the building and streets or parking areas where potential vehicle bombs could be detonated is one of the most effective means of minimizing damage from explosions. The cost of land, however, must be considered in this measure. Control of surrounding streets and adjacent off-site parking is ideal, but rarely available to civilian commercial building owners. As to the building itself, earlier chapters discussed some technically sophisticated tools, especially computer codes, for designing structures to respond acceptably to explosions.

The following discussion explores less technical design approaches that, when applied with common sense, can economically reduce the effects of an explosion on the people and contents of the building. Of course, hardening parts of a building may also be necessary. Many planning and design response options could be considered for a new building or retrofitting an existing structure.

All the following options could be applied to new or retrofit situations- identifying potentially hazardous functions, such as mail- and freight-receiving and handling facilities. If a letter or package in freight is considered a likely means of introducing a bomb into a building (such as buildings housing celebrities who might be targets and who receive large volumes of unsolicited mail), providing such facilities in either a hardened area or a remote location, perhaps off site, might be considered, even at the cost and inconvenience this might involve. (TM 5-853 addresses bombs introduced through mailed or shipped packages in considerable detail.) Controlling or eliminating hazardous material storage on site. Fuel storage, trash holding, paint shops, and pressure vessels can contribute to the fire and smoke generated in an explosion, and might be located remotely from areas vulnerable to the introduction of a bomb, from means of egress, and from life-safety systems such as fire pumps and locating vulnerable functions away from uncontrolled public traffic areas to minimize blast-effects on occupants.

High-profile potential targets (and facilities for the particularly vulnerable such as children, the elderly, or handicapped) might be placed in remote, inconspicuous locations rather than, say, at the front of the building over the entrance. Offices and other continuously occupied spaces including day care centers can be located, for example, on the sides of the building away from streets or on interior courtyards. Street frontages can be reserved for circulation, non-vital equipment, storage, or other uses that could even be sacrificed to an explosion and absorb the initial shock. (TM 5-853 addresses this strategy briefly.) Providing dispersed, concealed, and controlled access to utility service entrances, fuel delivery, and storage facilities, and providing decentralized internal electrical and telecommunications distribution centers.

Frequently, these important utilities enter buildings near one another, are easily identified, and are relatively easily accessed by unauthorized persons. An explosion in the area of the utility service entrances could destroy all services in one stroke if they are all close together. (TM 5-853 is concerned with the vulnerability of utility openings to forced entry or introduction of chemical and biological agents, but not with protection of the utilities themselves. Where it is impossible or not cost-effective to locate utilities out of harm's way entirely, redundancy of vital systems, such as switchgear, primary feeders, power generators, sprinkler mains, and fire pumps, may be advisable. Wherever possible, the alternative source should be located in a protected area and remote from the primary source.

Determine the practical applications of physical security system. A wide assortment of surveillance, access control, and access-denial products are available to use to reduce the risk of bomb deliveries by persons or vehicles. These products are identified in such manuals as TM 5-853 and in commercially available sources.

Enhancing of refuge areas. Modern multistory buildings are allowed by many building codes to use "horizontal exits" in addition to the usual exit stairways. This concept permits large floor areas to be compartmented by fire and smoke barriers, so that persons fleeing fire and smoke in one area may move horizontally to an adjacent area. Occupants can either continue to exit by stair or remain in the area of refuge as long as necessary. Incapacitated persons need not negotiate fire stairs, at least immediately. As a result of an explosion, lower floors and means of egress from the building may be so severely damaged or filled with smoke that refuge areas may be needed for some period of time before rescue can be attempted successfully. The construction of the walls and partitions surrounding such areas might be strengthened to resist breach by flying debris. Additional accommodations to this situation can include emergency medical equipment, blankets, toilets, drinking water, radios, and flashlights in a designated area of each compartment.

Continually assessing the existing conditions and the availability of new technologies to mitigate blasts-effects. Any building owner or occupant who believes the building may be a target for bombings should undertake systematic threat and vulnerability assessments periodically and decide on any new courses of action if new technologies are available. The Balanced Survivability Assessments technique developed for military applications by DNA would provide an excellent basis for this task after being adapted to civilian situations. Controlling or eliminating parking and loading under or within the building. Vehicle parking and loading operations within or under an occupied building pose a major hazard, since vehicle bombs can be very large and powerful. Vehicle bombs may also elude detection, especially in high-volume facilities where inspection of vehicles with any regularity or thoroughness may be operationally and financially unacceptable.

Where parking or loading cannot be excluded, limiting the number of vehicles, such as those of tenants only, and providing machine-readable identifiers, vehicle-weight sensors, and spot checks are often acceptable compromises. Having a well-developed emergency operations plan to aid occupants after an explosion. Essential components of an emergency plan are the appointment of trained wardens, conducting practice drills, and regular review and update of emergency procedures. These measures are seldom appreciated by occupants in a peacetime environment and in situations other than high alert. They are often neglected or abandoned as soon as the sense of real urgency is lost. Disaster planning and emergency operations are two areas which can potentially return enormous dividends in terms of lives saved and suffering averted. A sample of the considerable literature in this field is included with the references to this chapter. Relocating functions and installing or upgrading fire- and life-safety features such as smoke control and evacuation. Fire and life-safety code requirements are becoming more stringent, especially for new buildings in urban locations. Periodic review of a facility's fire- and life-safety features and upgrades to new building standards seem prudent in any case, but such measures are more urgent for a facility that could be a target of terrorism.

Avoiding architectural features that magnify blast-effects. If there are architectural features that focus or increase blast-effects, they should be identified and avoided. (TM 5-853 indicates that re-entrant corners tend to cause blast pressures to build up.) Research is needed in this area to determine what other building configurations may have these properties.

Incorporation of controlled venting and other measures to mitigate the effects of internal explosions. There is a considerable body of knowledge on techniques to mitigate the effects of an internal explosion which has been developed as protection against accidental explosion in military, explosive, and chemical environments. (For example, U.S. Department of the Army [1990] Technical Manual TM 5-1300 (Structures to Resist the Effects of Accidental Explosions) discusses the use of blast valves for the controlled release of blast pressure from accidental explosions; Air Force Engineering and Services Center [1989] ESL-TR-87-57, [Protective Construction Design Manual] discusses the same topic for blasts resulting from weapon detonations.) Other methods of blast-effects mitigation available are blow-out panels for pressure relief and the use of "frangible" or sacrificial elements designed to fail to reduce the amplification of shock pressures.

Temperature-reducing systems to retard the development of high overpressures are also available. Research on these techniques is needed to determine their applicability to civilian office structures where the survivability of the occupants is the paramount objective. Designing windows that minimize the effects of blasts or applying such technologies as high-strength glazing or fragment curtains. A number of studies have been done on security windows resistant to explosions. Recently, research has been exploring more-robust window assemblies, including glazing for resistance to hurricane-blown debris. High-strength glazing materials, including glass block, tempered glass, and polycarbonates, and laminated and film-backed glass and fragment-entrapping meshes for fragment control are already in use for both security and storm resistance, but more research is needed to develop better assemblies and distribution of impact loads.

Designing elevator and stair shafts to resist smoke penetration by pressurization or compartmentation. Elevator entrances and cabs are currently not resistant to smoke penetration. In a fire or explosion emergency, persons may be trapped in elevators and overcome by smoke. Research is needed to explore the possibility of sealing elevators against smoke penetration and to meet fire-resistance standards. At the present, the only option is isolation of shafts in smoke or fire compartments. Pressurization of stair shafts is a design problem, especially in tall buildings where shafts must be interrupted to decrease the height of pressurized chambers and to control pressure levels.

Special Considerations for Hardening Existing Buildings Since there are many more existing buildings than planned new buildings; it is understandable that building owners and management would be more interested in ways to protect existing buildings. Structural Design for Physical Security, "Retrofitting Existing Structures," discusses some approaches for possible improvements to existing structural systems. Sometimes little or nothing can be done to protect existing buildings from explosions, such as older wall load-bearing structures in congested urban settings where closing adjacent streets to vehicle traffic cannot be done.

Defensive precautions, such as threat and vulnerability assessments, access control, and good intelligence and law enforcement, are always useful, but there are limitations to what building technologies can offer, and in some of these cases, the only option may be relocation. In addition to the architectural planning techniques discussed above, there are other means to harden typical existing civilian buildings against terrorist attacks. One consideration in commercial structures is that hardening features may be quite apparent when installed after the fact in an existing building, and most commercial building occupants do not want the appearance or the function of the building to be changed or to advertise their presence, if they are potential targets, by obvious security measures. Hardening a monumental structure such as the U.S. Capitol Building without changing its appearance or function would be technically challenging and extremely costly. Of course, many federal buildings have large security systems including on-site enforcement personnel.

Yet the attack on the Murrah Federal Building in Oklahoma City demonstrates the vulnerability of most governmental buildings. Other prominent buildings, such as places of worship, communications centers, courthouses, and office buildings, are not as security conscious as airports, banks, and museums. In addition to the planning techniques discussed in the previous section, structural reinforcement of some building elements may be possible through the use of:

- Additional mass;
- Additional strength, through modification of boundary conditions (e.g., supports to walls or floors), reduction in spans, or reduction in loaded areas;
- Replacement of weak components;
- Redundancy of structure;
- Strengthening of exterior curtain wall (by attention to windows or doors); and
- Strengthening of interior partitions.

However, some of these techniques may present problems. For instance, consider the addition of mass. Loading from TNT is dynamic in nature, while adding mass to a building component has an effect where damage is caused by impulsive loading. Also, the addition of mass contributes to the weight of the building, which often places greater demands on the existing framing and foundations. It is usually difficult and expensive to add additional foundation capacity. Adding strength and stiffness to the structure is also difficult, especially when attempts are made to decrease spans. Such approaches usually require additional columns or walls and clearly are not suitable for inherently long-span structures such as courtrooms, trading floors, retail sales floors, convention centers, sports arenas, performing arts centers, museums, or worship areas. Reduction of loaded areas usually refers to earth beams placed against the exterior walls of the building.

This solution has possibilities, depending on the site conditions and the exterior wall material, but it is certainly not a universal solution. Modifying boundary conditions also has its limits, especially when dealing with reinforced concrete structures. Wall load-bearing buildings are sometimes easily brought down by localized damage. Structural load-bearing members may need to be examined for their participation in the load-bearing system and to ascertain that they exhibit reasonable redundancy.

Structural redundancy has potential, especially in pre-cast structures or masonry-bearing wall structures. The designer may ensure that, when certain key elements (columns or walls) of a structure are damaged or destroyed, alternate load paths are provided so that the building will not undergo progressive or total collapse. Often this retrofit procedure only requires additional means of tying the structure together. For significant blast resistance, substantial and compact structural forms—such as box-type construction, with strong walls, roof, and floor—are often preferred. The building material most commonly used throughout the world, because of its relatively low cost and ease of fabrication, is concrete.

Although concrete is a relatively brittle material, it is rendered ductile through steel reinforcing. For resistance to high pressures, care with the details of reinforced columns, connections, and walls is required; special reinforcing may include closely spaced ties throughout the element, with attention given to the reinforcing and tie-in to other walls and slabs at the edges where much of the resistance is developed. In some cases, the use of fiber-reinforced (metal or polymer) concrete can be effective. Quite obviously, anticipated loading conditions will influence the design, but reinforced concrete structures can be expected to be relatively thick (102 to 103 mm) to provide the mass and strength to resist blast pressures. Steel structures also need special attention where they are employed to resist intense blast loading or are expected to respond in an inelastic manner. Of particular concern are those connections that, if they fail, can lead to instability of the structure, and possibly collapse.

For both steel and concrete structures, the designer should consider redundancy in supporting members, to help ensure the survivability of the structure even if some columns or other critical members are severed. Although current design procedures provide guidelines on how to enhance the breaching resistance, it is often impractical to protect against breaching and direct shear effects by conventional means. Alternative reinforcement details should be employed when heavy shear (diagonal, punching, or direct) is expected. Special materials and combinations of materials (e.g., high-strength concrete, perhaps combined with fiber reinforcement, and layering with energy-absorbing material) might possibly be employed in such situations. Strengthening exterior curtain walls may be quite effective against a bomb placed outside a building. Assuming the structure can resist the loading from the bomb, substantial damage can be avoided by not letting the blast wave into the building.

Typically, doors and windows are the weak points. Windows can now be protected to some degree by several means: polyester fragment retention films, polyethylene terephthalate (PET) backing or interlayer, heat-strengthened and tempered glass, polycarbonate-sheet and urethane/glass composite glazing, and polyvinyl butyrate (PVB) interlayer or combined PVB-PET laminated glazing. Security windows and glazing are discussed in the U.S. Army Technical Manual TM 5-853 and Structural Design for Physical Security, (ASCE, 1995). Various available shutter designs can decrease blast loading on the windows, although they are only useful with advance notice of a threat. Nylon and Kevlar® mesh curtains can also be used inside the windows to contain blast fragments, or special blast windows can be purchased. Special blast doors are available, though they can be too massive for high-frequency applications. Security doors are generally marketed for ballistic and forced-entry resistance, and while these doors are suitable for regular high-frequency use, their performance under blast conditions is unknown. Although these solutions have some impact on appearance, they can often be acceptable. (Security doors are also discussed in TM 5-853.)

More research is needed on these assemblies, research that might also benefit design of windows and doors for protection from projectiles during high winds such as hurricanes. Selected metal stud and drywall interior partitions can be replaced with steel plate on hot-rolled steel framing. Steel-plate shear walls have been used in buildings before, to resist horizontal loads when thick, reinforced, concrete shear walls occupy too much space. Drywall interior partitions can also be replaced with reinforced masonry walls with a spray-on concrete/steel mesh or Kevlar or ballistic nylon. When these interior partitions are tied into the existing structure, they increase the stiffness of the building, with minimal impact on the appearance or function of the interior space. Because of the high cost of retrofitting existing buildings for blast-effects mitigation, developing improved methods of monitoring and controlling the flow of people into and out of facilities may prove to be the most cost-effective way to frustrate terrorist bombing attempts for the long term.

Vulnerabilities of Civilian Structures

The trend in new civilian building design for the last 50 years has been toward the use of lighter but stronger materials. This has led to more economical buildings, with the structure accounting for less of the floor area and lower first costs. During this same period of time, engineers have developed a greater understanding of building performance when a structure is subjected to dynamic horizontal and vertical forces associated with wind and earthquake. In a situation involving earthquake loading, the design forces decrease as the weight of the building decreases. Seismic design calls for the building to possess adequate strength (force and ductility-resistance characteristics) so as to resist the repetitive seismic motions in a manner that protects human lives and leaves the building usable, or, at the most, with damage that is easily repairable. When designing for wind and earthquake loads, therefore, it is advantageous, especially for the upper levels, to use lightweight non-structural building materials such as metal stud and drywall partitions instead of masonry.

The dynamic loading on buildings caused by explosions differs in important respects from dynamic loads imposed by earthquake and wind. These latter loads are of relatively low intensity, long duration (seconds to minutes), and essentially oscillatory (periodic in nature). Explosive loads, by comparison, are extremely large initially, act for very short durations of time (milliseconds), and are non-oscillatory (aperiodic). For explosive loads localized in the lower levels, characteristic of terrorist bombing incidents, the lower levels of a structure should be massive to effectively resist the large, short-duration loading. This goal is generally in keeping with seismic requirements where significant strength is called for in the lower levels. Sound engineering judgment, of course, should be used in the design of buildings to withstand short-duration explosive incidents.

During the design process, particular attention should be paid to the following factors, because under certain conditions, or in combination with other factors, they may positively or negatively impact building performance following an explosion:

- The use of lightweight materials—especially in nonstructural applications;
- The use of very long spans;
- The use of live-load reductions permitted by codes;
- The vulnerability, especially of pre-cast systems, to progressive collapse;
- The strength of the exterior cladding and its effect on the structural system;
- The effect of the loss of an individual column; and
- The behaviour of ductile framing systems.

A discussion of the design and behaviour of structural components typically used in modern civilian buildings subjected to a transient blast-wave form is contained of Structural Design for Physical Security (ASCE, 1995). Although not specifically addressed to blast-effects, design for lateral loading for wind and earthquake is the subject of two important military publications (U.S. Department of the Army, 1986, 1991; and two civilian publications (ASCE, 1993; FEMA, 1994) as well as the three Model Building Codes. Vulnerabilities of Nonstructural Building Systems Recent instances of buildings that have suffered the effects of an explosion, such as the World Trade Center, have demonstrated that if the structure of the building survives and does not progressively collapse, the greatest problems are experienced during evacuation and rescue, when fire and smoke control and other critical building systems may not provide the necessary support. Most buildings are designed to resist events of seismic origin, fire, flood, wind, snow, and similar natural and human-caused events.

Long experience with these perils has permitted rational codification of how a building and its systems must perform to achieve several critical goals to allow:

- The maximum number of occupants to escape,
- The minimum number of injuries and fatalities to be sustained,
- The protection of property, and
- Emergency personnel to control or prevent further destruction of the building while these objectives are accomplished.

Few civilian buildings in the United States are designed to withstand the effects of an explosion within or adjacent to the structure, although the design features for more common emergencies will also help to achieve the same objectives in the event of an explosion. After any disaster—fire, flood, or bomb explosion—a building's systems are major factors in the recovery period when evacuation, and, ultimately, reoccupancy and return to normal operation are the principal objectives. A modern building can be thought of as a set of interdependent systems and subsystems, rather than as a group of autonomous elements such as wall, floor, roof, and so forth. The structural system is probably the most vital, since failure of even part of this system may directly and immediately threaten all other systems. Extreme examples include the nearly total destruction of the Alfred P. Murrah Federal Building in Oklahoma City and the U.S. Marine barracks in Beirut.

The structural system and its protection have therefore been extensively studied, and technologies for designing this system to resist failure following an explosion are discussed in this report. Nonstructural building systems have been given less attention in blast-effects mitigation technology. However, the survival of some of these systems is essential to the rescue and evacuation of building occupants and to the recovery of the building to normal use. Therefore, the roles of these nonstructural systems in civilian buildings are addressed here. Three general types of nonstructural systems are defined for the present discussion.

The first type of nonstructural system consists of those systems that may be critical for survival and evacuation during and immediately after an explosion:

- The electrical system supports lighting to aid in evacuation, fans that may be designed for smoke exhaust, occupied elevators at the time of an explosion, fire pumps, and numerous control systems that may ensure the function of security and communications systems.
- Communications systems allow building occupants to be notified of the nature of the emergency and instruct them in evacuation and provide contact with outside rescue and emergency forces.

- Plumbing systems deliver water for extinguishing fires, provide for hygiene and drinking during entrapment situations, and are used in administering first aid.
- Ventilation systems provide pressurization and exhaust to control and contain smoke.
- Circulation systems, including corridors, stairs, doors, and ramps, provide the means for occupants to escape and emergency personnel to enter the building.

All of these systems must be operational and support each other in their various tasks to enhance the likelihood of survival of individuals not killed by the explosion itself. The second group of nonstructural building systems may not in themselves play active roles in survival or rescue activities following an explosion, but they may attenuate, propagate, or contribute to the effects of an explosion:

- Exterior wall systems consisting of interdependent subsystems: - wall construction—pre-cast panels, metal panels, masonry, framed, and so forth—that is basically supported by the structural system; - sash supported by the wall system; - glazing supported by the sash, although polycarbonate glazing could hold the sash together; - sun-control system supported by the sash or soffit which could contain glass fragmentation, if in the form of a film or mesh, or contribute fragments, if in the form of blinds.
- Interior partition system - metal runners and studs supported by the structural system; - drywall panels supported by the studs and perhaps holding them together following an explosion; - finish materials supported by the drywall, and, in the case of some fabrics, possibly holding the drywall together under the effects of an explosion.
- Interior ceiling system: - suspension grid supported from the structural system; - ceiling panels supported on the grid system; - lighting fixtures supported on the grid system:

- Interior mechanical and electrical distribution systems: - heating, ventilating, and air-conditioning terminal units and ductwork supported by the structural system and perhaps easily dislodged by an explosion; - electrical conduit usually hung under the structural system and possibly severed by structural failure or directly damaged by an explosion if it occurs nearby (exposed or ruptured power lines may pose a threat to occupants and emergency personnel, or contribute to fire); - piping for water and gas under pressure usually hung under the structure, and, like conduit, possibly destroyed by the structure if it fails or is breached by the explosion itself (loss of fire-fighting water not only loses the fire-extinguishing function, but can pose a threat of flooding to occupants, other systems, and rescue personnel).

These systems may perform in any number of ways in an explosion, either absorbing some of the shock, shielding people or property from fragments, or becoming lethal fragments themselves. In the case of an exterior explosion, loss of the exterior wall allows greater damage to the interior of the building. Strengthening the exterior wall and window systems has been studied, and design information is available in the TM 5-853 manual and elsewhere. However, little research appears to have been done on how these and other assemblies might be protected from the effects of an explosion in order to reduce the possibility of damage to critical systems. On the other hand, breach of any part of the building's envelope or of the enclosure of a space in which an explosion occurs will relieve pressures, possibly to the benefit of the building and its occupants. The effects of venting are discussed in the U.S. Department of the Army Technical Manual (1990) TM 5-1300. The BLASTX computer code provides computational methods to predict the effects of explosions in vented conditions.

The third type of system assures the continued functioning or rapid repair of certain building systems for the continued beneficial use of the structure after the building sustains serious damage. The definition of this type of system depends to some extent on the user's objectives and expectations, the type and location of the building, the season during which the event occurs, and what recovery-time interval is sought. Examples of this type of system include:

- Mechanical temperature conditioning, as may be essential for computers supporting other systems, for certain laboratories and medical functions, and for food or other low-temperature storage needs.
- Elevators.
- Water and sewer service.
- Security and perimeter control, such as may be needed to protect secure information, or sensitive or vital facilities, or to control inmates or prevent looting.

Additional choices will have to be made according to the circumstances, financial considerations, and priorities of the building user or owner. Below-Grade Vulnerabilities in Civilian Buildings Many modern buildings and complexes have parking, loading, and service areas within the building, and because vehicles are capable of surreptitious transport of large explosive charges, the location of critical systems in such areas as basements, where the above-mentioned functions are often placed, is a common vulnerability. This arrangement often reflects the desire to reserve above-ground building areas for occupancies that benefit from access to daylight, and in some cases, it also reflects the desire to maximize the above-grade envelope permitted by zoning. Primary electrical switchgear is commonly located in a below-grade room (which is at a garage level in many buildings) simply because large commercial electric service is usually delivered underground.

Although this equipment is housed in a separate, controlled access room, the enclosing construction is designed to meet fire codes only and is poorly equipped to withstand an explosion. If the room is located adjacent to or in the midst of the vehicle parking area, some of the main feeders from this equipment are also potentially exposed to an explosion from a vehicle bomb. If the building has a secondary power source from an alternative substation or even a power grid, the switchgear for that service is also typically placed in a similarly vulnerable location, if not in the same vicinity. If the building or complex has emergency power generation on site, the generator(s) might be located remotely from the main switchgear, but the generator controller and automatic-transfer switching equipment is typically mounted in the same room as the switchgear.

An explosion that breaches the switchgear room also renders the emergency system inoperable, leaving the building with neither primary nor backup electricity. The generators themselves are usually situated for ease of heat and exhaust rejection on an outside wall in an areaway or even in a separate structure. In some buildings, however, the generators are also located in basement areas, making them subject to the same vulnerabilities noted above. Generator and switchgear rooms below grade are also vulnerable to water damage or flooding if an explosion ruptures water piping in the vicinity and there is insufficient drainage or pumping capacity. Building control centers for refrigeration and other building operating systems may also be located below grade in or near the central mechanical equipment room, if it is also below grade. This arrangement is vulnerable to the same risks in the event of an explosion. If this control center also includes security, communications, fire alarm, and other systems, its loss could be catastrophic. Buildings with early (non-enhanced) fire-detection and annunciation systems may have the main fire-panel controller and power supply in the switchgear room also.

Buildings with enhanced systems have their fire-control panel located just inside the lobby doors for rapid access by fire officials, but in this location, the panel may be vulnerable to an explosion in the lobby area. As is typical of other commercial utilities, voice and data communications services usually enter a building underground, into a room that may also contain the main distribution frames. In some cases, this room also houses the electronic switching equipment that routes calls within the building and is the interface with the local telephone exchange. If the switching equipment is owned by a private telephone service provider, it may serve several adjacent buildings as well. A below-grade location adjacent to areas accessible to vehicles is vulnerable in the same way as the primary electric power service room. The main water and sewer services are also located below-grade level, and are usually co-located with the building's fire pump, Siamese connection, standpipe, and sprinkler manifolds.

This equipment may be enclosed in a room, but also may be placed behind a chain-link barrier that is intended only to discourage tampering and vandalism. Again, if this equipment is within or adjacent to vehicle parking areas, it may be lost in an explosion, and in addition to the loss of the services of water supply for fire and hygiene, the probability of flooding and interruption of other systems is high. Mechanical heating, cooling, and ventilation equipment may be located below-grade, at, or adjacent to, parking levels, especially if the building is subject to height or setback restrictions or other zoning constraints. This equipment and its attendant piping and ductwork are mostly in enclosed rooms, though the rooms are usually not resistant to blast-effects. However, air ducts are connected to the fan housings to bring outside air into the system and to distribute it into the building above and chilled and hot water lines pass into and out of the room.

Any of these ducts or pipes that traverse an area exposed to an explosive source is vulnerable to loss. Most modern buildings are totally dependent on mechanical systems, and the loss of these systems can jeopardize recovery of vital functions that permits rapid reoccupancy and resumption of the building's business. Shafts for utilities are typically adjacent to stair and elevator shafts and subject to many of the same vulnerabilities. Utilities can also be severed in these shafts by explosion-generated debris. The most serious damage to building systems, then, can probably be accomplished from a vehicle-transported bomb that is detonated in a building's basement areas, simply because a number of critical building systems are typically found in this location, as is much of their control and distribution equipment. A garage detonation also has significant potential for fire and smoke because of the large amount of combustible materials present in and on the vehicles that may be parked there.

Any basement vehicle parking areas, therefore, should be given particular attention when considering blast-hardening features or access control and detection, perhaps even at the expense of other measures when available funds are limited. Protecting Nonstructural Systems Blast-resistant, reinforced concrete walls can be constructed to decrease the effects of an explosion in or around buildings, including protection of many of the critical systems discussed above. Since little research has been done on the protection of systems or behaviour of common building assemblies following an explosion, the following discussion is limited to a few of the planning techniques available to design professionals to remove at least parts of these systems from harm's way. As a general principle, critical services should be decentralized and, wherever possible, separated from garages, loading docks, and vehicle routes.

Where emergency or alternative systems exist, they should be kept as remote as possible from primary systems. Although there are some first-cost economies in placing the electric switchgear, emergency generator controls, and fire panels in the same room, this practice places the building at greater risk of losing three critical systems in a single event. Physically decentralizing critical systems and their components may help one or more of these systems survive or may reduce the extent of damage to them, thus reducing the time needed to repair and restore them. Rooms containing critical systems may be placed behind or nested within other rooms deeper in the building to achieve greater distances from areas of vehicle access. Of course the same logic can be applied to non-critical systems as well. A design precaution may be to keep critical services away from exterior walls that face possible locations for a bomb at the building's exterior.

A more drastic solution would be to place as many services as possible in floor raceways or in access floors, where they would be less exposed to explosions. Some hardening at little or no cost can be achieved during building design by locating lower floor chases behind protective building elements where they are less likely to be in the line of an approaching blast wave. It may also be useful to orient the elevator lobby's lengthwise axis perpendicular to the anticipated location of an explosion, such as a parking place along the building's street frontage. Garage-level auxiliary rooms, such as those housing the primary electric service, are usually constructed of concrete masonry units that have poor resistance to side-loading, and it is doubtful that these assemblies could withstand a nearby explosion even if retrofitted with interior or internal bracing.

Blast-response technology may permit the design of a device, baffle, or room shape that can deflect the shock wave away and toward a less critical building component or a component that is known to successfully resist blast-effects, such as underground perimeter walls. Some protection can be afforded to elevators and stair shafts by not having them be continuous from upper stories to basement levels. Separate elevators and stairs can be provided for the below-grade floors. This design is often desirable for security reasons as well. However, existing buildings have few if any options other than to construct stand-off barriers to keep vehicles as far as possible from elevators and stair shafts.

Stack Effect in High-Rise Buildings

The vast majority of the injuries caused by the World Trade Center bombing were not the result of direct impingement of fire or explosion, but from smoke and dust inhalation. Smoke and dust were driven upward through both towers by stack action, filling the stair shafts and many of the floors. The stack effect in tall buildings is similar to the behaviour of a chimney: the colder, heavier air outside of the chimney pushes the warmer, lighter air inside of the chimney to the top; this action stops when the flue is closed. Each of the towers of the World Trade Center is like a chimney, with the warm air inside of the building pushed up by the cold air outside, generating an upward flow through the towers, particularly during the cold winter months.

To minimize this air flow, an air lock was constructed around each of the two towers. Passing through the revolving doors is, in effect, passing through the air lock. With the detonation of the bomb, much of the masonry wall along the south wall of the north tower at the basement level, where the explosion occurred, was blown into the building. Other masonry work surrounding the shuttle elevator shafts was blown into those shafts. (Similar but lesser damage was done to the south tower.) In this way, the air locks were breached, particularly for the north tower. With the loss of the air locks, the smoke- and dust-laden air from the bombed area was drawn into and upward through the towers by stack action. The problem was aggravated in areas where tenants broke windows.

It is conjectured that had the air locks survived the explosion, the smoke-laden air would have been confined to below-grade areas of the complex and would not have been forced into the towers, and perhaps several hundreds of millions of dollars of nonstructural damage would have been averted and personal injuries would have been greatly reduced. Much less smoke was found in the south tower where the air locks remained largely intact. Controlling stack effect in tall buildings is mechanically complex and worthy of further study. Economic Considerations It is reasonable to expect that blast-hardening a building will cost an owner additional money, whether the building is in the design stages or already exists. A blast-hardened building may cost more to operate and maintain as well, especially for increased security staff.

For a building still in the concept or design stage, additional first costs may include services of consulting experts, perhaps some testing or modeling, and the increased expense of nonstandard design, nonstandard construction practices, and, possibly, the purchasing and use of unusual materials. Existing buildings would entail these same costs plus the cost of retrofit demolition and perhaps the loss of some usable or rentable area occasioned by the relocation of subsystems or the creation of buffer spaces. For this discussion, properties may be divided into two broad classes: those constructed by an owner for the owner's use and those expected to perform as a financial investment. The economic factors in these two classes differ according to the owner's objectives. Buildings constructed by and for an owner include owner-occupied office buildings, such as corporate headquarters, warehouse and distribution facilities, process and production plants, and civilian government buildings. The facility typically does not need to compete financially directly with other similar facilities.

The owner does not expect a return on the investment through leasing or renting these facilities to a second party, although some building owners may reduce their own floor space needs and rent or lease out other portions to lower their costs. When such a facility is being planned, the concern for protecting it against attack is based on the owner's assessment of risk. This assessment may depend on the owner's potential attractiveness to an attacker, perhaps for offering a controversial product (tobacco) or service (abortion), or for suffering an unpopular public image (a petroleum company or a multinational corporation that operates in many foreign countries, where it must try to satisfy diverse and often conflicting social and cultural expectations). While any owner must weigh the costs of protection against the perceived threat, this type of owner may be more willing to install security, because in an owner-occupied building convenience or preference of the occupants are less of a concern than for a commercial building requiring access by the general public. Since ease of public access is not a major determining factor, in this case the owner is also more likely to emphasize physical security measures to intercept an attacker through access control.

Rather than taking measures to mitigate damage from a successful attack, this type of owner may be more interested in avoiding disruption of whatever processes are taking place at the facility. This type of owner may also not be as concerned with space utilization as a commercial owner would be, and may be able to make more use of design strategies such as buffer space against outside walls and increased stand-off distances. Since the degree of occupant satisfaction is a prerogative of the owner, fenestration and other fragile building components can be reduced or eliminated, which could, in fact, result in lower direct costs of construction, operation, and maintenance than would have been the case for a building of conventional design and construction. On the other hand, buildings constructed as financial investments are expected to provide a return on their costs by generating revenues as a direct result of their use by others.

Commercial office buildings, retail and mixed-use centers, and recreational facilities are typical of this class of structures. Moreover, these investments are made in a very price-competitive environment where even small-cost excursions can and do affect investment decisions. The discussion and accompanying cost models conclude that the construction premium for blast-hardening does not materially impact the financial performance of a commercial building. The committee believes that reasonable blast resistance can be accomplished for about a 5 percent premium in construction cost which equates to an increase of the lease premium of about 3.5 percent. However, there are still financial and other barriers to incorporating blast-hardening features in such buildings. Commercial developers and their investors are wary of anything that alters the traditional financial profile of a building or that injects an unknown element in its liquidity potential, refinancing value, or market position, or other factors that could in any way impact the property's performance as an investment. Since every element in the development of an investment-grade property must pass a rigorous cost/benefit analysis to ensure that the added element does not dilute the anticipated return on investment, the decision to add a non-revenue element, such as blast-resistant construction, to a building would be much more likely if there were some cost-recovery mechanism available.

Some of these mechanisms could be tax credits, reduced insurance costs, or more favorable lender terms. However, none of these mechanisms are available today, nor are they being contemplated. The most attractive and likely incentive for including blast protection in an investment property would be finding a long-term tenant, such as a government agency, that is sensitive to security issues and is willing to pay a higher rent for a blast-hardened building. Such a long-term lease would allow the developer to recover his costs. It also delays the time when it becomes necessary to find a replacement tenant with the same security concerns, or to compete for another tenant against properties with lower cost bases and operating expenses. Finding a tenant who is willing to pay higher rent may mean advertising or promoting the property as blast-resistant, and most developers would be reluctant to do this because the advertising could be interpreted as a challenge and might actually invite an attack on what otherwise is an unremarkable target.

Development and publication of security measures or blast-effects mitigating technologies may also carry the risk of liability potential, so the dissemination of technology may have to be done in a way that does not put the source at risk. Casualty insurers are most affected by damage to a property caused by an explosion, because of both repair costs and insured lost revenues. The potential for terrorist activity at a specific building can affect its insurability when an insurer believes that a tenant of the building is a high-profile target. A positive side of the economics of effective blast-hardening is the reduction in personal injuries or deaths with inevitable claims and the reduction in repair costs and lost revenues following an explosion. To the extent that the structure and its systems are able to resist blast-effects, occupants are better protected, repairs are more easily made, and the time the building is nonfunctional is reduced, along with the revenue losses to the occupant businesses. Additional benefits are possible to the extent that blast-hardening features improve a building's resistance to accidental explosions, which can result from the improper storage of chemicals, or fuel or gas leaks, for example.

Representatives of the building industry, such as the Building Owners and Managers Association, generally corroborate the observation that there is a low level of continuing public concern about terrorist attacks on commercial buildings in the United States. In the case of the World Trade Center, public attention and concern were very high in the months that followed, only to subside as time passed. Time will tell if interest in the Oklahoma City bombing will be brief, or if a sustained level of concern will develop into widespread demand for blast-resistant measures in commercial buildings. Agents for Technology Transfer Successful transfer of relevant military technology to the civilian sector must overcome several significant barriers: inadequacy of professional education, inaccessibility of information, and lack of financial incentives. Agents for affecting this technology transfer must be selected with these barriers in mind and the specialized knowledge and resources are required to effectively realize the blast-effects mitigation potential for commercial buildings.

Today, a select number of architect-engineer firms specializing in hardened military design and construction are also engaged in civilian building design and thus possess the requisite capabilities. Many of the design-oriented computer programs described in were developed by research-oriented firms who frequently assist architect-engineer teams in the application of their design tools. However, if these technologies are to gain widespread acceptance, a major effort must be made to broaden the educational and experiential base within the profession. The agents for technology transfer are many and normally take months or years to be developed and disseminated. Past experience suggests that documents or reports that address certain aspects of the problem will become available; an example is the ASCE (1995) document currently being developed. Over time, if demand is sufficient, a series of such guideline documents could be expected.

The sponsors for such documents could be technical societies, governmental laboratories, or contracted documents could be supported and funded by any number of sources. These guideline documents, even though not referenced in building codes, can normally be used in building design or retrofit. The guideline provisions normally far exceed code requirements, however, the professional would have to be sure that adopted procedures are not in violation of any building code procedures or other local, state, or federal ordinances. In time, such material will naturally find its way into texts and special courses in universities and colleges. This evolutionary process has occurred in many sub disciplines. In the civil engineering field, such design topics as wind, earthquakes, and other natural phenomena, offshore platforms, major pipelines, and criteria for nuclear power plants have evolved in this general manner. The schools of architecture, construction, and engineering in our country's universities have a unique ability to transfer technology through education, and they must be part of the process.

So too must the professional societies, such as the American Institute of Architects, the American Society of Civil Engineers, the National Society of Professional Engineers, the American Society of Heating, Refrigerating, and Air Conditioning Engineers, the Association of General Contractors, the Association of Building Contractors, and the American Society for Industrial Security. Federal and state governments are also good candidates as agents of technology transfer, since they have a long-term concern to protect their own commercial office buildings. They are not subjected to all of the code issues that pertain to the private sector, and hence could incorporate blast-effects mitigation technology in their office buildings at a faster rate than the private sector. Also, the initial additional cost is not as great a concern when balanced against long-term objectives. Because the same designers typically work on both government and civilian office buildings, technology transfer would be much quicker. This same transfer technique is being used to introduce the metric (SI) system of units into civilian design and construction. Government agencies are requiring the SI units for their building projects and hence building designers who want to do the work are quickly making the necessary conversion.

4

Illegal Firearm Acquisition

Firearms are bought and sold in markets, both formal and informal. To some observers this suggests that one method for reducing the burden of firearm injury is to intervene in these markets so as to make it more expensive, inconvenient, or legally risky to obtain firearms for criminal use. As guns become more expensive to acquire or hold, it is hypothesized that criminals will reduce the percentage of their criminal careers in which they are in possession of a gun. However, the pervasiveness of guns and the variety of legal and illegal means of acquiring them suggests the difficulty of keeping firearms from people barred by law from possessing them. The goals of this chapter are to provide a systematic analytic framework linking interventions to the outcomes of interest and to describe what is known about the effectiveness of those interventions.

We also suggest a research agenda that addresses the major unanswered questions. Market-based interventions intended to reduce criminal access to guns include taxes on weapons and ammunition, tougher regulation of federal firearm licensees, limits on the number of firearms that can be purchased in a given time period, gun bans, gun buy-backs, and enforcement of laws against illegal gun buyers or sellers. Other interventions that may have market effects—for example, storage requirements (such as trigger locks or the placement of firearms in secure containers) and mandating new technologies that personalize guns so only lawful owners can fire them—are dealt with in detail elsewhere in the report. While these new technologies may make new guns less attractive relative to older secondhand guns and thus reduce the attractiveness of guns in aggregate to offenders, the potential market effects are probably secondary to other mechanisms by which these interventions may lower firearms injuries, such as preventing children from accidentally hurting themselves or others.

Little is known about the potential effectiveness of a market-based approach to reducing criminal access to firearms. Arguments for and against such an approach are based largely on speculation rather than research evidence. There is very little of an analytic or evaluative nature currently available in the literature on market interventions. Even on most descriptive topics (e.g., gun ownership patterns, types of guns used in crimes), there are only a few studies, often not well connected, that have been adequately summarized in existing papers). We begin with a brief discussion of legal and illegal firearms commerce, followed by a summary of what is known about the methods by which offenders acquire guns. We then present an analytic framework to understand the effects of specific interventions on gun markets. The next section reviews the literature evaluating various interventions. The final section presents the committee's views about high-priority research activities.

The relationship of firearms acquisition and markets to suicide is quite different and is discussed in the chapter on suicide. We note that the interventions discussed here may impose costs on legitimate users of firearms. A waiting period law inconveniences hunters and others who use firearms in legitimate fashion. In addition to delays, the system may generate errors, causing unnecessary embarrassment or worse. Some interventions putatively have no such effects and may even facilitate the activities of legitimate owners; for example, gun buy-backs can only help by providing another outlet for individuals wishing to dispose of existing weapons with minimal inconvenience. No research has explored these effects, although they may be important in forming attitudes toward gun control proposals.

Offenders Obtain Firearms

In the United States, there are some 258 million privately owned firearms, including nearly 70 to 90 million handguns. Some 4.5 million new firearms, including about 2 million handguns and about 2 million secondhand guns, are sold each year in the United States. Legal firearms commerce consists of transactions made in the primary firearms market and in the largely unregulated secondary firearms market. Acquisitions (other than theft) of new and secondhand firearms from federal firearms licensees (FFLs), whether conducted properly or not, form the primary market for firearms. Retail gun stores sell both new and secondhand firearms and, in this regard, resemble automobile sales lots.

FFLs are required to ask for identification from all prospective gun buyers and to have them sign a form indicating that they are not prohibited from acquiring a firearm; the FFL must also initiate a criminal history background check of all would-be purchasers. FFLs are also required to maintain records of all firearms transactions, report multiple sales and stolen firearms to the Bureau of Alcohol, Tobacco, and Firearms (BATF), provide transaction records upon request to BATF; when they go out of business, they are required to transfer their records to BATF. A privately owned gun can be transferred in a wide variety of ways not involving FFLs, such as through classified ads in newspapers, gun magazines, and at gun shows (which include both licensed and unlicensed dealers). Transfers of secondhand firearms by unlicensed individuals form the secondary market, for which federal law does not require transaction records or criminal background checks of prospective gun buyers.

Using household survey data, Cook and Ludwig estimate that about 2 million transactions per year (30-40 percent of all gun transactions) occur in the secondary market. Primary and secondary firearms markets are closely linked because many buyers move from one to the other depending on relative prices and other terms of the transaction. Since states vary greatly in their requirements on secondary firearms market transfers, another way to think about firearms commerce is to distinguish between regulated and unregulated transfers. In Massachusetts, for example, all firearms transfers must be reported to the state police and secondary markets can be regulated through inspection of these transfer records. In neighboring New Hampshire, however, sales of guns by private citizens are not recorded, and even legitimate transfers in the secondary market cannot be monitored. In this report we use the primary/secondary distinction because it is standard, but regulation is probably the critical distinguishing feature.

Through theft, firearms can be diverted to criminals and juveniles at any stage of commerce. Guns can be stolen from manufacturers, importers, distributors, licensed dealers, and private citizens. Cook et al. estimated that some 500,000 guns are stolen each year. This estimate, derived from National Crime Victimization Survey data for the years 1987 to 1992, suggests that 340,700 thefts occurred annually in which one or more guns were stolen; separate data from North Carolina suggest that on average 1.5 guns are stolen per theft. This figure is also consistent with a similar estimate calculated for the Police Foundation, which used data from a telephone survey of a nationally representative sample of 2,568 adults in which those who were gun owners reported firearms theft and the number of firearms stolen per theft. Braga et al. also identify three broad mechanisms through which criminal consumers acquire firearms from licensees without theft: straw purchase, "lying and buying," and buying from a dealer who is willing to ignore regulations.

A straw purchase occurs when the actual buyer, typically someone who is too young or otherwise proscribed, uses another person to execute the paperwork. Lying and buying refers to prohibited persons (e.g., felons and juveniles) who purchase firearms directly by showing false identification and lying about their status. And in some cases the seller is knowingly involved and may disguise the illegal transaction by falsifying the paper record of sale or reporting the guns as stolen. The available research evidence suggests that gun-using criminals go through a number of guns during the course of their short careers. The population of active street criminals is characterized by brief careers (typically 5 to 10 years) and many interruptions through incarceration and injury. Each year a substantial fraction of current offenders are released from prison and may have to acquire new weapons in order to continue their criminal career; others will have just begun their careers and must obtain guns from somewhere.

Survey research on criminally active populations suggests that gun offenders buy, steal, borrow, sell, and otherwise exchange guns quite frequently. Young offenders have been noted as active in illegal markets both as sellers and buyers of guns through their informal networks of family, friends, and street sources. Using data from self-administered questionnaires completed by 835 male inmates in six correctional facilities in four states between November 1990 and February 1991, Sheley and Wright found that 86 percent of juvenile inmates had owned at least one firearm at some time in their lives, 51 percent reported having personally dealt with many guns before being incarcerated, and 70 percent felt that they could get a gun "with no trouble at all" upon release. Wright and Rossi found that 75 percent of incarcerated adult felons had owned at least one firearm at some time in their lives and, for those who did report ownership, the average number of guns owned prior to their current incarceration was approximately six.

For incarcerated felons who reported stealing at least one gun, 90 percent also reported that they had sold or traded a stolen gun at least once in the past, and 37 percent had done so many times. It is also important to recognize that guns have value in exchange as well as in use. Based on interviews with youth offenders, Cook and his colleagues suggest that guns were valuable commodities for youth to trade for services, money, drugs, or other items such as video games, VCRs, phones, and fax machines. Guns are not costly when compared with other durable goods but may constitute a large asset in the portfolio of drug users or of youth. The retail prices of guns vary greatly based on the type, manufacturer, model, caliber, and age. For example, the suggested retail price of a new high-quality 9mm semiautomatic pistol is about $700, while a secondhand low-quality one can retail for as little as $50. The proximate source of a gun can also influence its price for prohibited persons. Sheley and Wright's) survey research suggests that juveniles paid less for guns acquired from informal and street sources than for guns acquired through normal retail outlets, such as gun stores and pawnshops: 61 percent of the juvenile inmates and 73 percent of the high school students who acquired their guns from a retail outlet paid more than $100, while only 30 percent of the juvenile inmates and 17 percent of the high school students who acquired their most recent gun from an informal or street source paid more than $100. We do not know whether this is driven by differences in the quality of the guns purchased or in the costs of distribution in the two sectors.

Gun Sources

There are three main types of evidence on the origins of guns for criminals and juveniles: survey research, BATF firearms trace data, and BATF firearms investigation data. Each provides different insights into the means by which offenders acquire firearms. Survey Research A number of inmate surveys has documented the wide variety of sources of guns available to criminals and youth. Precise patterns are sometimes difficult to discern because different definitions and questions are used to elicit similar information. Nevertheless, survey research has documented a wide variety of sources of guns and methods of firearm acquisition used by criminals and youth. Guns referenced in these surveys come from a variety of sources, including family members, friends, the black market, and direct theft. Wright and Rossi's 1992 survey of 1,874 convicted felons serving time in 11 prisons in 10 states throughout the United States, for example, revealed a complex market of both formal and informal transactions, cash and non-cash exchange, and new and used handguns.

Felons reported acquiring a majority of their guns from non-retail, informal sources. Only 21 percent of the respondents obtained the handgun from a retail outlet, with other sources including family and friends (44 percent) and the street (that is, the black market), drug dealers, and fences (26 percent). Moreover, the majority of handguns were not purchased with cash. Of the surveyed felons, 43 percent acquired their most recent handgun through a cash purchase, while 32 percent stole their most recent handgun. The remainder acquired their most recent handgun by renting or borrowing it, as a gift, or through a trade. Finally, almost two-thirds of the most recent handguns acquired by felons were reported as used guns, and one-third were reported as new guns. Illicit firearms markets dealt primarily in secondhand guns and constituted largely an in-state, rather than out-of-state, market.

Most recent handgun—incarcerated juveniles 32%, straw purchase 12%, theft 90% from friend, family, street, drug dealer, drug addict, house or car from a 1991 Bureau of Justice Statistics (BJS) survey of some 2,280 handgun-using state prison inmates support Wright and Rossi's observation that the illicit firearms market exploited by criminals is heavily dominated by informal, off-the-record transactions, either with friends and family or with various street sources. The 1991 survey found that only 27 percent of the inmates who used a handgun in crime that led to their incarceration reported they obtained the handgun by purchase from a retail outlet. In contrast to the Wright and Rossi findings, the BJS survey found that only 9 percent of inmates who used a handgun in a crime had stolen it.

More recently, Decker and colleagues' analysis of arrestee interview data (i.e., the Arrestee Drug Abuse Monitoring Survey) revealed that 13 percent of arrestees admitted to having a stolen gun. Among juvenile males, one-quarter admitted to theft of a gun. Sheley and Wright's survey of high school students and incarcerated juveniles suggested that informal sources of guns were even more important to juveniles. More than 90 percent of incarcerated juveniles obtained their most recent handgun from a friend, a family member, the street, a drug dealer, or a drug addict, or by taking it from a house or car. Sheley and Wright found that 12 percent of juvenile inmates had obtained their most recent handgun by theft and 32 percent of juvenile inmates had asked someone, typically a friend or family member, to purchase a gun for them in a gun shop, pawnshop, or other retail outlet.

When juveniles sold or traded their guns, they generally did so within the same network from which they obtained them—family members, friends, and street sources. BATF Firearms Trace Data BATF firearms trace data, have been used to document that firearms recovered by law enforcement have characteristics suggesting they were illegally diverted from legitimate firearms commerce to criminals and juveniles. Trace data, reflecting firearms recovered by police and other law enforcement agencies, have revealed that a noteworthy proportion of guns had a "time to crime" (the length of time from the first retail sale to recovery by the police) of a few months or a few years. For example, Cook and Braga report that 32 percent of traceable handguns recovered in 38 cities participating in BATF's Youth. In addition to the incarcerated juvenile sample described above, Sheley and Wright also surveyed 758 students enrolled at 10 high schools in 5 large cities that were proximate to the juvenile correctional facilities they surveyed between 1990 and 1991.

Crime Gun Interdiction Initiative (YCGII) was less than 3 years old. Cook and Braga also report that only 18 percent of these new guns were recovered in the possession of the first retail purchaser, suggesting that many of these guns were quickly diverted to criminal hands. Recovered crime guns are relatively new when compared with guns in public circulation. Pierce et al. (2001) found that guns manufactured between 1996 and 1998 represented about 14 percent of guns in private hands, but they accounted for 34 percent of traced crime guns recovered in 1999. Wright and Rossi found that criminals typically use guns from within-state sources, whereas the 1999 YCGII trace reports suggest that the percentage of crime guns imported from out of state is closely linked to the stringency of local firearm controls.

While 62 percent of traced YCGII firearms were first purchased from licensed dealers in the state in which the guns were recovered, this fraction was appreciably lower in northeastern cities with tight control—for example, Boston, New York, and Jersey City—where less than half of the traceable firearms were sold at retail within the state. A noteworthy number of firearms originated from southern states with less restrictive legislation, for example,

Virginia, North Carolina, Georgia, and Florida. Moreover, by examining the time-to-crime of out-of-state handguns in the trace data, Cook and Braga concluded that the process by which such handguns reach criminals in these tight-control cities is not one of gradual diffusion moving with interstate migrants; rather, the handguns that make it into these cities are imported directly after the out-of-state retail sale.

In contrast, Birmingham (AL), Gary (IN), Houston (TX), Miami (FL), New Orleans (LA), and San Antonio (TX), had at least 80 percent of their firearms first sold at retail in the state in which the city was located. Kleck attempts to explain the interstate movement of crime guns by simply observing that, according to the U.S. Census Bureau, 9.4 percent of the United States population moved their residence across state lines between 1985 and 1990. These migration patterns, however, do not necessarily explain the big differences in import and export patterns across source and destination states as well as the overrepresentation of new guns that show up in tight-control cities from other loose-control states. BATF Investigation Data While analyses of BATF trace data can document characteristics of crime guns that suggest illegal diversions from legitimate firearms commerce, trace data analyses cannot describe the illegal pathways through which crime guns travel from legal commerce to its ultimate recovery by law enforcement. BATF also conducts numerous investigations both in the course of monitoring FFL and distributor compliance with regulations and following detection of gun trafficking offenses.

Analyses of BATF firearms trafficking investigation data provide insights on the workings of illegal firearms markets. To date, the most representative look at firearms trafficking through a comprehensive review of investigation data was completed by BATF in 2000. This study examined all 1,530 investigations made between July 1996 and December 1998 by BATF special agents in all BATF field divisions in the United States. They involved the diversion of more than 84,000 guns.

This does not include simple Armed Career Criminal or Felon in Possession cases. The BATF study found that 43 percent of the trafficking investigations involved the illegal diversion of 10 guns or fewer but confirmed the existence of large trafficking operations, including two cases involving the diversion of over 10,000 guns. Corrupt FFLs accounted for only 9 percent of the trafficking investigations but more than half of the guns diverted in the pool of investigations. Violations by FFLs in these investigations included "off paper" sales, false entries in record books, and transfers to prohibited persons. Nearly half of the investigations involved firearms trafficked by straw purchasers, either directly or indirectly. Trafficking investigations involving straw purchasers averaged a relatively small number of firearms per investigation but collectively accounted for 26,000 guns.

Firearms were diverted by traffickers at gun shows and flea markets in 14 percent of the investigations, and firearms stolen from FFLs, residences, and common carriers were involved in more than a quarter of the investigations. Interpreting the Data Braga et al. suggest that the three sources of data on illegal gun markets are not directly comparable but broadly compatible. Each data source has its own inherent limitations and, as such, it is difficult to credit the insights provided by one source over another source. None of the three sources of data contradicts the hypothesis that stolen guns and informal transfers (as opposed to transfers from legitimate sources) predominate in supplying criminals and juveniles with guns.

However, they also clearly suggest that licensed dealers play an important role and that the illegal diversion of firearms from legitimate commerce is a problem. In their review of these three sources of data, Braga and his colleagues suggest that, in the parlance of environmental regulation, illegal gun markets consist of both "point sources"—ongoing diversions through scofflaw dealers and trafficking rings—and "diffuse sources"—acquisitions through theft and informal voluntary sales. As in the case of pollution, both point sources and diffuse sources are important. Braga and his colleagues also speculate that the mix of point and diffuse sources differs across jurisdictions depending on the density of gun ownership and the strictness of gun controls.

Analytic Framework

General Model Real interventions in gun markets tend to target particular types of firearms or sources. If policy raises the difficulty (cost, time, risk) of obtaining a particular type of gun or using a particular type of source, the effect inspection process, some 13,271 missing guns could not be accounted for by 202 licenses, and 16 FFLs each had more than 200 missing guns. More than half of the licensees had record-keeping violations only. The focused compliance inspections identified sales to more than 400 potential firearms traffickers and nearly 300 potentially prohibited persons, resulting in 691 referrals sent to BATF agents for further investigation. This reinforces the impression that a relatively small number of dealers systematically violate rules in ways that allow for leakage of guns to prohibited persons. In a recent paper, Koper examined the effects of the nearly 70 percent reduction in FFLs following the 1993 and 1994 federal licensing reforms on the availability of guns to criminals.

Using a data base of all active gun dealers in summer 1994 and the number of BATF gun traces to each dealer since 1990, Koper examined whether "dropout" dealers were more likely to be suppliers of crime guns than were "survivor" dealers. He concluded that it was not clear whether guns sold by the dropout dealers had a higher probability of being used in crime or moved into criminal channels more quickly when compared with active dealers. This study, however, used national BATF firearms trace data from 1990 through 1995, before the adoption of comprehensive tracing practices in most major cities and prior to BATF nationwide efforts to encourage law enforcement agencies to submit guns for tracing. National trace data from this time period are not representative of guns recovered by law enforcement, so it is difficult to interpret the findings of Koper's analysis of the impact of federal licensing reforms on the availability of guns to criminals. Some states and localities have imposed additional regulations on gun dealers. In 1993, North Carolina found that only 23 percent of dealers also possessed its required state license.

Non complying dealers were required to obtain a state license or forfeit their federal license. Alabama also identified FFLs who did not possess the required state license; 900 claimed not to know about the state requirements and obtained the license; another 900 reported that they were not currently engaged in the business of selling firearms; and 200 more could not be located. Alabama officials scheduled the licenses for these 1,100 dealers for cancellation. The Oakland (CA) Police Department worked with BATF to enforce a requirement for all licensed dealers to hold a local permit that required dealers to undergo screening and a criminal background check. This effort caused the number of license holders in Oakland to drop from 57 to 7 in 1997.

Officials in New York found that only 29 of 950 FFLs were operating in compliance with local ordinances. In cooperation with BATF, all local license applications were forwarded to the New York Police Department, which assumed responsibility for screening and inspections. The increased scrutiny reduced the number of license holders in New York from 950 to 259. These state-level and local initiatives have not been rigorously evaluated to determine whether they have affected criminal access to guns and rates of gun misuse. Limiting Gun Sales Federal law requires FFLs to report multiple firearms sales to BATF. A few states, including Virginia, Maryland, and California, have passed laws that limit the number of guns that an individual may legally purchase from FFLs within some specified time period. Underlying this intervention is the idea that some individuals make straw purchases in the primary market and then divert these guns to proscribed persons or others planning to do harm.

Trace data analyses conducted by BATF suggest that handguns that were first sold as part of a multiple sale are more likely than others to move rapidly into criminal use. If multiple sales were limited, then the volume of new guns available to criminals might decline. In the language of supply and demand, this is a supply-side intervention aimed at raising the price of new guns to criminals. In principle this sort of intervention holds promise. However, in order for this intervention to work—in the sense of reducing violence—not only must the intervention make it more difficult for criminals to get new guns but also the substitution possibilities must be limited; that is, comparably harmful guns cannot be available from comparably accessible sources. In July 1993, Virginia implemented a law limiting handgun purchases by any individual to no more than one during a 30-day period. Prior to the passage of this law, Virginia had been one of the leading source states for guns recovered in northeast cities including New York, Boston, and Washington, DC.

Using firearms trace data, Weil and Knox showed that during the first 18 months the law was in effect, Virginia's role in supplying guns to New York and Massachusetts was greatly reduced. For traces initiated in the Northeast, 35 percent of the firearms acquired before one-gun-a-month implementation took effect and 16 percent purchased after implementation were traced to Virginia dealers. This study indicates a change in the origin of traced crime guns following the change in the law. In this sense, the law change had an effect. However, the law may have been undermined by a substitution from guns first purchased in Virginia to guns first purchased in other states. An important question not addressed by this study is whether the law change affects the ultimate outcome of interest—the quantity of criminal harm committed with guns—or even the intermediate questions of the law's effects on the number of guns purchased or owned.

Screening Gun Buyers Enacted in 1994, the Brady Handgun Violence Prevention Act required FFLs to conduct a background check on all handgun buyers and mandated a one-week waiting period before transferring the gun to the purchaser. A total of 32 states were required to implement the provisions of the Brady act. The remaining states and the District of Columbia were exempted because they already required a background check of those buying handguns from FFLs. In 1998, the background check provisions of the Brady act were extended to include the sales of long guns and the waiting period requirement was removed when, as mandated by the initial act, it became possible for licensed gun sellers to perform instant record checks on prospective buyers. The policy intent was to make gun purchases more difficult for prohibited persons, such as convicted felons, drug addicts, persons with certain diagnosed mental conditions, and persons under the legal age limit (18 for long rifles and shotguns, 21 for handguns). In 1996, the prospective purchasers with prior domestic violence convictions were also prohibited from purchasing firearms from FFLs.

Theoretically, by raising the cost of acquisition, this procedure reduces the supply of guns to would-be assailants and to some persons who might commit suicide. Several BJS studies have demonstrated that Brady background checks have created obstacles for prohibited persons who attempt to purchase a gun through retail outlets. The Bureau of Justice Statistics (2002) reported that, from the inception of the Brady act on March 1, 1994, through December 31, 2001, nearly 38 million applications for firearms transfers were subject to background checks and some 840,000 (2.2 percent) applications were rejected. In 2001, 66,000 firearms purchase applications were rejected out of about 2.8 million applications.

Prospective purchasers were rejected because the applicant had a felony conviction or indictment (58 percent), domestic violence misdemeanor conviction or restraining order (14 percent), state law prohibition (7 percent), was a fugitive from justice (6 percent), or some other disqualification, such as having a drug addiction, documented mental illness, or a dishonorable discharge (16 percent) (Bureau of Justice Statistics, 2002). The 19 remaining states include: California, Connecticut, Delaware, Florida, Illinois, Indiana, Iowa, Maryland, Massachusetts, Missouri, Nevada, New Jersey, New York, Ohio, Oklahoma, Oregon, South Carolina, South Dakota, and Virginia.

These figures suggest the possibility that the Brady act might be effective in screening prohibited purchasers from making gun purchases from FFLs. Based on descriptive studies revealing heightened risks of subsequent gun offending, some researchers suggest extending the provisions of the Brady act to a wider range of at-risk individuals, such as persons with prior felony arrests and misdemeanor convictions. Wright et al. compared the gun arrest rates of two groups in California. The first consisted of persons who were denied purchases because they had been convicted of a felony in 1977. The second was purchasers who had a prior felony arrest in 1977 but no conviction. Even though the former group would reasonably be labeled as higher risk, they showed lower arrest rates over the three years following purchase or attempt to purchase. It is important to recognize that the group of convicted felons who attempt to purchase through legal channels may be systematically lower risk than the entire felony population, precisely because they did attempt to use the prohibited legitimate market; the finding is suggestive rather than conclusive Wintemute et al. also recognize that extending the provisions of the Brady act would greatly complicate the screening process.

Moreover, while this policy seems to prevent prohibited persons from making gun purchases in the primary market, the question remains what, if any, effect it has on purchases in the secondary market, on gun crimes, and on suicide. Using a differences-in-differences research design and multivariate statistics to control for state and year effects, population age, race, poverty and income levels, urban residence, and alcohol consumption, Ludwig and Cook compared firearm homicide and suicide rates and the proportion of homicides and suicides resulting from firearms in the 32 states affected by Brady act requirements (the treatment group) compared with the 19 states and the District of Columbia (the control group) that had equivalent legislation already in place.

Ludwig and Cook found no significant differences in homicide and suicide rates between the treatment and control groups, although they did find a reduction in gun suicides among persons age 55 and older in the treatment states. This reduction was greater in the treatment states that had instituted both waiting periods and background checks relative to treatment states that only changed background check requirements. The authors suggest that the effectiveness of the Brady act in reducing homicides and most suicides was undermined by prohibited purchasers shifting from the primary market to the largely unregulated secondary market. While the Brady act had no direct effect on homicide rates, it is possible that it had an indirect effect, by reducing interstate gun trafficking and hence gun violence in the control states that already had similar laws.

Cook and Braga document the fact that criminals in Chicago (a high control jurisdiction) were being supplied to a large extent by illegal gun trafficking from south central states, in particular Mississippi, and that a modest increase in regulation—imposed by the Brady act—shut down that pipeline. However, this large change in trafficking channels did not have any apparent effect in gun availability for violent acts in Chicago, as the percentage of homicides with guns did not drop after 1994. Moreover, the authors found that the percentage of crime handguns first purchased in Illinois increased after the implementation of the Brady act, suggesting substitution from out-of-state FFLs to instate FFLs once the advantage of purchasing guns outside Illinois had been removed. Gun buy-back programs involve a government or private group paying individuals to turn in guns they possess. The programs do not require the participants to identify themselves, in order to encourage participation by offenders or those with weapons used in crimes.

The guns are then destroyed. The theoretical premise for gun buy-back programs is that the program will lead to fewer guns on the streets because fewer guns are available for either theft or trade, and that consequently violence will decline. It is the committee's view that the theory underlying gun buy-back programs is badly flawed and the empirical evidence demonstrates the ineffectiveness of these programs. The theory on which gun buy-back programs is based is flawed in three respects. First, the guns that are typically surrendered in gun buy-backs are those that are least likely to be used in criminal activities. Typically, the guns turned in tend to be of two types: (1) old, malfunctioning guns whose resale value is less than the reward offered in buy-back programs or (2) guns owned by individuals who derive little value from the possession of the guns (e.g., those who have inherited guns).

The Police Executive Research Forum (1996) found this in their analysis of the differences between weapons handed in and those used in crimes. In contrast, those who are either using guns to carry out crimes or as protection in the course of engaging in other illegal activities, such as drug selling, have actively acquired their guns and are unlikely to want to participate in such programs. Second, because replacement guns are relatively easily obtained, the actual decline in the number of guns on the street may be smaller than the number of guns that are turned in. Third, the likelihood that any particular gun will be used in a crime in a given year is low. In 1999, approximately 6,500 homicides were committed with handguns. There are approximately 70 million handguns in the United States. Thus, if a different handgun were used in each homicide, the likelihood that a particular handgun would be used to kill an individual in a particular year is 1 in 10,000.

The typical gun buy-back program yields less than 1,000 guns. Even ignoring the first two points made above (the guns turned in are unlikely to be used by criminals and may be replaced by purchases of new guns), one would expect a reduction of less than one-tenth of one homicide per year in response to such a gun buy-back program. The program might be cost-effective if those were the correct parameters, but the small scale makes it highly unlikely that its effects would be detected. In light of the weakness in the theory underlying gun buy-backs, it is not surprising that research evaluations of U.S. efforts have consistently failed to document any link between such programs and reductions in gun violence. Outside the United States there have been a small number of buy-backs of much larger quantities of weapons, in response to high-profile mass murders with firearms. Following a killing of 35 persons in Tasmania in 1996 by a lone gunman, the Australian government prohibited certain categories of long guns and provided funds to buy back all such weapons in private hands.

A total of 640,000 weapons were handed in to the government (at an average price of approximately $350), constituting about 20 percent of the estimated stock of weapons. The weapons subject to the buy-back, however, accounted for a modest share of all homicides or violent crimes more generally prior to the buy-back. Unsurprisingly, Reuter and Mouzos were unable to find evidence of a substantial decline in rates for these crimes. They noted that in the six years following the buy-back, there were no mass murders with firearms and fewer mass murders than in the previous period; these are both weak tests given the small numbers of such incidents annually. Banning Assault Weapons in 1994, Congress enacted the Violent Crime Control and Law Enforcement Act, which banned the importation and manufacture of certain military-style semiautomatic "assault" weapons and ammunition magazines capable of holding more than 10 rounds. Assault weapons and large-capacity magazines manufactured before the effective date of the ban were grandfathered and thus legal to own and transfer. These guns are believed to be particularly dangerous because they facilitate the rapid firing of high numbers of shots. While assault weapons and large-capacity magazines are used only in a modest fraction of gun crimes, the premise of the ban was that a decrease in their use may reduce gunshot victimization, particularly victimizations involving multiple wounds or multiple victims.

A recent evaluation of the short-term effects of the 1994 federal assault weapons ban did not reveal any clear impacts on gun violence outcomes. Using state-level Uniform Crime Reports data on gun homicides, the authors of this study suggest that the potential impact of the law on gun violence was limited by the continuing availability of assault weapons through the ban's grandfathering provision and the relative rarity with which the banned guns were used in crime before the ban. Indeed, as the authors concede and other critics suggest, given the nature of the intervention, the maximum potential effect of the ban on gun violence outcomes would be very small and, if there were any observable effects, very difficult to disentangle from chance yearly variation and other state and local gun violence initiatives that took place simultaneously. In a subsequent paper on the effects of the assault weapons ban on gun markets, Koper and Roth found that, in the short term, the prices of assault weapons in both primary and legal secondary markets rose substantially at the time of the ban, and this may have reduced the availability of the assault weapons to criminals.

However, this increase in price was short-lived as a surge in assault weapon production in the months prior to the ban and the availability of legal substitutes caused prices to fall back to nearly preban levels. The ban is also weakened by the ease with which legally available guns and magazines can be altered to evade the intent of the ban. The results of these two studies should be interpreted with caution, since any trends observed in the relatively short study time period (24-month follow-up period) are unlikely to predict long-term trends accurately. District of Columbia Handgun Ban bans on the ownership, possession, or purchase of guns are the most direct means available to policy makers for reducing the prevalence of guns. The District of Columbia's Firearms Control Regulations Act of 1975 is the most carefully analyzed example of a handgun ban.

This law prohibited the purchase, sale, transfer, and possession of handguns by D.C. residents other than law enforcement officers or members of the military. Note, however, that individuals who had previously registered handguns prior to the passage of this law were allowed to keep them under this law. Long guns were not covered by the ban. One would expect the passage of the District's handgun ban to have little impact on the existing stock of legally held handguns but to greatly reduce the flow of new handguns to law-abiding citizens. Over time, the number of legally held handguns will decline. It is less clear how the illegal possession of guns will be affected. The flow of new guns to the illegal sector may be reduced to the extent that legal guns enter the illegal sector through resale or theft from the legal stock in the District. Theory alone cannot determine whether this handgun ban will reduce crime and violence overall.

One would expect that the share of crimes in which guns are used should decline over time if the handgun ban is effective. The empirical evidence as to the success of the Washington, DC, handgun ban is mixed. Loftin et al. used an interrupted-time-series methodology to analyze homicides and suicides in Washington, DC, and the surrounding areas of Maryland and Virginia before and after the introduction of the ban. They included the suburban areas around Washington, DC, as a control group, since the law does not directly affect these areas. Using a sample window of 1968-1987, they report a 25 percent reduction in gun-related homicides in the District of Columbia after the handgun ban and a 23 percent reduction in gun-related suicides. In contrast, the surrounding areas of Maryland and Virginia show no consistent patterns, suggesting a possible causal link between the handgun ban and the declines in gun-related homicide and suicide.

In addition, Loftin et al. report that non gun-related homicides and suicides declined only slightly after the handgun ban, arguing that this is evidence against substitution away from guns toward other weapons. Britt et al. however, demonstrate that the earlier conclusions of Loftin et al. are sensitive to a number of modeling choices. They demonstrate that the same handgun-related homicide declines observed in Washington, DC, also occurred in Baltimore, even though Baltimore did not experience any change in handgun laws. Thus, if Baltimore is used as a control group rather than the suburban areas surrounding DC, the conclusion that the handgun law lowered homicide and suicide rates does not hold. Britt et al. also found that extending the sample frame an additional two years (1968-1989) eliminated any measured impact of the handgun ban in the District of Columbia.

Furthermore, Jones discusses a number of contemporaneous policy interventions that took place around the time of the Washington, DC, gun ban, which further call into question a causal interpretation of the results. In summary, the District of Columbia handgun ban yields no conclusive evidence with respect to the impact of such bans on crime and violence. The nature of the intervention—limited to a single city, non experimental and accompanied by other changes that could also affect handgun homicide—make it a weak experimental design. Given the sensitivity of the results to alternative specifications, it is difficult to draw any causal inferences.

We have documented what is known about how people obtain firearms for criminal activities and identified the weaknesses of existing evaluations of interventions. There is not much empirical evidence that assesses whether attempts to reduce criminal access to firearms will reduce gun availability or gun crime. Most research has focused on determining whether prohibited persons illegally obtain firearms from legitimate commerce (legal primary and secondary markets) or whether crime guns are stolen or acquired through informal exchanges. Current research evidence suggests that illegal diversions from legitimate commerce are important sources of guns and therefore tightening regulations of such markets may be promising. There also may be promising avenues to control gun theft and informal transfers (through problem-oriented policing, requiring guns to be locked up, etc.).

We do not yet know whether it is possible to actually shut down illegal pipelines of guns to criminals or what the costs of such a shutdown would be to legitimate buyers. Answering these questions is essential. We also provide an analytic framework for assessing interventions. Since our ultimate interest is in the injuries caused using guns and not how guns are obtained, the key question involves substitution. In the absence of the pathways currently used for gun acquisition, could individuals have obtained alternative weapons with which to wreak equivalent harm? Substitution has many dimensions; time, place, and quality are just some of them. For example, that crime guns tend to be newer than guns generally indicates that criminals prefer new guns, even though old guns are generally as easy to get and are cheaper. This may be strictly consumer preference, or it may be to avoid being implicated, through ballistics imaging, in other crimes in which the gun was used.

Would offenders currently using newer guns use older guns—or any guns—if access to newer guns became more limited? If particular dealers account for a disproportionate share of crime weapons, then we are left with yet another version of the substitution question: Would the criminals have obtained other guns, with similar harmful effects, from other sources, including other FFLs? How long would this process of substituting from new to old or from one source to another take? What data are needed to determine the extent of substitution among firearms? Much could be learned from individual-level data from a general population survey on the number of guns owned by length of time, along with detailed individual characteristics of the individual (age, demographic characteristics, psychiatric history, other high-risk behaviours), along with type of gun owned (if any) and the method of acquisition (retail purchase, legal purchase of used gun, illegal purchase of stolen gun, borrowed through informal network). In addition, one would want measures of the availability of firearms of each type to potential buyers of each type in each locale.

For adults without criminal records, for example, there are established, observable prices of new guns at retail outlets. Similarly, there are active markets in used guns, for which there are (at least in principle) prices. The prices are individual specific in the sense that, for example, juveniles and felons cannot purchase guns at Wal-Mart. In effect, they face an infinite price of guns through this channel. Beyond this information one would also need a source of exogenous variation on the difficulty of obtaining guns through different channels. While guns available to legal buyers through retail outlets have literal prices, the measures of the difficulty of gun acquisition through some other channels are prices only in a metaphorical sense. When a city undertakes an intervention at a particular point in time, for example to make it more difficult for juveniles to get guns from interstate traffickers in new guns, then (provided that the policy has some effect), it is as if the price of guns to juveniles has risen.

Provided that the timing of the intervention is independent of the time pattern of local gun use, we could treat it as an exogenous increase in the metaphorical price of a gun to juveniles; money prices may fall as other costs rise because this increase in no money costs shifts the demand curve down. What happens to the tendencies for juveniles to obtain guns; do they substitute purchases of guns stolen from homes for the new guns they had previously purchased from traffickers? Is the substitution complete? That is, is the volume of juvenile gun use as high in the presence of the intervention as it was in the absence of the intervention? The biggest potential problem with this framework, however, is the assumption of an exogenous intervention. No real intervention is likely to be exogenous; that is, unrelated to changes in gun crimes. It might be more realistic to think about exogeneity conditional on some specified set of covariates, but the prospects for finding consensus on the correct set of covariates to credibly maintain this independence assumption are unknown.

Alternatively, researchers may be forced to rely on other methodological approaches and data. The committee has not attempted to identify specific interventions, research strategies, or data that might be suited for studying market interventions, substitution, and firearms violence. The existing evidence is of limited value in assessing whether any specific market-focused firearm restrictions would curb harm. Thus, the committee recommends that work be started to think carefully about the prospects for achieving "conditional exogeneity," the kinds of interventions and covariates that are likely to satisfy this independence requirement, how one could gather the data, the potential for building in evaluation at the stage of policy change, and other possible research and data designs. Future work might begin by considering the utility of emerging data systems; described in this report, for studying the impact of different market interventions, this type of effort should be taken place in collaboration with a group of survey statisticians, social scientists, and representatives from the Bureau of Justice Statistics and the National Institute of Justice.

5

Violent Crimes and Right-to-Carry Laws

This chapter is concerned with the question of whether violent crime is reduced through the enactment of right-to-carry-laws, which allow individuals to carry concealed weapons. In all, 34 states have right-to-carry laws that allow qualified adults to carry concealed handguns. Proponents of these laws argue that criminals are deterred by the knowledge that potential victims may be carrying weapons and therefore that the laws reduce crime. However, it is not clear a priori that such deterrence occurs. Even if it does, there may be offsetting adverse consequences. For example, increased possession of firearms by potential victims may motivate more criminals to carry firearms and thereby increase the amount of violence that is associated with crime. Moreover, allowing individuals to carry concealed weapons may increase accidental injuries or deaths or increase shootings during arguments. Ultimately, it is an empirical question whether allowing individuals to carry concealed weapons generates net social benefits or net social costs. The statistical analysis of the effects of these laws was initiated by John Lott and David Mustard and expanded by Lott and Bronars and Lott (hereinafter referred to simply as Lott). Lott concludes that the adoption of right-to-carry laws substantially reduces the prevalence of violent crime. Many other researchers have carried out their own statistical analyses using Lott's data, modified versions of Lott's data, or expanded.

The laws are sometimes called shall-issue laws because they require local authorities to issue a concealed-weapons permit to any qualified adult who requests one. A qualified adult is one who does not have a significant criminal record or history of mental illness. The definition of a nonqualified adult varies among states but includes adults with prior felony convictions, drug charges, or commitments to mental hospitals data sets that cover the more recent time period not included in the original analysis. Because the right-to-carry issue is highly controversial, has received much public attention, and has generated a large volume of research, the committee has given it special attention in its deliberations. This chapter reviews the existing empirical evidence on the issue. We also report the results of our own analyses of the data. We conclude that, in light of (a) the sensitivity of the empirical results to seemingly minor changes in model specification, (b) a lack of robustness of the results to the inclusion of more recent years of data (during which there are many more law changes than in the earlier period), and (c) the imprecision of some results, it is impossible to draw strong conclusions from the existing literature on the causal impact of these laws.

Researchers studying the effects of right-to-carry laws have used many different models. However, all of the analyses rely on similar data and methodologies. Accordingly, we do not attempt to review and evaluate each of the models used in this literature. Two other general responses to Lott's analysis deserve brief mention. First, some critics have attempted to discredit Lott's findings on grounds of the source of some of his funding (the Olin Foundation), the methods by which some of his results were disseminated (e.g., some critics have claimed, erroneously, that Lott and Mustard, 1997, was published in a student-edited journal that is not peer reviewed), and positions that he has taken on other public policy issues related to crime control. The committee's view is that these criticisms are not helpful for evaluating Lott's data, methods, or conclusions. Lott provides his data and computer programs to all who request them, so it is possible to evaluate his methods and results directly. In the committee's view, Lott's funding sources, methods of disseminating his results, and opinions on other issues do not provide further information about the quality of his research on right-to-carry laws.

A second group of critics have argued that Lott's results lack credibility because they are inconsistent with various strongly held a priori beliefs or expectations. For example, Zimring and Hawkins argue that "large reductions in violence [due to right-to-carry laws] are quite unlikely because they would be out of proportion to the small scale of the change in carrying firearms that the legislation produced." The committee agrees that it is important for statistical evidence to be consistent with established facts, but there are no such facts about whether right-to-carry laws can have effects of the magnitudes that Lott claims. The beliefs or expectations of Lott's second group of critics are, at best, hypotheses whose truth or falsehood can only be determined empirically. Moreover, Lott has argued that there are ways to reconcile his results with the beliefs and expectations of the critics. This does not necessarily imply that Lott is correct and his critics are wrong. The correctness of Lott's arguments is also an empirical question about which there is little evidence. Rather, it shows that little can be decided through argumentation over a priori beliefs and expectations. Instead, we describe the common data used and focus on the common methodological basis for all of them.

Data

The basic data set used in the literature is a county-level panel on annual crime rates, along with the values of potentially relevant explanatory variables. Early studies estimated models on data for 1977-1992, while more recent studies use data up to 2000. Between 1977 and 1992, 10 states adopted right-to-carry laws. A total of 8 other states adopted right-to-carry laws before 1977. Between 1992 and 1999, 16 additional states adopted such laws. The data on crime rates were obtained from the FBI's Uniform Crime Reports (UCR). Explanatory variables employed in studies include the arrest rate for the crime category in question, population density in the county, real per capita income variables, county population, and variables for the percent of population that is in each of many race-by-age-by-gender categories. The data on explanatory variables were obtained from a variety of sources. Although most studies use county-level panels on crime rates and demographic variables, the actual data files used differ across studies in ways that sometimes affect the estimates. The data set used in the original Lott study has been lost, although Lott reconstructed a version of the data, which he made available to other researchers as well as the committee. This data set, which we term the "revised original data set," covers the period 1977-1992. More recently; Lott has made available a data set covering the period 1977-2000 that corrects acknowledged errors in data files used by Plassmann and Whitley.

There is some disagreement over when and whether particular states have adopted right-to-carry laws. Lott and Mustard, for example, classify North Dakota and South Dakota as having adopted such laws prior to 1977, but Vernick and Hepburn code these states as having adopted them in 1985. Likewise, Lott and Mustard classify Alabama and Connecticut as right-to-carry states adopting prior to 1977, yet Vernick codes these states as not having right-to-carry laws. There are 3,054 counties observed over 16 years in the revised original data. In the basic specifications, there are a number of sample restrictions, the most notable of which is to drop all counties with no reported arrest rate (i.e., counties with no reported crime). This restricts the sample to approximately 1,650 counties per year (or approximately 26,000 county-year observations). In specifications that do not involve the arrest rate, Lott treats zero crime as 0.1 so as not to take the log of 0. Black and Nagin further restrict the sample to counties with populations of at least 100,000, which limit the sample to 393 counties per year. In some regressions, Duggan and Plassmann and Tideman estimate models that include data on the over 2,900 counties per year with no missing crime data. We term this file the "revised new data set." We make use of both of these data sets in our replication exercises.

Dummy Variable Model

For expository purposes it is helpful to begin by discussing the dummy variable model without "control" variables. The model allows each county to have its own crime level in each category. Moreover, the crime rate is allowed to vary over time in a pattern that is common across all counties in the United States. The effect of a right-to-carry law is measured as a change in the level of the crime rate in a jurisdiction following the jurisdiction's adoption of the law. Any estimate of a policy effect requires an assumption about the "counterfactual," in this case what would have happened to crime rates in the absence of the change in the law. The implicit assumption underlying this simple illustrative dummy variable model is that, in the absence of the change in the law, the crime rate in each county would, on average, have been the county mean plus a time-period adjustment reflecting the common trend in crime rates across all counties. Dummy variable models estimated in the literature are slightly more complicated than the above-described model. First, they typically include control variables that attempt to construct a more realistic counterfactual.

For example, if crime rates vary over time with county economic conditions, then one can construct a more credible estimate of what would have happened in the absence of the law change by including the control variables as a determinant of the crime rate. Most estimates in the literature use a large number of control variables, including local economic conditions, age-gender population composition, as well as arrest rates. Second, some estimates in the literature model the time pattern of crime differently. In particular, some studies allow each region of the country to have its own time pattern, thereby assuming that in the absence of the law change, counties in nearby states would have the same time pattern of crime rates in a crime category. We term this the "region-interacted time pattern model," in contrast to the "common time pattern" dummy variable model above. These data were downloaded by the committee from www.johnlott.org on August 22, 2003. This no-control model is often used as a way to assess whether there is an association between the outcome (crime) and the law change in the data. The committee estimates and evaluates this model below.

The interpretation of the "trend" model is slightly complicated, since the model already includes year effects to accommodate the time pattern of crime common across all counties. To see what this model does, consider a more flexible model with a series of separate dummy variables, for each number of years prior to—and following—the law change for adopting states. The coefficient on each of these variables shows how adopting states' time patterns of crime rates move, relative to the national time pattern, surrounding the respective states' law adoption. Note that the time pattern in question is not calendar time but rather time relative to local law adoption, which occurs in different calendar years in different places.

Statistical Analyses of Right-to-Carry Laws

In this section, we review the basic empirical findings on the effects of right-to-carry laws. Lott finds that where they have been adopted, right-to-carry laws have reduced homicide by about 8 percent, rapes by about 5 percent, and aggravated assaults by about 7 percent. Lott also finds that adoption of right-to-carry laws may increase the rates of nonviolent property crimes (burglary, larceny, auto theft). In theory, this is possible, as criminals substitute away from crimes that involve contact with victims toward crimes that do not involve encounters with victims.

The regressions use the covariates and specification from the original Lott and Mustard models that do not control for state poverty, unemployment, death penalty execution rates, or regional time trends. The controls include the arrest rate for the crime category in question (AOVIOICP), population density in the county, real per capita income variables, county population (POPC), and variables for the percentage of the population that is in each of many race x age x gender categories (e.g., PBM1019 is the percentage of the population that is black, male, and between ages 10 and 19). The "no controls" specification includes county fixed effects, year dummies, and the dummy for whether the state has a right-to-carry law close and consistent with the conclusion that right-to-carry laws reduce the incidence of murder.

The estimates from these revised data are substantially different from those originally reported by Lott. In the dummy variable model, the magnitude of the estimated reduction in the rates of violent crime and aggravated assault was reduced, the estimated reduction in the murder rate increased, and the sign of the estimated effects of right-to-carry laws on robbery reversed. Moreover, the effects of right-to-carry laws on violent crime are no longer statistically significantly different from zero at the 5 percent significance level. Finally, the estimated increase in the rates of ail property crimes increased substantially.

These new results tend to show larger reductions in the violent crime trends than those found using the revised original data. Other Statistical Evaluations of Right-to-Carry Laws Researchers have estimated the effects of right-to-carry laws using Lott's or related data and models. Many of these studies have found that the use of plausible alternative data, control variables, specifications, or methods of computing standard errors, weakens or reverses the results. The committee does not endorse particular findings or consider them to provide better estimates of the effects of right-to-carry laws than do Lott's results. Moreover, the committee recognizes that several independent investigators have used alternative models or data to obtain results that are consistent with Lott's. These investigators include Bartley and Cohen and Moody. We focus on the conflicting results in this section because they illustrate a variability of the findings that is central to the committee's evaluation of their credibility.

The regressions use the covariates and specification from the original Lott and Mustard models that do not control for state poverty, unemployment, death penalty execution rates, or regional time trends. The controls include the arrest rate for the crime category in question (AOVIOICP), population density in the county, real per capita income variables (RPCPI RPCUI RPCIM RPCRPO), county population (POPC), and variables for the percentage of the population that is in each of many race × age × gender categories (e.g., PBM1019 is the percentage of the population that is black, male, and between ages 10 and 19).

Control Variables and Specification

The most common modifications to Lott's original analyses of right-to-carry laws have been to assess the sensitivity of the findings to variation in the control variables or the specification of the model. Lott's basic model relies on dozens of controls, but concerns have been raised that some controls may be missing, others may be unnecessary, and still others may be endogenous (that is, related to the unobserved determinates of county crime rates). Duggan for example, raises concerns that county-level control variables may not be precisely measured on an annual basis and that the arrest rate control variable, which includes the crime rate in the denominator, may bias the estimates. In response to these concerns, Duggan estimated a simple dummy variable model that controls only for year and county fixed effects. Duggan drops all other covariates from the model. When estimated on all county-year observations with no missing crime data, this reduced the magnitude of the estimated reduction in the rates of murder and aggravated assault, and it reversed the signs of the estimated effects of right-to-carry laws on rape, robbery, and all violent crime. That is, according to Duggan's estimates, adoption of right-to-carry laws increases the frequencies of rape, robbery, and violent crime as a whole.

Duggan also changed the coding of the dates of adoption of right-to-carry laws, although this had only a minimal effect on the estimates. According to Duggan and others, there is an inconsistency in the coding used by Lott and Mustard. Duggan finds that in 8 of the 10 right-to-carry states, the adoption date is defined as the year the law was passed, but in 2 states, Florida and Georgia, the adoption date is set to the calendar year after the law was passed. Lott, in personal communications, maintains that the dates are coded correctly. The committee does not take a stand on which coding is correct.

Moreover, Duggan found there is no statistically significant effect of right-to-carry laws on violent crimes (at the 5 percent significance level). Other researchers have varied the specification of the model, allowing for the effects of right-to-carry laws to be more heterogeneous. Black and Nagin for example, estimated a dummy variable model in which the effects of right-to-carry laws are allowed to vary among states (that is, the coefficient ä is allowed to take different values for different states). The results from these analyses, which vary the way in which right-to-carry laws can affect crime, are highly variable, with some suggesting that the laws increase crime, others suggesting that they decrease crime, and many being statistically insignificant. In Black and Nagin for example, only Florida has a statistically significant decrease in the murder rate following adoption of a right-to-carry law, and only West Virginia has a statistically significant increase in murder rate.

This is a particularly important concern because states that pass right-to-carry laws are not representative of the nation as a whole on important dimensions (e.g., percentage rural) that are correlated with rising crime in the 1977-1992 period and falling crime in the years 1993-2000. The specifications estimated are identical to the original model, with the only difference being that the number of years has been expanded. Compared with the model estimated on the original (1977-1992) sample period, the results have now changed rather substantially. Only the coefficient on murder is negative and significant, while seven coefficients are positive and significant (violent crime overall, aggravated assault, robbery, property crime overall, auto theft, burglary, and larceny). The dummy variable results that were apparent with the earlier data set and earlier sample periods almost completely disappear with the extension of the sample to 2000. The committee views the failure of the original dummy variable model to generate robust predictions outside the original sample as important evidence of fragility of the model's findings.

These results are also substantially different from those found when using the expanded set of control variables first adopted by Lott 9.1. As described above, Ayres and Donohue estimate a dummy variable model using the revised new data. As in Lott and Plassmann and Whitley they modify the original specification to include additional covariates (i.e., state poverty, unemployment, and death penalty execution rates) and region-interacted time patterns, as opposed to a common time trend used in the original Lott models. These seemingly minor adjustments cause sub- 12 in light of the variability in the estimates, statistical tests might aid in determining whether particular specifications can be rejected by the data. It is not possible to test empirically whether a proposed set of explanatory variables is the correct one. It is possible to test for specification, given a set of controls. None of the models examined by the committee passes a simple specification test.

In the first exercise, we replace the right-to-carry dummy with a series of dummies for each of the possible numbers of years prior to—and following—adoption. We summarize the estimated coefficients in three figures. These figures show the estimated coefficients normalized on the year of adoption and multiplied by 100 (so the y-axis is a percentage), and the associated 95 percentage confidence intervals. The vertical line marks the adoption year, while the horizontal line marks 0. For years preceding adoption, violent crime is increasing in ultimately adopting states (relative to the national time pattern). Following adoption, the increase relative to trend continues, reverses, and then reverses twice again. The obvious striking feature of these figures is that the big reductions in crime occur roughly 9 years after adoption. Otherwise, the post adoption estimates are generally small and sometimes positive and are, in general, both statistically insignificant and statistically indistinguishable from the pre adoption estimates. The trend model essentially fits a line with constant slope through the post adoption portions of these graphs, and the line's slope is affected by years long after adoption.

These time patterns raise serious questions about whether the reductions in crime documented in the trend model are reasonably attributed to the change in the law. In the second exercise, to further explore the sensitivity of the trend model estimates, we re-estimate the baseline trend model using revised new Lott data on the period 1977-2000.

Subsequent rows include observations that occur in certain numbers of years after the law change. These estimates show that including 5 years or fewer reverses the signs of the estimated effects of right-to-carry laws on murder and property crime (from negative to positive) and reduces the magnitude of the estimated reduction in the rates of rape, aggravated assault, robbery, and violent crime. Moreover, there are fewer statistically significant changes in crime trends. One needs to include at least 6 years following the pre-law-change period to find statistically significant reductions in the violent crime and murder trends.

These estimates tell us how crime has changed in states that have adopted the right-to-carry laws before and after the law change, relative to national time patterns in crime. It is important to stress that the committee is not arguing that excluding all socioeconomic and demographic covariates is an appropriate method of identifying the effects of right-to-carry laws. Rather, we are simply assessing whether such laws are associated with a decline in the level of crime. If not, then detecting the effect, if any, of right-to-carry laws.

The trend results rely on changes in crime trends occurring long after the law changes, again raising serious questions about whether one can requires controlling for appropriate confounding variables and thereby reliance on a model such as those used by Lott and others. The results without controls are quite different. Using the earlier sample period and the new data, one finds three negative coefficients, only one of them statistically significant. When the sample is extended to 2000, only one of nine coefficients is negative, and it is insignificantly different from zero. For example, the violent crime coefficient with controls is 4.1 percent, while it is 12.9 percent without controls. These results show that states that passed right-to-carry laws did not on average experience statistically significant crime declines relative to states that did not pass such laws. There are two points to make about the no-controls results.

First, the no-controls results provide a characterization of the data that shows that, if there is any effect, it is not obvious in the dummy variable model. What do estimates from that model mean? The model says that crime rates differ across counties and, moreover, that they change from one year to the next in the same proportionate way across all counties in the United States. Over and above this variation, there is a one-time change in the mean level of crime as states adopt right-to-carry laws. So these estimates indicate that, for the period 1977-1992, states adopting right-to-carry laws saw roughly no change in their violent crime rates and 8.5 percent increases in their property crime rates, relative to national time patterns. Estimating the model using data to 2000 shows that states adopting right-to-carry laws saw 12.9 percent increases in violent crime—and 21.2 percent increases in property crime—relative to national time patterns.

The first-blush evidence provided by these no-controls models is thus not supportive of the theory that right-to-carry laws reduce crime. A final lesson to draw from the no-controls dummy variable results is that the results are sensitive to the inclusion of controls. That is, whether one concludes that right-to-carry laws increase or decrease crime based on models of this sort depends on which control variables are included. Such laws have no obvious effect in the model without controls (and therefore no clear level effect in the raw data). Moreover, as demonstrated above, seemingly minor changes to the set of control variables substantially alter the estimated effects. Given that researchers might reasonably argue about which controls belong in the model and that the results are sensitive to the set of covariates, the committee is not sanguine about the prospects for measuring the effect of right-to-carry laws on crime. Note that this is distinct from whether such laws affect crime. Rather, in our view, any effect they have on crime is not likely to be detected in a convincing and robust fashion. Estimates from the trend model are less sensitive to the inclusion of controls.

The trend model without controls shows reductions in violent and property crime trends following the passage of right-to-carry laws for both sample endpoints. For murder, however, the results are positive when using the 2000 end point, negative when using the 1992 end point, and statistically insignificant in both cases. The literature on right-to-carry laws summarized in this chapter has obtained conflicting estimates of their effects on crime. Estimation results have proven to be very sensitive to the precise specification used and time period examined. The initial model specification, when extended to new data, does not show evidence that passage of right-to-carry laws reduces crime.

The estimated effects are highly sensitive to seemingly minor changes in the model specification and control variables. No link between right-to-carry laws and changes in crime is apparent in the raw data, even in the initial sample; it is only once numerous covariates are included that the negative results in the early data emerge. While the trend models show a reduction in the crime growth rate following the adoption of right-to-carry laws, these trend reductions occur long after law adoption, casting serious doubt on the proposition that the trend models estimated in the literature reflect effects of the law change. Finally, some of the point estimates are imprecise. Thus, the committee concludes that with the current evidence it is not possible to determine that there is a causal link between the passage of right-to-carry laws and crime rates.

6

Political Violence and Contexts of Terrorism

As seems inevitable, when ambiguous and alarming events occur and unfold, many single and oversimplified explanations appear, and these represent, in part, attempts to reduce uncertainty and anxiety. Thus, the causes of terrorism suggested include "poverty," "inequality," "globalisation," "technology," "energy," "oil," "Islam," "Islamic fundamentalism," and "psychopathy," among others. There are also widespread challenges to each of these causes on both scientific and ideological grounds.

In approaching the daunting questions of origins and contexts we are guided by the following first principles:

- The search for a single or even a few causes is misguided. The factors influencing contemporary terrorism are a blend of historical, economic, political, cultural, motivational, and technological factors, to name only the most obvious.
- The logic of cause-followed-by-effect is inappropriate to the understanding of origins and contexts of terrorism. Causes differ qualitatively in their generality as determinants. Some are remote background conditions, others are facilitating circumstances, others are precipitating factors, and still others are inhibitory

factors. The most appropriate way to organize these factors is in a nesting or combinatorial way. Each adds its value at a different level and significance to work toward more complete accounts and explanations.

At the very least it is essential to separate the origins and context issue into two distinguishable levels: (a) the historical, social, political, and cultural conditions that constitute a favorable soil in which terrorism can take root and grow, provide a continuously changing mix of support and discouragement for terrorism, and constitute one of the main audiences for terrorists and (b) the immediate motivational, ideological, group, and organizational determinants of terrorist activities themselves. The explanations at each level are separate, though they overlap and articulate with one another as one regards the total picture. We employ this distinction in our own account, treating the more general conditions first and the immediate ones afterward.

The impulse for territorial expansion, conquest, and domination is as old as history itself. The ways in which this impulse has expressed itself, however, reveal vast differences. For comparative purposes, we mention three variations. *Imperialism* is, above all, a system based on military conquest, territorial occupation, and direct governmental/military control by the dominant imperial power. This characterization clearly applies to the classical Roman, Ottoman, Spanish, and Soviet empires, and it is also evident but not so unequivocal in other cases, such as the Austro-Hungarian Empire. The political sovereignty of occupied regions is not a salient issue; that notion does not apply to militarily occupied and controlled territories.

Imperial powers are also dominant economically, but the mechanisms are extraction and exploitation of resources through the mechanisms of expropriation, direct control of economic activities, and coercion (including slavery in some cases). If we regard the eighteenth-, nineteenth-, and twentieth-century European cases as the major referents, *colonialism* overlaps with but is distinguishable in important ways from imperialism. Military conquest, settlement, territorial acquisition, and administrative rule—sometimes military, sometimes civil—is the essence, but in practice the administrative rule varied from direct rule resembling imperialism to indirect rule involving a symbiotic relationship between colonial rulers and indigenous authorities. Nineteenth- and twentieth-century colonialism also involved more striking economic contrasts between the technological and industrial superiority of the (developed) colonial powers and the (undeveloped) colonial countries. The resultant pattern was the extraction of primary products necessary for industrial production (e.g., cotton from India and Egypt) or for consumption in the colonizing countries (e.g., tea, sugar, coffee, spices).

After the effective demise of British, French, Dutch, and Belgian colonialism in the decades after World War II, there was acceleration in the development of the form of international organization described as *globalization*. Globalization is something of a misnomer, because economic, political, and cultural penetration around relevant parts of the globe is observable through several millennia. Since the collapse of the Soviet bloc in 1989-1990, the world system has also been called "the American hegemony." This is also misnamed, because the dominant powers are a complex combination of North American, West European, and East Asian powers. Nevertheless, the role of the United States is paramount. The contemporary global mode is one of economic influence, realized through greater economic productivity (and its concomitant, wealth) based on a superior, science-based technology. This influence is realized and exercised by the mechanisms of trade among nations, capital and financial investment, and power in the international monetary system.

There is also an aspect of military domination, but this is primarily realized not through military conquest and administration of occupied territory, but through a technologically superior arsenal of weaponry, occasional wars and "peacekeeping" interventions, and, above all else, military intimidation. American hegemony also has a less tangible political-ideological ingredient, namely, a conviction of the moral superiority of a particular (American) version of democracy and its accompanying characteristics of personal liberty, constitutional rights of citizens, and mass political participation. This ideological dimension affects U.S. foreign policies toward other nations, generally favoring nations like it politically and distancing it from or applying pressures on nations unlike it. The final aspect is a cultural one, consisting mainly of the effective export of cultural and materialist values through the worldwide American domination of the mass media, especially television.

In that part of the world that currently commands the nation's special attention—referred to variously as the Arabic or Islamic world—we observe a long period of interaction, penetration, and conflict with the West. Especially in the late eighteenth century, there was exposure to and borrowing of Western military and other technology and such ideas as democracy, nationalism, and the rights of women, as travel, commercial activity, and communication increased. The forces of modernization, however they may be defined, are thus several centuries old; an informative account of the historical process is found in Lewis. Of special subsequent significance was the century-long (1830 through the end of World War I) colonization and political control of North Africa and the Near East countries of Syria, Lebanon, and modern Iraq, Jordan, and the Palestine mandate. In the twentieth-century, commercial and cultural penetration and influences have accelerated, dramatically in the case of the exploitation of oil but more generally as well.

Impacts on Receiving Societies

The general impacts of the complex of influences imposed by more powerful societies are both to dislocate and to provide alternatives to the traditional ways of life in the affected societies. Economic production is transformed, systems of wage labour increased, existing patterns of inequality altered, economic expectations stirred, and political institutions modified or displaced. Traditional and authoritarian political values and institutions are shaken by exposure to ideas of freedom, rights, and democracy. Competing religious forces, especially nonreligious secularism, are introduced. And especially recently, commercial and cultural penetration has exposed the world, and notably the non-Western world, to a range of materialistic values and aspirations that are evidently unattainable in those societies in the historical short run.

A political corollary of these modernizing influences is that, under conditions of domination by and acculturation to a more powerful society, the receiving society experiences an increase in the growth, complexity, and magnitude of political divisions. Some of these are "class" in nature, as new groups—for example, a new middle class, a paid labouring class, or the unemployed—come into being and develop interests in common. Other divisions are cultural in nature, as groups crystallize along the dimension of how much and in what ways they want to be modernizers (e.g., democratic, capitalistic, secular) and how much and in what ways they want to preserve a traditional way of life.

All these impacts are observable in dramatic form in the world's Islamic societies. They combine with several additional features of these societies to make for very high levels of discontent and combustibility. Almost all of the Islamic societies in the world fall into the category of rapidly growing populations that have relatively high proportions of young people compared with those of working age, but low proportions of elderly people. The Muslim population is the most rapidly growing religiously defined category in the world, doubling perhaps every 25 years at current rates. These populations have been growing on an average of more than 3 percent per year, although fertility is declining in many of them. These patterns yield large families in which younger siblings in particular are likely to suffer from lack of parental investment of resources and emotional care.

Such societies have few resources to devote to education, so their high numbers of young people cannot be trained to participate in advanced economic activities. It is hard for such countries to guarantee employment for their youth, who experience high rates of unemployment, engage in criminal activity or gang violence, or must otherwise migrate to the richer countries, where they work in low-level jobs. Such poor countries are also often obliged to spend substantial sums on police control and national defense against neighboring poor countries, in which they employ local youth in low-level military jobs.

The majorities of the world's Muslims are poor and live in countries characterized by great inequalities of wealth. The ratio of children to workers in the Muslim world is very high, especially because there are so few women in the labour force, so the actual ratios of children to workers are almost double the child to adult ratio. Finally, high growth ratio produces large numbers of children in families, and this may spread the family's financial and emotional resources. Some research suggests that later-born children in families are more rebellious. This suggests the possibility that in a population in which many families have many children, the level of rebelliousness in the society may be higher.

The relevance of these outcomes to an understanding of social unrest is clear. Unemployed young males with poor local prospects will feel angry and frustrated. They can seek a future in military endeavors, emigrate to take menial work, or become involved in criminal activity in a foreign and often culturally inhospitable environment. Sexual frustration may also be part of the picture. Marriage is often a high-cost matter in these countries because it requires substantial outlays for parents and elaborate ceremonies. Young women have restricted choices in the local marriage market because of the male exodus and little hope of employment themselves unless they also emigrate (especially if local customs deter them from entering the labour market).

Looking at these demographic and economic realities, it is clear that the majority of Muslims in the world experience a high level of absolute poverty. These poor compare themselves with the rich in their own societies and with an unrealistic view of Western culture gleaned from films and television, and thus they also experience a high level of relative deprivation. This combination is a sure recipe for social unrest in general. Insofar as these conditions are blamed on the United States and the West in general—as they typically are—they also provide a favorable atmosphere for supporting violence against these enemies, as well as a potential recruiting ground for recruits to this cause. To note this is not to argue that poverty causes terrorism, but that it is one ingredient in a volatile mix of causes.

Reactions to Impacts

It is a reasonable historical generalization that those who are dominated—or who believe themselves to be dominated—by stronger outside powers come to resent and oppose their oppressors. Especially under conditions of imperialist and colonial domination, in which direct force is used against the population, this discontent can often be held in check, at least temporarily. When societies experience economic and cultural domination without direct military occupation and political control, the opportunities to express discontent publicly are usually more readily available.

This rejection of outside domination is not surprising and can be readily appreciated. It is not as frequently appreciated that the hatred of outside domination is typically only half the picture. The other half is conveyed by the idea of *ambivalence*. To bring the point closer to home, anti colonial ideologies are mainly negative toward the colonial powers. But they also contain the seeds of positive attraction. A remote but telling instance of this is found in the cargo cults, a widespread religious phenomenon mainly in colonial Melanesia. These movements, were millenarian, envisioned the end of the world accompanied by the arrival of Western ships or airplanes loaded with tinned foods, transistor radios, and other Western items. At the millenarian moment, too, white Westerners would be destroyed, and the true believers would survive in a world of Western plenty.

Further evidence of this type of ambivalence is provided by the fact that colonial societies, once independent, frequently establish institutions and retain political and other values resembling those of their former conquerors. A similar ambivalence toward the United States is now found throughout the world, including (perhaps especially) Muslim societies. On one hand there is America the demon, the rich, godless, morally and sexually corrupt, imperialist country that has come to its wealth by exploitation, a power that dominates the world and forms alliances with the ruling elites in their own societies, a nation that is hypocritical in its assertions of equality when it is plagued with racism and poverty, and the power that is primarily responsible for the existence and support of Israel. Side by side with this, however, is a utopian America, as the immigrant communities of Detroit, Brooklyn, and Los Angeles typify. America is a place to come to, a place of wealth and consumption where the payoff for hard work is leisure and opportunity, and where freedom is buttressed by myriad choices in both the market and in the polity.

This positive side of the ambivalence, moreover, stands in stark contrast to what almost all Muslims can realistically aspire to in their own societies. Typically, it is psychologically difficult to hold both sides of an ambivalent attitude at the same time, and it usually is resolved by rigidly accentuating one side to the exclusion of the other. In anti-American Muslim ideologies this appears to be the case, with vitriolic hostility as the conspicuous and exclusive element and the admiration and envy suppressed. Insights that take account of this element of ambivalence signal a potential chink in the armor of what appear to be exclusively hostile attitudes, yield a more realistic grasp of the social psychology of protest and resentment, and instruct Americans as to the half-truth of the question asked by some in the wake of September 11: "Why do they hate us so much?"

The complex of economic, political, and cultural penetration does not occur in a vacuum. It is always interpreted and reacted to in the framework of the cultural milieu it affects—accepted, altered, synthesized, or rejected, all in complex ways. An inevitable accompaniment of the process is the widespread perception that the domestic culture is under threat of extinction. The reactions to this perception are, as indicated, multiple, but, in light of the religious character of much of recent terrorism, we take special note of what have been called revivalist or fundamentalist reactions. This variant of terrorism in particular has developed in the context of a wider Islamic revival.

Revivalist or fundamentalist movements are efforts to restore an often-imagined indigenous culture, especially its religion, to a pure and unadulterated form. Their elements have been found in American Indian movements such as the ghost dance and peyote religion, revivalist cults, nationalist movements in colonial societies, revivalist and fundamentalist Christian movements, and in some extreme Western political movements such as fascism. The typical ingredients of such movements are:

- A totalistic worldview rooted in a sacred religious system.
- A profound sense of threat, angst, and apprehension about the destruction of their society, culture, and way of life.
- A specification of certain agents who are assigned total responsibility for this deterioration.
- An unqualified, and absolute, sense of rage that is felt to be morally legitimate.

A utopian view of their own culture and society—perhaps referring to an imagined, glorious past—standing in point-by-point opposition to the decaying and threatening world they confront. The historical picture in many Muslim societies is not different from this general pattern. The analogy is not between cults and terrorism as such, but between nativity movements and Islamic revivalism, which provides a fertile ground for religiously based terrorism.

The penetration of Muslim societies by Western values during the past few centuries has occurred in the context of Islam, one of the world's great religions, dedicated to the transcendence of God and the observance of Islamic law. It is also a religion with a proselytizing tradition and a centuries-long history of both conquest of and humiliation by Western Christian and Eastern Orthodox powers—a history actively remembered in detail in Muslim societies to this day. It is, finally, a religion with a keen sense of infidels, both inside and outside Islam. All these features have conditioned the reactions to the West in Muslim societies, including the Islamic revival.

Revivalist-like movements of a totalistic sort—i.e., to "Islamize" the religious community by imposing Islamic norms throughout all spheres of life—antedate deep Western influences. Among these is the Safavid movement that eventually became the basis of the Shiite state in Iran. There were also a number of nineteenth-century antecedents, and the early twentieth century witnessed the rise and consolidation of the Muslim Brotherhood in Egypt and its subsequent underground offshoots.

The widespread Islamic revival in contemporary times partakes of elements of these earlier movements but has added new and different ingredients. Some of these ingredients include: (a) It expresses the feelings of humiliation at the loss of the supremacy of Islam, the imposition of European commercial and colonial power, and the Euro-American domination in world affairs. Its enemies are foreign infidels, non-Muslims in their midst, representatives of more moderate forms of Islam, and secular dictatorial regimes in their own societies. (b) It expresses a fear of cultural extinction by the spread of an American consumerist lifestyle, and of individualistic values disrespectful of the old hierarchies of society. (c) It typically takes hold in countries ruled by regimes that repress even legitimate forms of domestic political opposition.

On the more constructive side, the goal of the revivalist movements is the creation of an ideal Islamic society, in which morals are pure and the community just, and all live in a state that protects a Muslim way of life, defends it against enemies, and aggrandizes the domain of Islam. Revivalists regard this envisioned society as a comprehensive alternative to nationalism or capitalism. In the main, the movements are carried by self-declared charismatic teachers, ideologues, community organizers, and political activists. The followers are diverse, consisting of petit bourgeois *bazaaris* (small businessmen, peddlers, craftsmen, and workers) and *maktabis* (clerks, teachers, and students) and sometimes the professional middle classes. The movements have become extensively institutionalized in schools, mosques, clinics, study groups, women's auxiliaries, and economic enterprises.

Some groups take the form of political lobbies and parties, and some have paramilitary forces. They constitute opposition movements to domestic governments, as in Turkey, Egypt, Algeria, and Indonesia, or to foreign rulers or occupiers, as in Palestine, Chechnya, Xinjiang, and Kashmir. The revivalist movements represent a small part of Islam in general. It is not difficult to appreciate, however, why Muslim terrorists have taken on the ideology of militant revivalism as their major guiding belief system. It provides a meaningful account of what is wrong in their world and legitimizes their extreme and violent political actions.

To say this is neither to assert that Islam "causes" terrorist behaviour nor to say that terrorists are simply "exploiting" Islamic beliefs to rationalize their destructive ends. Rather, the presence of extreme Islamic fundamentalism, like the demographic, economic, and political realities found in most Muslim societies, is part of the fertile seedbed in which a particular ideologically based brand of terrorism finds a supportive audience and some recruits. We emphasize, however, that Islam-inspired terrorists are a minority of terrorists, considered worldwide, and that the vast majority of Islamic peoples have no connection with and do not sympathize with terrorism.

Recent terrorist activity in general and the particular organization of Al Qaeda have cemented the view that the "new terrorism" involves a distinctive asymmetry: a stateless and no territorially bounded organization that wages war against a state, and vice versa. In domestic terrorism the terrorist organization typically operates within a state but itself is not a state. In international terrorism, the organization may operate within the confines of a single state, but it typically involves a far-flung organization or network of organizations, operating out of the territories of whatever states will harbor, tolerate, or cannot detect it.

Corollaries of this view are: (a) that these organizations are out of range of institutions of truce, international diplomacy, alliances, and treaties, all of which are peaceful alternatives to warlike violence; (b) that, unlike states, these organizations do not face the "conservatizing" influences imposed by the state's necessity to maintain law and order and manage politically negotiated relationships among diverse groups (except in the most totalitarian of societies, and to a limited degree in these); and (c) that they are relatively unreachable militarily because they are moving and semi visible targets, forever changing their form and moving from state to state and from place to place within states. This view contains much truth, but it must be qualified in two ways: first that all "states" are not states as we understand them, and, second, that the relations between states and terrorist organizations are highly variable.

The standard Western model of a state is that it is a discrete, territorially bounded, politically sovereign unit with a legal monopoly over force and violence, responsible for law and order in its domestic population, and the focus of the solidarity, culture, and identity of its citizens. Regarding the panoply of states and other organizations in the contemporary world, we must conclude that the state is not a unitary thing that is either present or absent but is a continuum. The West still has many states that approximate the model—despite the intrusions of globalization on all states—but Afghanistan, Algeria, Colombia, Rwanda, Somalia, Sudan, the former Yugoslavia, and Zaire, while in the United Nations as states, do not, for various reasons, meet the understood conditions. Much has been made recently of the notion of "failed states" to describe the non-development of modern states in the non-Western (including the Muslim) world in the political science literature. Finally, many "non state actors" take on state-like roles—United Fruit in Honduras, Aramco in Saudi Arabia—as did the East India Company in an earlier era of British colonialism.

In addition, whatever their approximation to the standard model, states have variable, not fixed, relations with terrorist networks. At one extreme there is the Taliban, which had supportive, hand-in-glove relations with Al Qaeda. Pakistan has had a vacillating relationship with terrorist organizations. Egypt has allowed their terrorists to leave to fight as terrorists in other places but curtailed their activities radically at home. Finally, when Libya at its inception entered the United Nations as a state, it had almost no attributes of a state and has only slowly developed those characteristics. Its international capriciousness during the first two decades of the regime of Muammar al Qaddafi—including some "state terrorism"—drew military attacks from the United States and sanctions from the international community.

Since the end of the cold war, Libya has evolved more toward statehood and membership in the world of states. No longer a pawn in the cold war and facing internal threats from Islamic opposition groups, Libya is not now considered a major part of the worldwide terrorist threat and, indeed, actively collaborated with the United States in the wake of the September 11 attacks. To realize this double variability—of states themselves and of state-terrorist relations—is at one level heartening. Since all states maintain some kind of relations with terrorist organizations if they are in their midst—supporting, neglecting, opposing, suppressing—this means that foreign policy exercised through state-state relations has variable potential to operate as one form of constraint, albeit uncertain, against terrorism and terrorist activities.

Motivations for Terrorism

We now shift from an emphasis on the broader origins and contexts of terrorism to individual terrorists in their group and organizational settings. We have already touched on background reasons for supporting or joining terrorism, such as economic desperation, political repression, and the ready presence of a framing religious ideology. We now turn to more immediate psychological motives, while fully aware of the slipperiness of this exercise. The perils are that (a) human variation is such that there is no single, "typical" terrorist psychology; (b) many terrorists are psychologically inaccessible and when accessible often secretive and none yielding; and (c) Western psychological concepts and assessments often are not readily exportable and applicable to cultures very different from their own.

Individual Motivations

With respect to motivational profiles, work by Jerrold Post and others has suggested some similarities among members of given terrorist organizations, as well as some differences among the prototypical membership of different organizations. For instance, members of the German Red Army Faction and the Italian Red Brigades were likely to come from broken homes, and members of the Basque ETA group have come disproportionately from mixed Spanish-Basque parentage. "Comparable data are not available for Shi'ite and Palestinian terrorists, but specialists share the impression that many of their members come from the margins of society and that belonging to these fundamentalist and nationalist groups powerfully contributes to consolidating psychosocial identities at a time of great societal instability and flux".

In all events, generalizations of this sort must always be tempered by the recognition that the composition of terrorist organizations is diverse and that well-educated and wealthy individuals are also represented, particularly in leadership ranks. More recent research on terrorists has rejected the idea that psychopathy is a key feature of terrorist motivations. Leaving aside considerations of pathology or normality, the identity conferred by participating in a terrorist organization can be quite glamorous and appealing. As Post observed about one youthful recruit of a terrorist organization, "Before joining the group, he was alone, not particularly successful. Now he is engaged in a life and death struggle with the establishment, his picture on the 'most wanted' posters. He sees his leaders as internationally prominent media personalities. Within certain circles he is lionized as a hero".

Glorification of and personal salvation through violence is not limited to Islamic terrorists. Salvation as a voluntary martyr to violence or suffering has a religious history with roots in the theology of Christianity, Judaism, and Islam, as well as analogs in Buddhism. It is only because terrorists and their source populations on one hand, and target populations on the other, *share* these cultural precepts that such acts have the psychological impact that they do. Self-fulfillment through perpetration of violence also has a history, going back at least to nineteenth-century anarchists, early elements of Soviet communism, and some elements of the cowboy culture.

Similarly, utopian visions achieved through apocryphal transformation are not limited to Islam but are common both in mainstream and sectarian aspects of Christianity and Judaism. They are also found in cultures outside the province of the three major Near Eastern religions, although it is not always clear that they have appeared entirely independently of their influence (examples are Melanesian cargo cults and the ghost dance of American Indians). The glamour of the terrorist identity depends to a large extent on the terrorists' success. For example, following the tremendous media attention accorded the Palestinian cause in the wake of the killing of Israeli athletes at the Munich Olympics by the Black September faction of the Palestine Liberation Organization, thousands of Palestinians rushed to join the terrorist organizations.

It is evident that joining a terrorist group is not related uniquely to any given motivational profile. The search for identity is probably important, but so is the venting of anger, the power motive, and the glamour and aura of heroism and martyrdom—all operating in the context of situational opportunities.

The Process of Becoming a Terrorist

Why do individuals relinquish the societal values they have been brought up to cherish and adopt an extremist value system that may condone the killing of innocents? Studies of brainwashing, religious conversion, cults, as well as of terrorist groups per se provide a likely answer. It has to do with extreme forms of group influence and social pressures for conformity. The objectives are to isolate the individual from other belief systems, to delegitimize and dehumanize potential targets, to tolerate no uncertainty in rejecting or even killing skeptics, and to adore a leader. All these, taken together, create a separate, closed minded social reality at variance with the social reality of origin or the social reality of alternative cultures.

As Ehud Sprinzak notes: "Ideological terrorism does not emerge from a vacuum or from an inexplicable urge on the part of a few unstable radicals to go berserk...In the main, the process does not involve isolated individuals who become terrorists on their own because their psyche is split or they suffer from low esteem and need extravagant compensation. Rather, it involves a group of true believers. An understanding of this group process seems to be much more important than an understanding of individual terrorists' personal psychology". Once in the grasp of the group, it matters less what motivation may have brought the individual there in the first place.

An extreme illustration of this process is suicide bombing. Ariel Merari, an empirical investigator of suicide terrorism in the Middle East and Sri Lanka, writes:

The key to creating a terrorist suicide is the group process. Terrorist suicide is an organizational rather than an individual phenomenon. To the best of my knowledge, there has not been a single case of suicide terrorism which was done on the suicide's personal whim. In all cases, it was an organization that decided to embark on this tactic, recruited candidates, chose the target and the time, prepared the candidate for the mission, and made sure that he/she would carry it out (often via a back-up detonation device activated via remote control in case the would-be terrorist got cold feet after all). The three critical elements in the preparation are boosting motivation, group pressure (e.g., mutual commitment), and creating a point of no return (public personal commitment) by videotaping the candidate declaring that he is going to do it and having him write last letters to family and friends.

Terrorism as a Public Phenomenon

One intrinsic objective for terrorists is the drawing of attention to themselves or their cause, not only among their supportive constituencies but also from the whole world. News of terrorists in the media and in public awareness is omnipresent. It is inconceivable to think of a public event—the Olympics, an economic summit, any official gathering—without worrying about security and the threat of terrorist activity. The amount of publicity and literature devoted to terrorism in the past six months is unprecedented. Osama bin Laden was a contender for *Time* magazine's "Man of the Year" status, which was ultimately awarded to New York Mayor Rudolph Giuliani. The basis for inclusion was related to terrorism in both cases.

The tremendous attention-getting potential of terrorism may have given rise in the 1990s to a new brand of terrorism that Ehud Sprinzak recently called "the megalomaniac hyper terrorist," by which he means "self-anointed individuals with larger-than-life callings: Ramzi Youssef (the man behind the 1993 World Trade Center bombing), Shoko Asahara (leader of Aum Shinrikyo and architect of the 1995 gas attack in Tokyo subway station), Timothy McVeigh (the

1995 Oklahoma City bomber), Osama bin Laden (likely planner of the September 11 carnage)," Igal Amir, who assassinated Itzhak Rabin—all manifesting in some degree a desire to use catastrophic attacks in order to write a new chapter in history.

Whereas attention-getting in and of itself may be gratifying to terrorist leaders, successful terrorism sometimes advances terrorists' real-world objectives. High-casualty suicidal terrorist attacks on U.S. and French targets in Lebanon contributed to the decisions of those countries to withdraw their forces. Hezbollah, or the Party of God, is regarded in Lebanon (nearly universally) as the successful vanquisher of the Israeli occupation. Perhaps not coincidentally, 18 months after the slaughter of the Israeli athletes in Munich, Yasser Arafat was invited to address the UN General Assembly. Attention to Islam and Muslim values and traditional Islamic ways is on the rise among young generations of Muslims worldwide. The interest in Islam as a culture is rising, and the call for reexamination of U.S. foreign policy in regard to Muslim countries is no doubt related to attention that terrorist attacks have drawn to these issues.

Terrorism Networks

The preferred organizational form for terrorism is organizational networks or, perhaps better, networks of network-based organizations. Like other aspects of terrorism these networks are relatively unfamiliar to those who study organizations, who have focused more on formal organizations, such as corporations, hospitals, universities, civil service bureaucracies, voluntary organizations, and organizations that direct the activities of social movements. As a result, there are only some, mainly indirect insights about terrorist organizations from the literature on formal organizations.

The characteristics of terrorist organizations can be understood by tracing out the implications of the fact that terrorism must be simultaneously invisible and at the same time coordinated for preparing and executing terrorist activities. Consistent with these purposes, terrorist organizations must maintain extreme secrecy, avoid record-keeping, and minimize any paper trails that could reveal their internal movements, plans, and intentions. The last is extremely difficult to ensure completely, because of the necessity to rely on computer and telephone—in addition to handwritten and face-to-face—communication as a part of organizational coordination, and the necessity to rely on financial transaction institutions to shift resources from place to place and on credit cards to facilitate movements of their personnel by cars, buses, trains, and airplanes.

The foreign affairs or external political exigencies of terrorist organizations are limited and concern mainly their relations with the host states in which they are located. If they are unknown to those states—rarely if ever the case—then questions of foreign relations with them are moot, because terrorist organizations avoid routine interactions with governing regimes. However, host states usually know about, tolerate, protect, or promote terrorist organizations for their own political purposes. This means establishing relations with terrorist organizations, taking an interest in and perhaps influencing their activities, thus forcing the terrorist organizations to observe and perhaps play along with various state-related realities.

Because much of the glue of terrorist organizations is commitment to an extreme ideology in a group with extreme solidarity, this generates a special range of issues of maintaining internal control. They must recruit those whom they regard as ideologically committed and ideologically correct. While there have been news reports that claim to trace associations between individual terrorists and specific schools or other social ties, the panel is not confident that these purported ties are sufficient evidence to make conclusive statements.

Regardless of where recruits come from, the leaders must dedicate some of their organizational activities to maintaining that loyalty and commitment and preventing backsliding among members who are frequently living in societies with values, ways of life, and institutions that are different from their own and may be found seductive. The need to maintain various kinds of discipline through intense personal ties, hierarchical control, and surveillance is very strong. Organizations must ensure that information flows but also that it is kept secret. They must coordinate extremely complex activities of destruction. And they must ensure steadiness of ideological commitment.

There are several associated points of vulnerability of terrorist organizations, many of which involve failures of information flow, security of information, and coordination of activities. One additional vulnerable, characteristic of all ideologically extreme and rigid organizations, is the constant danger of schismatic ideological tendencies from within. Demanding extreme conformity, such organizations constantly face problems of internal deviation, mutual accusations among both leaders and followers that they are less than true believers, the splitting off of factions based on ideological differences, and the political intrigues that are involved in preventing such splits and dealing with them once they have occurred.

Direct knowledge about these organizational dynamics is very frail, mainly because it is so difficult to study organizations that are bent on secret operations and concealment of information. Such knowledge must usually come from defectors, detainees who cooperate, and agents who have been able to infiltrate. However, the world has experienced many other kinds of secret, network-based organizations, and a base of knowledge about them and their operations has accumulated. Among these organizations are spy networks, gang rings such as the Mafia, drug-trafficking organizations, Communist cells, sabotage operations undertaken during wartime and during the cold war period, and extremist social and political movement organizations.

In addition, network analysis as a field of study in sociology, social psychology, and elsewhere has yielded a great deal of theoretical and empirical knowledge during recent decades, and some aspects of this general knowledge might also be brought to bear. We conclude this long section on origins, contexts, motives, and organization of terrorism by noting a number of potential limitations on and vulnerability of contemporary terrorism: (a) their partial dependence on "domestic" friendly audiences, whose support and applause can wane if the terrorists appear to be inept or gratuitously excessive in their activities; (b) their dependence on states within which they operate—variable in terms of their precise relationship with those states—which may constrain their activities in light of their own "state" interests in the international arena; (c) extreme ideological/religious rigidity and backsliding, both of which have the potential to generate schisms within the terrorist organizations; (d) motivational failings, reversals, and defections, always a possibility when so much psychic energy is invested in an extreme cause; and (e) organizational failures, especially in flows of information in a dispersed, secretive network.

Responses to Terrorism

The targets of terrorist attacks are multiple and diverse. This fact constitutes an advantage for terrorists, because it is one facet of the uncertainty on which they capitalize—where and when will an attack occur and what kind of attack will it be? Some targets of terrorist attacks are human beings themselves, for example, assassinations, the bombing of large human assemblies, and biological and chemical poisoning and contamination. Others do not attack humans at all but aim to disrupt some vital economic or institutional functioning, for example, disruption of financial institutions or computer networks. No matter what the attack, however, there is always a human response to it. In this chapter we summarize much of what is known about these responses from research in the behavioural and social sciences.

Preparedness and Warning

Throughout its history, the American nation has been relatively free from anxieties about attacks on its homeland, except for a few wartime situations (including the cold war). The "age of terrorism," however, with us for some time but dramatically imposed by the events of September 11, has led to a heightening of multifaceted anxiety. This is especially difficult to dispel, largely because of the irreducible quotient of uncertainty involved. A condition of high anxiety, moreover, leaves a population skittish and prone to extreme reactions, mainly rumors and exaggerated fears. Preventive measures may be sought at five points in the terrorist process: (a) long-term efforts to modify the demographic, economic, political, and cultural background of terrorism; (b) prevention at the source, that is, by seeking out and disrupting terrorist activities—in the present case, in staging areas in the several countries that knowingly harbor terrorists and to some extent in countries that do not wish them there; (c) prevention at the end of the line, by erecting defenses at the locus of known or conceivable targets, such as dams, public buildings, mass assemblages of people, and so on; (d) along the way between source and event, by controlling the movements of people and weapons at the national borders and other points of entry; and (e) after an attack, by having in place a response-and-recovery apparatus that will minimize its effects.

A few comments on the middle three measures are in order. On one hand, the attractiveness of the at-the-source alternative is that, if successful, it prevents all sorts of terrorism. On the other hand, intelligence and military operations of this sort are very costly and constitute a significant drain on the nation's resources; it is also impossible to ensure that eradication efforts will ever approach anything like completeness, given the secrecy and mobility of terrorists and their networks. In addition, even if eradicated, terrorist activities and organizations can re-grow. Finally, aggressive ferreting poses certain perils of unilateralism and the peeling away of allies and friends if the pursuit appears to them to be too aggressive. The attractiveness of along-the-way strategies is similar in that they intercept persons with a possible diversity of purposes, but in this case as well, both the cost and the impossibility of completeness are evident, given the mass movement of things and people that global commerce and tourism entails.

The attractiveness of the end-of-the-line strategy is security but, given the multiplicity of targets and the adaptive capacity of terrorists to change them and invent new ones, it also raises the questions of cost and the impossibility of completeness. Considerations of strategic prudence and the force of national public opinion probably dictate that the country will pursue all three lines of prevention. Preparedness for attacks should be organized at two levels—responsible authorities and the general population. At the level of government and community officials, preparation should be both exhaustive and contingent—anticipating every kind of attack, understanding the probable ripple effects, thinking in terms of multiple attacks, preparing proper responses for agents who give out information in crisis situations, detailing the roles of first-line response agencies such as police and rescue agencies, and developing a whole range of backup responses to contain damage and minimize future damage. These measures will also call for new levels of cooperation among government, the media, schools, businesses, hospitals, churches, and other types of organizations, as well as households.

Applied research, conducted in advance, on all these aspects of preparedness is necessary. At the level of the populace the effort is both educational and instructional. As much unambiguous information as possible should be disseminated about the nature of different kinds of attacks—information that is clear, placed in context, repeated, and authoritative. Training and drills for behavioural responses for each generally increase the sense of mastery and reduce anxiety before the attack and reduce both chaos and human death and suffering in the event of attack. Readiness and preparedness involve a number of delicate equilibrium, however. If attacks do not occur for a long period of time, public apprehension diminishes and knowledge about responding properly erodes. Recall the high-profile, sometimes hysterical movement to protect against fallout in the wake of a nuclear attack in the 1950s and 1960s. Despite encouragement by both government and the media, only 1 in every 100,000 people actually built some sort of fallout shelter.

The desired equilibrium is to keep public consciousness high without whipping up public anxiety. Overtraining and over drilling, moreover, can generate public indifference, irritability, and criticism of responsible authorities. Warning systems also create a delicate balance. Authorities should strive to make warnings free from ambiguity, directed to all those at risk (wherever they may be), and communicated through multiple channels (public warning devices such as sirens, radio, television, and Internet) (National Science and Technology Council, 2000). False alarms and misdirection of warnings to people not at risk, however, tend to generate public apathy and hostility.

Behavioural and social science research carried out mainly, but not exclusively, during World War II and the civil defense era of the 1950s and 1960s (e.g., Wallace, 1956) yields a reliable store of knowledge about behaviour during and after disaster situations. We detail below a typical scenario: An initial response of disbelief, denial, and emotional numbing. A wildfire spread of information, both factual and fictional (mainly rumors) as a part of the process of comprehending and assigning meaning to the events; much of this is by word-of-mouth and telephone (if possible), but over time the mass media have taken over a decisive role in the structuring of cognitive and emotional reactions. The appearance of a mix of intense emotional reactions, including fear, anxiety, and terror, as well as rage, guilt, grief, and serious mental disturbances in a small proportion of the affected population; some research indicates that many of the extreme reactions occur among individuals already suffering from mental disorders.

The occurrence of a mix of collective behaviour reactions, such as rare episodes of collective panic, rapid movement of people in an effort to join and help loved ones, some disorganized behaviour, and some "derived" behaviours, such as looting and crime in the context of a temporary breakdown of social order. Research on hurricane disasters has shown that, even when warned, households make their own assessments of risk and actively decide whether or not to evacuate, depending on such factors as level of risk perceived, job circumstances, concern for personal property, and family situation. A rush to the scene of a disaster ("convergence effect") of agencies formally designated to respond to crisis situations (police, firefighters, and military personnel, as well as rescue and relief agencies), along with individual and group rescue activities; at the same time, the occurrence of failures of communication and coordination in these responses, as well as some conflict and jurisdictional squabbling among the agencies. One of the most common vulnerabilities of responses to disaster is the uncertainty of mission and communication among different response agencies.

The development of a notable social solidarity, including a pulling-together of the affected community to respond to the crisis; altruistic and heroic behaviour; an increase in trust of other individuals, groups, and authorities; an augmented spirit of cooperation and good will; and the spread of euphoric feelings as a kind of collective offset to the negative emotional responses. The simultaneous appearance of scapegoat reactions, directed primarily at individuals believed to be responsible for permitting the disaster to occur and for failures in responding to the crisis. A gradual return to the routine and the normal, including the management and diminution of intense affective reactions by way of adaptive processes akin to mourning; the restoration and recreation of broken social ties, a return to familiar rounds of activities, and the completion of recovery and reconstruction efforts. In the aftermath of the catastrophic events of September 11, 2001, every one of these ingredients appeared. Yet limited comfort can be taken from these observations and insights, because the contemporary terrorist situation, as it has evolved, does not correspond to "normal" disaster reactions. It is more complex than these, calling for a correspondingly increased complexity in efforts to comprehend and respond to it.

To begin with the most basic differences, terrorism involves intended and manipulated disasters, as contrasted with acts of God and accidental misfiring in complex systems of industrial, transportation, and economic organizations. This element of deliberateness, moreover, involves maximizing the surprise, uncertainty, novelty, and diversity of assaults, thus limiting the effectiveness of discrete efforts to anticipate, prepare for, and respond to single types of terrorist attacks. The contemporary terrorist situation thus dictates that one abandon any conception that there is a single and unified disaster syndrome and incorporate complexity, contingency, and continual adaptation and revision of thinking about, readying for, and preventing terrorist events and situations.

As we now understand it, terrorism involves great variations along the following, overlapping lines: Discrete types of targets, including buildings, food and water supplies, electrical and other energy systems, transportation systems, information and communication systems, large human populations (including bombings as well as chemical and biological poisoning), currency and financial systems, and governmental structures. Degree of localization (e.g., explosion) or dispersion (e.g., biological contamination) of assault to which targets are symbolically charged (rail-road tracks at one extreme, sacred symbols such as the Statue of Liberty at the other). Whether attacks are single or multiple one-time or recurrent, and if recurrent, how erratic or "random" in pattern, the agent of attack is known, suspected, ambiguous, unknown, or unknowable.

As should be evident from this listing, the mix and multiplicity of responses in the ideal-typical disaster syndrome is highly variable. Localized attacks, especially if they involve the closing of escape routes, are more likely to occasion collective panic reactions. Generalized attacks, such as contamination and poisoning, are likely to cause reactions of mass hysteria but not localized panics. Widespread terror—a generic objective of terrorist attacks—is more likely to occur when attacks are dispersed, multiple, unpredictably recurrent, and by ambiguous or unknown agents. And converging rescue and relief operations are qualitatively different for localized bombings than they are for attempts to poison or sicken large numbers of people. Finally, the mix of reactions will differ widely according to whether human casualties result from the attack and whether the attack is immediately recognizable or is perceived as having invisible or unknown dimensions.

It is instructive to comment on the September 11 attacks on the World Trade Center and the Pentagon in this context. Widespread terror was not the most salient feature of the immediate response to the events. Rather, September 11 created an intense reaction of moral outrage against a readily identifiable and "evil" enemy and a reaction of exceptional collective resolve to unite, mobilize, and retaliate—violently and with perceived legitimacy—against that enemy. In that limited sense, the attacks present an appearance of miscalculation. (The sense of uncertainty created by the assaults, however, has generated a persistent level of anxiety in the population.) As such, the September 11 attacks, like Pearl Harbor 60 years earlier, were a "natural" for American society and national character—which includes a sense of ambivalence and inhibition in initiating aggression but a great capacity to respond morally and collectively when unequivocally provoked by an act of aggression from outside.

Some insights about the anthrax mail episode a few weeks later can be generated as well. As passing and amateurish as those events seemed to be, they nevertheless had a potential to be very terror-inducing. This lay in the many kinds of uncertainty surrounding the episodes. The agents were unknown. The fatal effects of widespread exposure could be extensive. And mail, like currency, is something that everyone regularly handles. The episode left room for feelings of danger for everyone—that it could strike anywhere, any time—however unrealistic such fears may have been. The press also played a role, scarcely deliberate, in magnifying the threat, bringing what were essentially a series of highly localized events to the attention of a vast population of viewers and readers.

Normalisation

As indicated, the natural history of recovery from disaster involves a diminution of emotional responses, the setting in of a certain denial of the possibility of recurrence, and a return to routine activities, events, rhythms, and conflicts. These are, by and large, reasonable and adaptive responses on the part of a population because of the rarity of specific kinds of catastrophic events in life. It is not psychically economical for people to worry about them all the time. Discrete acts of terrorism, if not soon repeated, should be expected to show the same tendency toward routinisation. Indeed, there were messages from government and public leaders exhorting the public to return to normal activities in the wake of terrorism:

The September 11 attacks, while at the same time stressing the need for vigilance and even warning of impending attack. Should additional major attacks on the homeland occur, the whole routinisation process would be thrown in the air and a new situation created? Many of the emotional and behavioural symptoms of the disaster syndrome would recur, but in a different context of public memory of the earlier attacks. Scapegoat of governmental and other agencies and persons singled out as lax or irresponsible would become more salient because of expectations that vigilance and security should have increased as a result of the previous attacks. Subsequent attacks would also probably lead to even more tightening of homeland security, along with all the psychological and political consequences that would ensue. If, down the line, a dreadful scenario of multiple, repeated, and continuous terrorist attacks should unfold, one would expect the emergence of, among other things, a certain routinisation of disaster reactions, including an inuring and hardening of public outlooks and behaviour reminiscent of what has been witnessed over time in places like Northern Ireland, Israel, and Lebanon. Because the attacks of September 11 were such a dramatic and profound wound to the nation, they qualify as what social scientists and humanists recently have been calling a cultural trauma. Within a matter of days after the assault, it was appreciated in all quarters that these events would embed themselves deeply in the nation's memory and endure indefinitely. Unlike some other cultural traumas that are mainly negative—regicides and assassinations of national leaders, holocausts, and episodes of ethnic cleansing—September 11 already emerges not only as a deep scar on the nation's body, but also as a moment of extreme heroism and pride. In the wake of the events, the nation has simultaneously experienced both deep mourning and a not altogether expected season of celebration. A cultural trauma of this type can be expected to manifest a number of known characteristics: The event is indelible, not only not forgotten but unable to be forgotten; It is sacred, not in any specific religious sense, but as a monumental instant in the history of the nation; There are deliberate efforts to remember the event and its heroes collectively, through commemorative ceremonies, public observation of anniversaries, and the erection of monuments; and There is sustained public interest in the remembering process, including, down the line, some contestation among politically interested groups over how the remembering should be concretized. These are a few of the threads involved in the process of public normalization. More will emerge in the final two sections of this chapter on political and economic aspects of terrorism.

7

Political Aspects of Recovery

A post-attack development of political solidarity parallels the burst of social solidarity noted above. Citizens experience an increase in trust and support of political leaders, which can endure for long periods of time if a sense of crisis continues and it is perceived that leaders are dealing with the crisis well. The most dramatic evidence of this effect is the report of polls of black Americans in late December 2001, which revealed a figure of 75 percent support for President George W. Bush among a segment of the population that had cast only 10 percent of their votes for him one year earlier. Such support does not last indefinitely, however, as the fate of President George Bush after the Gulf War demonstrates. Political leadership also pulls together in such times of crisis, particularly if the crisis involves an attack on the nation as a whole. This effect is not necessarily seen in other types of crises—such as an economic collapse of the domestic economy and major political scandals—which typically set off both class and party conflicts. Partisan politics are quick to return, however, even in areas that have some connection with the crisis. It was less than two months after September 11 when Democrats and Republicans split along recognizable lines over the issue of whether airline security personnel should be federal employees or remain as private-sector employees.

By December 2001, the New York Times, in summarizing the national situation, quipped that "the Democrats and Republicans are fighting about everything but terrorism". Apparently this effect is a general one. In 1689, after the semi forced departure of the Catholic King James II and the succession of William of Orange, a Whig political leader observed that "fear of Popery has united [Whigs and Tories]; when that is over, we shall divide again". We mention four other political possibilities: Tension between the exigencies of national security and the preservation of civil liberties. This tension seems real and perhaps inevitable in times of political crisis. The two sets of considerations pull in opposite directions. Three foci of tension after September 11 were the issues of (a) detention of immigrants, (b) the use of military tribunals for trying apprehended terrorists, and (c) the continuing controversy over the practice — and negative repercussions—of ethnic profiling in checking and searching for suspects. This tension between vigilance and liberty is of special significance and is likely to be a running sore in the context of American democracy, because of the nation's commitment to civil liberties.

Discrimination against and scapegoat of relevant minority groups in the domestic population are sometimes encouraged or even executed by the government. The negative actions taken against German Americans during World War I and the more drastic measures taken against Japanese Americans in World War II are cases in point. In the present crisis, neither the government nor the populace has turned against Muslim Americans in the same overt way, except for some local incidents. The crisis created uneasiness and ambivalence in that sector of the population, however, despite exhortations for tolerance in government and media circles. A sense of comfort and pride can be gained from the posture of moderation on the part of the government, the press, and the public. It should not be supposed, however, that the issue is permanently closed. In the future, successful terrorist attacks, especially major ones, or evidence or suspicion of terrorist activities on the part of Muslim Americans could quickly turn the picture around and stimulate explosive group antagonisms. One aspect of political solidarity and the diminution of partisanship during national crises of the sort now being experienced is that opposition parties and groups extend unusual trust of, and cooperation with, top national leaders.

The engine that drives this is patriotism—love of nation. Two features of this unusual type of political situation may make for a muting of political opposition: (a) a temptation of the leaders and party in power to play their political trump card by insinuating or claiming that political opposition is tainted with a lack of loyalty and (b) the tendency for opposition voices to drift toward a self-imposed muteness, out of apprehension that voters in their own districts may also confuse opposition with lack of loyalty. The optimal resolution of these tendencies is the recognition of the right to oppose responsibly and legitimately in the context of an appreciated loyalty to the nation, but this is a matter of delicate equilibrium, not automatically guaranteed.

Extremist Political Movements

An extension of these three tendencies can result in nationally disruptive political movements that evoke accusations of disloyalty in periods of realistic or exaggerated threats. There is nothing inevitable about the development of such movements, but it is worth recalling two disturbing episodes of stereotyping and group punishment in the twentieth century: (a) the red scare of the early 1920s, in which government intimidation and actual raids were carried out in the context of a great national fear of Bolshevism and (b) McCarthyism in the late 1940s and early 1950s, which occurred in the context of a state of high national anxiety over the development of nuclear explosives and weaponry by the Soviet Union and the fall of mainland China to communism in 1948. Both movements, while limited in duration, seriously compromised the civil liberties and livelihood of some citizens, and both left ugly scars on the body politic. Raising these four possibilities is in no way to predict that any or all will materialize as the nation continues to struggle with its current situation.

We cannot unambiguously predict political movements, even though social scientists understand a good deal about the conditions under which movements develop. Some potential terrorist targets are economic in nature. The disruption or destruction of the stock market, the paralysis of credit systems, and the contamination of currency with toxic and infectious agents come to mind. While potentially very disruptive in the short run, these types of attacks—except perhaps the last—are such that reasonably rapid recovery can be envisioned. Other direct economic consequences are the costs of rebuilding what has been damaged or destroyed. Depending on the scope and success of the attacks, these costs can be very significant. The full cost of replacing the World Trade Center (including compensation for survivors) and the damaged portion of the Pentagon are enormous, as would be the costs of replacing destroyed dams and severely damaged electrical supply systems. Once capital resources are raised and put to work, however, reconstruction projects take on the same stimulating significance for the economy as some public works projects. Assessment of the indirect and derived economic consequences of terrorist attacks is a more complicated matter, in part because of the great diversity of possible targets.

The overall economic losses generated by the September 11 attacks, while evidently severe, are difficult to establish, all the more so because the national economy had already entered a period of downturn. Temporary and selective economic dislocations, however, are readily traceable; some of these were mentioned above. In general, economic dislocations resulting from discrete terrorist activities should be expected to obey the laws of routinisation—however slowly in some cases—as people in the affected parts of the economy gradually return to their normally preferred lines of activity and expenditures. Another economic effect that appears over time in the wake of national traumas is the process of capitalizing on public crisis and turning it in the direction of private gain.

The plea on the part of airlines for financial relief is not exactly a case in point, because the losses they suffered after September 11 were genuine; nevertheless, the possibilities of turning relief into gain are always present. The need to gird up for prevention, retaliation against, and aggressive pursuit of terrorism inevitably sets off a scramble for government contracts in relevant parts of the economy. This pattern is observable in wartime situations and was evident throughout the cold war, and it is to be expected to reappear during the coming years. Other, more trivial examples of small-time entrepreneurial activity could also be cited, such as the manufacture and sale of patriotic t-shirts, hats, sweaters, and souvenirs.

The economic question of who pays will be a continuous one. Even under normal circumstances, American politics are fraught with ambiguities and conflicts over the respective costs to be borne by federal, regional, state, and local authorities. The defense against terrorism promises to make the uncertainties even more salient. Given the number and diversity of possible attacks, the prospect of terrorism is simultaneously national, regional, and local. Furthermore, while the fight against terrorism is manifestly a public and governmental responsibility, many if not most of the targets of terrorism are in the private sector. Given all these intersections, who prepares and who pays? More rational and less rational solutions to these dilemmas can be designed, but the nation must expect a significant residue of tugging and hauling, jockeying for position, and resentment of perceived off-loading. Two final sets of derived consequences of uncertain dimensions also lie on the horizon.

The first is the impact of a continuous, quasi-wartime effort on the balance and strength of the American economy. Such an effort will involve significant reallocation of public expenditures and capital among different industrial sectors (especially those connected with defense), the prospect of governmental budgetary deficits, and some impact on the pattern of imports and exports, and perhaps a greater sensitivity to periods of inflation. The second is the prospect of giving lower priority to some expenditure for programs in education, health, welfare, and other areas in consideration of the more urgent demands for military and home defense expenditures. War efforts typically slow the progress of social programs (demands for which often follow wars in a flurry). The quasi-wartime exigencies associated with counterterrorist activities promise to be no exception. It is also possible that the economically relevant aspects of environmental protection will fall from salience as well, unless special efforts are made to sustain them. Environmental efforts involve costs to the nation, and they could come to be seen as competitive with more urgent expenditures.

8

Experience and Lessons in Eliminating Terrorism

Moscow is the capital of the Russian state and the spiritual center of the Russian land. It is the center of the scientific and cultural life of the country, with a significant portion of the national wealth concentrated within its territory. It is a unique historical and architectural monument of world culture. It represents the largest concentration of financial and information flows and has a substantial influence on the development of the state. It is Russia's largest industrial city, making a significant contribution to the country's overall economic indicators. Moscow has the country's most developed energy and public utility networks. Our city is the country's most important transportation hub, on which the functioning of the entire Russian transportation system depends. Furthermore, unique tall buildings are being constructed and put into service in the city, and new metro stations are being built along with underground shopping and entertainment centers, tunnels, and parking garages.

Thousands of industrial enterprises are located in the city. Disruption of their normal operations, and especially terrorist acts and accidents at their facilities, could present a significant danger to every resident. Despite the measures being undertaken, Muscovites have been confronted with inhumane and antihuman manifestations of terrorism in recent years. Therefore, we understand and share the pain and suffering of other peoples that have suffered from extreme situations of any nature. We recall the seizure of hostages during the theatrical show Nord-Ost, as well as the bombings at the shopping center in Manezh Square; in the underground pedestrian passage at the Pushkinskaya Metro Station; outside the National Hotel and the Rizhskaya Metro Station; during the concert at the Tushino Airfield; and in a metro train car in the Paveletskaya Station, all of which resulted in more than 3,000 victims, about 700 of whom were killed. These events demonstrated that terrorist acts are increasingly moving from the realm of potential threats into that of actual extreme situations.

In our opinion it was the lack of the appropriate reaction from the world community to the fall 1999 terrorist acts in Moscow that led to the tragic events of September 11, 2001, in the United States, events that once again showed that terrorism has no nationality, that it is international in nature, and that no state is insured against it. In addition, accidents at facilities that use dangerous chemical substances in their production processes represent another serious potential danger for the city. Indeed, accidents at such facilities could lead to the chemical contamination of large sections of the city. For example, on April 26, 2004, an accident involving the release of ammonia into the atmosphere occurred at one of the city's dangerous facilities.

Subsequently analyzing the causes of the accident, one may conclude that it occurred due to the most egregious violations of the rules of technological safety. In the interests of obtaining the greatest possible profits, the management of the enterprise neglected to carry out mandated work and maintenance on systems and utility lines at the facility. An explosion resulted, and the production facilities were destroyed. Only the wise actions of the city's response services and favorable meteorological conditions prevented the contamination cloud from spreading over neighboring enterprises and residential blocks. In contrast, our greatest efforts were required to eliminate the consequences of the bombings of the apartment buildings on Guryanov Street (September 9, 1999) and Kashirskoe Shosse (September 13, 1999) and to extinguish the fire in the Ostankino television tower (August 27, 2000).

Using these examples, I would like to explain the organization of the system of efforts to eliminate the consequences of extreme situations. From the moment that the first search-and-rescue units and fire crews arrived on the scene, the Main Operational Headquarters for Eliminating the Consequences of Emergency Situations in the City of Moscow deployed its personnel and organized cooperation with the local authorities, the Moscow City Commission on Eliminating the Consequences of Emergency Situations, the city emergency services, the Russian Ministry of Emergency Situations, and other federal agencies. Thus, a two-level management system has been organized and has proven its effectiveness. Fire crews and search-and-rescue units from the Moscow Main Administration for Civil Defense and Emergency Situations, personnel and resources from the Russian Ministry of Emergency Situations, and the city emergency services were directly deployed for rescue operations.

This created a group including a total of more than 1,000 persons and 200 pieces of equipment. Efforts were organized in shifts. In extinguishing the fire at the Ostankino television tower, we encountered the need to apply new tactics in conducting rescue operations. When the fire broke out on the fifth floor of the television transmitter section of the television tower (which has a total height of 540 meters), preliminary information indicated that the fire occurred as a result of a short circuit in vertical cable lines in a room housing receiving-transmitting feeder devices. Based on the results of an analysis conducted by investigators, tactics were worked out and the optimal personnel and equipment were selected to carry out search-and-rescue operations and extinguish the fire at the focus of this emergency situation.

The following objectives were established: cutting cables covering the interiors of the cable shafts with sheets of damp asbestos to prevent the fire from spreading organizing a search for the elevator on which the cables had been severed within the tower ensuring security for personnel and removing some of them to a zone at a safe distance involving specialists from the Moscow City Trust for Geologic, Geodesic, and Cartographic Work to maintain constant watch over any deviations of the tower from the vertical axis. The experience gained in eliminating the consequences of these emergency situations has shown that the most serious attention must be devoted to matters regarding the management and comprehensive execution of rescue efforts. In conducting these efforts, the personnel involved were provided with continuous, 24-hour meal service at two mobile food distribution points and one cafeteria.

During the emergency situation, about 30,000 hot meals and cold sandwich meals were served. A system was also established for refueling all equipment and vehicles involved. More than 7.5 metric tons of fuel, oil, and lubricants were used. The emergency response group was also provided with the necessary expendable supplies and tools. The personnel involved in the emergency situation were able to warm themselves in special inflatable modules and buses. Heavy equipment, including cranes, loaders, and dump trucks to remove structural debris, was put into action from the very first hours of the emergency situation. This equipment arrived from facilities located around the city of Moscow. Experience amassed in cleanup efforts after building demolitions has shown that in such major emergency situations it is most expedient and efficient to use heavy cranes with a load capacity of 50 metric tons and a 20–40 meter swing-away jib. Cranes with a load capacity of up to 300 metric tons were subsequently used to bring down structures in danger of collapse.

Medical support was organized in accordance with the action plan of the Moscow City Center for Urgent Medical Care in Emergency Situations. Victims were sent to 13 different treatment facilities in the city. Ambulance brigades were put in place around the perimeter of the emergency zone to provide medical care on site and take the injured to city hospitals. The entire effort involved 80 ambulance brigades and 3 brigades for the transportation of the dead (the bodies were delivered to official morgues on orders from a representative of the city Medical Examiner's Office). A group of psychologists was organized to work in hospitals and clinics and a hotline was established for relatives of the victims.

Because operations went on 24 hours a day, we had to resolve questions regarding how to illuminate the work area during the hours of darkness. During the first hours (which occurred at night), the area in which rescue efforts were being carried out was lit by individual lighting devices belonging to the search-and-rescue units of the Moscow Main Administration for Civil Defense and Emergency Situations. Lighting was subsequently organized by a special unit of the Moscow city government, which set up powerful lighting equipment. The efforts organized and undertaken made it possible to ensure that there was sufficient light in the areas where work was under way. Experience shows that success in carrying out rescue efforts largely depends on how the efforts are organized in the initial hours. The primary organizational task in this regard is determining the most important areas in which to focus the work, the number of people and pieces of equipment needed at the given stage, and their placement around the site. It is also important to register personnel and equipment upon their arrival and establish a shift schedule for people and equipment over the course of the operation.

Security and Prevention

It must be noted that ensuring security against emergency situations and terrorist acts is a complex and multifaceted problem, and its successful solution may be achieved only through the active participation of all city structures, federal ministries, and agencies. Therefore, an effective emergency prevention and response system has been in operation in the city since 1996. Its operations are led by the mayor of Moscow through the City Government Commission on Emergency Situations and Fire Safety, which coordinates the activities of all services. The Main Administration for Civil Defense and Emergency Situations is the operating arm of the commission. Since the system was created we have done a certain amount of work aimed at ensuring the security of the capital's residents and territory. This work includes the creation of a regulatory and legal base that relies on international and federal experience.

The Law on Protecting the Population and Territory of the City of Moscow from Natural and Non-Natural Emergency Situations and the Concept for the Security of Moscow have both been ratified. These documents defined the system of views of the city's leadership for ensuring the security of its residents. In the process of developing them, several programs were worked out, including Moscow's Radiation Security, Moscow's Chemical Security, Moscow's Fire Security, the Program for the Development of the Moscow City System for Emergency Prevention and Response, and the Program for the Construction of Rescue and Treatment Complexes on the Water. At present, more than 100 regulations and legal acts govern the activities of executive branch agencies, local government entities, and the city's organizations and institutions with regard to protecting the population against emergency situations.

These documents have laid the foundation for resolving problems associated with reducing the risk of various types of emergency situations. Regarding the construction and renovation of structures, primary attention is focused on the implementation of modern technical means of ensuring safety. Work is being done at facilities that use dangerous chemical substances to equip them with automated emergency emissions control systems capable of detecting the onset of an emergency at its early stages and providing a solution to deal with the situation without any human involvement. At the city level, a light detection and ranging-based automated system for remote monitoring of the condition of the city's air basin has been created and is currently functioning and being further developed.

This system makes it possible to automatically detect the initiation of a crisis situation (fire, explosion with release of poisonous substances, contamination of the atmosphere by vehicles and industrial enterprises, and so forth), monitor its development in real time, and predict its effect on neighboring areas. City government agencies are devoting special attention to ensuring the security of residents in areas where large numbers of people gather and in the city's underground spaces, especially on the metro and in tunnels. Given that a large quantity of special cargo (gasoline, reagents for refrigeration units, and so forth) is transported through Moscow, as in other cities throughout the world, we have instituted stricter controls over their shipment via truck and rail within the city limits.

Furthermore, we have begun creating comprehensive vehicle inspection stations at entry points to the city, with their tasks being as follows: checking vehicles for contamination with hazardous substances decontaminating vehicles contaminated with hazardous substances monitoring the environment. However, practice shows that even with the most perfect monitoring systems, it is impossible to fully rule out the possibility of accidents and guarantee the safe operation of a particular facility. Therefore, in order to reduce the degree of risk, in addition to measures aimed at preventing accidents, we must consider a range of measures to reduce the risk that they will occur. Technical and organizational measures should be taken into account.

For example, after the tragic bombing in the underground walkway at the Pushkinskaya Metro Station, we discovered that 80 percent of the victims were injured by flying building fragments or pieces of glass. With this in mind, as part of international cooperation efforts, the Moscow city government is purchasing a unique protective coating for glass that prevents it from breaking. This coating is being installed in areas where large numbers of people gather. The creation, training, and development of emergency personnel hold an important place in the operation of the system. With the support of the Russian Ministry of Emergency Situations, the city has created a modern rescue service, which it maintains at its own expense. About 14,000 firefighters, rescue personnel, and other specialists of the Main Administration for Civil Defense and Emergency Situations are working to ensure the security of Muscovites as they go about their daily affairs. Each day, about 1,700 people report for 24-hour duty shifts, of whom more than 1,500 are firefighters, rescue workers, and support specialists.

Current world experience in resolving the problem of preventing and responding to emergency situations in large cities indicates that achieving an optimal result is impossible without the use of aviation technologies. Therefore, the city has created its own aviation structure, which in times of heavy traffic congestion on the main roads will make it possible to deliver rescuers to the emergency zone in a timely fashion and evacuate the injured to the city's health care facilities. In conclusion, I would like to say that in eliminating the consequences of emergency situations we have gained bitter but nevertheless practical experience in working under extreme conditions. The Moscow city government is devoting a great deal of attention to issues regarding the prevention of emergency situations and the creation of a security system. We are prepared to share this experience and render the necessary assistance in this regard.

The Search for a Sustainable Strategy

The scientific and research policies of the U.S. government were profoundly transformed by the cold war in response to a military strategy of technological superiority. Only the shock of the September 11, 2001, attack on the World Trade Center, the Pentagon, and one other unknown target forced a restructuring to meet the threat of catastrophic terrorism. This paper addresses the nature of that threat and the role that science and technology can play in mitigating the risk and the consequences of such attacks. The conclusion summarizes the impact on science and technology policy that may result. A serious constraint on that policy is the need for a sustainable and affordable strategy, which the private sector as well as government will adopt and which the public will support for many years into the future.

This presentation addresses four questions:

How different is the current threat from that for which the institutions of government are primarily structured? How can science and engineering contribute to making the nation safer against the threat of catastrophic terrorism? Where will the responsibility lie for defining those responses, investing the needed resources, and implementing the strategies? How can a strategy for mitigating the threat of catastrophic terrorism be sustainable in a democratic society whose political system is known for its short attention span? Given the reality that most of the targets of terrorism are privately owned, and many of the vulnerabilities are the result of firms maximizing efficiency at the expense of security externalities, how can a public-private balance between private efficiency and public vulnerability be found?

The Terrorist Threat Today

To understand how science and technology might contribute to countering terrorism, we must evaluate the nature of the threat, the vulnerabilities of targets in civil society, and the availability of technical solutions to address the vulnerabilities that are most likely to be exploited by terrorists. India and the United States, the world's two largest democracies, are both vulnerable to terrorist attacks. As an Indian participant in the workshop said, "The most vulnerable states are those with open societies that tolerate dissent." So far, India and the United States have faced rather different forms of terror attacks. Let me distinguish two forms of terrorism, which I shall categorize as tactical and strategic. Tactical terrorism is characterized by the use of conventional small arms weapons plus explosives (often in the form of car or truck bombs) against individuals in an attempt to put political pressure on a government that has proved intransigent regarding the political objectives of the terrorists.

India has experienced a great deal of this kind of terrorism, as has Israel, and the United Kingdom (from the military wing of the Irish Republican Army). Strategic or catastrophic terrorism, on the other hand, seeks to inflict maximum damage against targets that are ideologically despised by the terrorists. In this case the terrorists wish to draw attention to their cause, to inflict maximum damage on the legitimacy of a government, and to inflict major economic penalties on the nation or nations in question. The attack on the World Trade Center by al Qaeda fit this pattern, as did the attack in the Tokyo subway by the Aum Shinrikyo. Such terrorists do not seek to shock a government into making concessions through negotiation. Thus the U.S. concern for catastrophic or strategic terrorism is different—and presents a broader spectrum of opportunities for science and technology to reduce the nation's vulnerability—than is the case today in India. However, given the demonstration of catastrophic destruction in the September 11, 2001, attack in New York City, India, like the United States, a nation that plays an important role in the world, must assume that the day will come when such attacks might be inflicted upon her.

There is, of course, no clear line between these two types. Guy Fawkes's attempt to blow up the Houses of Parliament in London in 1605, the destruction of the Reichstag, attributed to Hitler's brown shirts, and the Chechen attack on the "Palace of Culture" in Moscow in October 2002, lie somewhere in between these two types. United States may also find itself the victim of suicide bombers and truck bombs (as indeed it was in the attack on the Alfred P. Murrah building in Oklahoma City in April 1995). Terrorists possess some advantages, despite their small numbers. First, their actions are largely unpredictable, since their objectives, at least those of ideological terrorists such as al Qaeda and Aum Shinrikyo, are largely idiosyncratic and obscure. Second, the terrorists must be assumed to have some part of their number in covert residence within the societies they plan to attack.

Third, terrorists appear to be very patient. They decide when they will strike. As a result, those defending against terrorism must be alert at all times, despite the apparent absence of visible terrorist activity. Finally, terrorists may have international bases of operations, and quite possibly enjoy the sponsorship and assistance of a rogue state. This combination of stateless terrorists who infiltrate target societies, supported by the resources of an irresponsible but technically competent foreign government, is a particularly dangerous combination. The U.S. government identified the Taliban government of Afghanistan as such a state. The U.S. administration was obviously concerned that the Baathist government of Iraq might also represent such a state, although there is no credible evidence that Saddam Hussein had anything to do with the September 11, 2001 attack.

Notwithstanding the terrorist threat, modern industrial societies have some offsetting advantages. Their global intelligence services and military presence, especially when they cooperate with one another, may keep the terror networks off balance, and may be able to damage some of them and interfere with their communications and money flows. Military action, or the threat of it, may discourage rogue states from supporting the terrorists. Nevertheless, highly efficient economies also acquire vulnerabilities and reduced resilience from the private sector's reluctance to sacrifice efficiency to reduce catastrophic risks whose likelihood is difficult to estimate. One area in which both India and the United States enjoy impressive capability is research and innovation. Through the application of available or new technologies, states can make targets less vulnerable, thus less attractive. They can limit the damage that may result from an attack, increase the speed of recovery, and provide forensic tools to identify the perpetrators. However, terrorist networks such as al Qaeda are led by well-educated and well-financed people who may also enjoy advanced technical skills.

If supported by a government whose military establishment has developed weapons of mass destruction, these skills may be greatly amplified. Any technical strategy for responding to the threat of catastrophic terrorism must address this fact. Politically motivated terrorists, such as the Irish Republican Army, may have a specific goal, which, if achieved, might bring an end to their attacks. We can imagine an attempt to negotiate an end to their terrorism. This is not the case for the al Qaeda terrorists who carried out the September 11, 2001 attack on New York City and Washington, D.C. Gerald Holton anticipates just such a combination of individual terrorists supported by a rogue government in a paper presented at a terrorism conference at the Hoover Institution in 1976 and published at that time in Terrorism, an international journal. He called this threat Type III Terrorism.

Any strategy for employing technical knowledge and systems to reduce the likelihood or consequence of catastrophic terrorism must be able to estimate the terrorists' goals and priorities the most vulnerable targets among those priorities the weapons most desired by and available to the terrorists and the consequences of their use the effectiveness of available means to either deter an attack or reduce its consequences Terrorists' Goals and Priorities The targets selected by terrorists will depend on their goals and opportunities. Terrorists may be expected to choose among six objectives: inflict extensive loss of human life destroy important, difficult-to-replace physical facilities exact severe economic damage for a persistent time disrupt the institutions of government attack the symbols of civil culture most detested by the terrorists boost the morale and enhance recruiting of terrorist groups.

The September 11, 2001 attack by al Qaeda was designed to create significant damage in all six areas and succeeded in doing so. However, their primary goal seemed to be a combination of the first and fifth objectives. Their success in wreaking economic havoc in the U.S. airline industry and in the economy as a whole appears to have been an unanticipated bonus. The physical facilities in which large numbers of people are concentrated are primarily in big cities. So too are many of the industrial facilities whose destruction might inflict both economic damage and human injury if toxic substances are released. These buildings and factories are largely owned by private businesses, especially in the United States. Transportation facilities—airports, bridges, dams, tunnels, and so forth——are typically owned by municipal, state, or national authorities. Thus, the responsibility for protecting the primary targets is shared among private and government owners, and on the government side, among national, state, county, and municipal authorities.

The targets of catastrophic terrorist attacks may be organized into these seven categories:

people who are vulnerable to infectious disease, toxic chemicals, or radiation delivered either directly or through contamination through food, currency, postage stamps, or other means of distribution to individuals communications and information services, especially those services essential to command and control centers, and to protection and recovery of complex industrial systems, energy systems (power plants, refineries, and both fuel and energy distribution systems) transportation systems (air, sea, and land, both mobile and fixed infrastructure for transportation—tunnels, bridges, harbors) cities and fixed infrastructure and the people who inhabit them (office buildings, water supplies, dikes) facilities where many people may be congregated at high density (as in athletic venues and theaters) indirect impact on economies through disruption of critical infrastructure services in a modern industrial society, how vulnerable are these targets? Both "critical infrastructure" service industries and structures housing large numbers of people are vulnerable. These are not created by the terrorists, but may be exploited by them. They are, instead, created by the quest for increased efficiency in a competitive, market economy. The competitive drive for commercial efficiency not only creates vulnerabilities in each critical service industry but also creates linkages among these critical infrastructure industries—energy, transportation, communications, food production and distribution, public health, and financial transactions are all interdependent. The mechanisms through which the quest for industrial efficiency may threaten industry's resilience to catastrophic terrorism include single-point failures, where costs of adding redundant elements are high and risks from small perturbations are low, such as ultra-high-voltage transformers in electric power distribution excessive concentration in the quest for scale economies (concentration of chicken meat processing and distribution in a handful of large firms; aggregation of fuel and passengers in ever larger commercial air transports such as the Airbus 380 with up to 850 passengers, and ever larger ocean liners such as the new cruise ship under construction for Royal Caribbean Cruise Lines, designed for 6,400 passengers) coupling of critical infrastructure systems to leverage their scale economies (dependence of transportation safety on availability of electric power and secure computer networks; the dependence of the electric power system on the integrity and security of computer networks). The single-point failures of some critical industrial infrastructures are vulnerable to widely available, conventional weapons, such as explosives, assault rifles, and rocket-propelled grenades. Others may be attacked with more potent weapons made from the very products, materials, and systems of a modern industrial economy.

Terrorists' Weapons

The weapons terrorists might use are divided into two classes: weapons of mass destruction (WMD) and weapons derived from the very economy under attack. WMD can, in principle, be fabricated by technically skilled terrorists, but more probably will originate in rogue states covertly supporting the terrorists or perhaps are stolen from military supplies of more advanced nations. These WMD are nuclear, biological, and chemical weapons designed initially for military use, and restricted (but not eliminated) by a series of treaties among many but not all nations. There are no more urgent issues for the future of civilization than the effective means for reducing the number and proliferation of WMD, the sequestering of those that remain, and the control of the materials from which they can be easily fabricated. However, we must bear in mind that while weapons of mass destruction are generally the most lethal, they also tend to be the most inaccessible to terror organizations that are not assisted by a technically competent but irresponsible government. The terrorists who attacked the World Trade Center in September 2001 certainly created mass destruction, but the weapons used (fully fuelled airliners used as cruise missiles) were technically, at least under U.S. law, not WMDs.

The other class of weapons, those derived from the civil economy of the nation under attack, are more diverse, more numerous, and more accessible to terrorists. Examples include the nitrogen fertilizer (ammonium nitrate) and fuel oil such as that used in the April 1995 attack on the Alfred J. Murrah building in Oklahoma City, tank cars of chlorine being shipped to water supply utilities and other chemical plants, crop dusters that might be used to disperse chemical agents, and fully fuelled aircraft such as used in the September 11, 2001 attack. A more complete list of terrorists' weapons includes fissile nuclear materials, tactical nuclear weapons, and radiological materials pathological organisms (human, plant, and animal) military-type toxic chemical weapons inflammable, toxic, and explosive chemicals and materials in industrial use cyber attacks and electromagnetic pulse (EMP) attacks on electronic targets (telecoms, data, or command and control centers) transportation systems used as delivery systems for weapons explosives, either conventional or derived from fuel oil and nitrogen fertilizer (ammonium nitrate), for example "Rogue" is used loosely here to refer to states that make WMD available to terrorists, either through deliberate policy or through failure to protect their stocks of weapons (and the talent for making them) from losses through theft and corruption. In the United States the legal definition of weapons of mass destruction includes not only fissile materials and nuclear explosives but also radiological weapons. However, radiological weapons (so-called dirty bombs) are weapons of mass terror, as the destruction caused by a detonation would be largely confined to the explosives used to disperse the radioactive material.

Protecting Non-governmental Infrastructure

Who will pay to harden non government-owned critical infrastructure and the critical services it supports? There are a variety of possible policies to motivate private investments in hardening of critical infrastructure. Some of them are compulsion through regulation (which may require congressional legislation) subsidies of the research and development to design the hardening strategies through public-private research and development partnerships (but this still leaves industry with the capital expense for implementing the strategy) voluntary commitments with antitrust exemption (the chemical industry in the United States has an excellent record of voluntary standards for plant safety, which might become a model for protection from terrorism, although the industry has lobbied hard, and effectively, against mandatory regulation for security) inducing the insurance industry to set a sliding scale of rates for terrorism loss insurance, reflecting the extent to which client firms have adopted hardening measures Unfortunately, little progress has been made by the U.S. federal government toward defining the tools to be used in each of the areas of critical industry.

The U.S. government is now proceeding on a case-by-case basis, focusing primarily on how to motivate the large pharmaceutical companies to manufacture vaccines for which there is no "peacetime" market. But no general strategy for the permanent hardening of the U.S. economy has been adopted. In a limited number of cases, firms may be able to devise hardening strategies that also reduce costs or improve product or service value so that the total costs are minimized or are even negative. The manner by which many firms responded to the Y2K threat offers some encouragement for this notion. Such a dual-use strategy is needed to increase the likelihood that industry will invest in hardening critical infrastructure, to create a more sustainable public commitment to the costs and inconveniences of national efforts against terrorist threats, and to integrate homeland security research and development with the rest of the societal research and engineering base to ensure a fully national effort of high-quality results. Because most of the targets and many of the weapons are imbedded in the civilian economy, security issues cannot be neatly separated from the daily life of the civilian population.

The strategy for gradually restructuring many of our physical facilities, production processes, means of providing food distribution, and the like, will have to reflect a complex balance of public-good investments (for which government will have to take the initiative), and commercial investments aimed at competitive success. The political economy of the United States is not designed to make this marriage of conflicting interests and responsibilities easy; India, European nations, and some Asian economies are more accustomed to this balance in their economies. However distasteful the phrase ideologically, the U.S. government needs a counterterrorism industrial policy. Examples of civilian benefits that might result from such a strategy are revitalization of the public health service for serving the normal health needs of communities technical capability to respond even faster and more effectively to natural biological threats such as Severe Acute Respiratory Syndrome (SARS), West Nile virus, and monkey pox virus reduction in the number of illnesses caused by infection or poisoning of the food supply more reliable electric power and other services, especially in the face of hurricanes, floods, and earthquakes further improvements in the safety standards of the chemical industry reduced incidence of cyber attacks by hackers and financial systems made more secure against theft and malicious damage more efficient and timely tracking of goods in transit and billing for their content reduced risk to fire, police, and emergency health professionals.

Making the Nation Safer made more than 130 recommendations for ways to prevent and respond to terrorist attacks. Listed here are a few examples of specific threats and the corresponding recommendations for the use of science and technology to address those threats. Nuclear and Radiological Threats If terrorists with a minimal level of scientific knowledge can acquire enough highly enriched uranium (HEU), they may be able to assemble an inefficient but effective nuclear weapon for detonation in a major city. The United States and Russia are now cooperating in safeguarding fissile material and blending down stocks of HEU, but progress is far too slow. Even more dangerous is the possible availability to terrorists of finished nuclear weapons either stolen and sold from nuclear states or provided by rogue states capable of making them. The U.S. public must be educated on the nature of radiological threats, both from Radiation Dispersal Devices (dirty bombs) and from damaged nuclear electric power plants and radioactive waste storage.

Americans are perhaps more nervous than their friends in India about the political instability of the Pakistani government and the possible consequences should Pakistani nuclear weapons or weapons materials find their way into the hands of terrorists hostile to the United States. Today, attention is shifting to North Korea and Iran as potential sources of weapons or materials, both of which apparently obtained technology from Pakistan. Public ignorance about radiation hazards may induce a level of panic much more destructive than the radiation from which people may be fleeing. The technical task of detecting fissile materials being covertly shipped into a target state is a daunting task, and is receiving a high level of research attention in the United States, but can never be depended upon to stop the import of material for a single weapon. Only control at the source will suffice.

Biological Threats to People and their Food Supply

Research on pathogenesis of infectious agents, and particularly on means for early detection of the presence of such pathogens before their symptomatic appearance, is important. Nations will stockpile vaccines against known diseases, but the threat of genetic modification—while perhaps beyond the capability of most terrorists but not of rogue states—requires a vigorous research effort to find solutions for detection, evaluation, and response. In the United States the Center for Disease Control and Prevention (CDC) provides a robust capability in epidemiology, but there is no equivalent epidemiological response capability for possible biological attacks on agriculture and farm animals. Thus, measures to protect the food supply, and to provide decontamination after an attack, must have high priority. Toxic Chemicals, Explosives, and Flammable Materials, some highly lethal chemicals, such as those made for military applications, are relatively easily made from widely available materials. There is even greater risk from industrial chemicals, which are widely accessible as they move in commerce. Dangerous chemicals in transit should be tracked and identified electronically.

To ensure that only first responders, and not terrorists, know what the tank cars contain, the rail cars should be equipped with encrypted electronic identification. Sensor networks are required to detect and characterize dangerous materials, particularly when they are airborne. Self-analyzing filter systems for modern office buildings whose windows cannot be opened can not only protect the inhabitants but also detect and report the first presence of materials (such as aerosols) that may be trapped in improved filters. An example of long-range, basic research that could be highly beneficial would be the discovery of olfactory biosensors than can reach dog levels of sensitivity, some 10,000 times that of humans.

Energy Systems

The hazards associated with fossil fuel storage, shipment, and its use is well known. Perhaps less apparent are the vulnerabilities of a modern electric power grid. Many of these systems have vulnerable, unique extra-high-voltage transformers for which there are no spares and thus represent a single-point failure. A solution recommended in making the Nation Safer is the production of more portable and safely stored midsized transformers specifically designed to be reconfigurable in combination to replace a failed high-voltage transformer. Other vulnerable results from the replacement of operating engineers in power distribution control rooms with computer systems running Supervisory Control and Data Acquisition (SCADA) systems. These computer-based software systems are generally produced abroad; it is difficult to guarantee their integrity. In addition, while some electric utilities use encrypted traffic on fiber optics to communicate among the SCADA computers, others use clear traffic on the Internet, vulnerable to a cyber attack. An experienced hacker might gain control of the SCADA system and use it to damage the power distribution system. From a longer time frame perspective, adaptive power grids should be developed to make them both harder to attack and make recovery after attack much easier and quicker.

Communications and Information Systems

In the United States the most urgent issue is to reconfigure first responder communications so that police, fire, and medical personnel can communicate with one another and with the emergency operations centers. Inability to do so greatly aggravated loss of life, especially among firefighters, in the World Trade Center attacks. The main worry about cyber attacks is the possibility of their use, perhaps with electromagnetic pulse devices as well, to amplify the destructive effect of a conventional physical or biological attack. Cyber security is one of the top priority areas for research investment because private industry was, before September 11, 2001, largely content with the level of computer and network security available to it. A quite inadequate level of sophisticated talent is devoted to the goal of fully secure operating systems and networks. Transportation and Borders Sensor networks for inspection of goods and passengers crossing the nation's borders will be a research priority.

The primary technical challenge will not be the design of sensors themselves, although much progress is needed in this area, but in the systems engineering of the networks of sensors together with data fusion and decision support software. Biometrics for more secure identification of individuals' shows promise, and systems superior to the driver's licenses and passports used by most travelers are promising. The range of threats to the transportation networks of a modern state is very great, and careful systems analysis is essential to identifying the weak points and finding the most effective and economical means of protecting them. The Emergency Operations Centers (EOC) in many large U.S. cities are quite vulnerable, not only to a destructive physical attack but to more indirect attacks on their ability to access data and to communicate through a cyber attack or electromagnetic pulse attack. Remedying these vulnerabilities must have high urgency; in many cases the centers will have to be relocated. Tragically, the EOC in New York City was located in a known target, the World Trade Center. Much research is already under way to analyze the structural characteristics of high-rise buildings that may make them much more vulnerable than necessary.

Without waiting for this research to result in revised building codes, the expert panel recommended immediate adoption and extension, where appropriate, of European standards for fire and blast, which were much improved following World War II. As already noted, air intakes for large buildings need to be less accessible and equipped with better air filters, perhaps with chemical analysis sufficient to determine if a toxic material is present. Instrumentation to allow first responders to detect toxic and hazardous materials; special provisions for protecting harbors, bridges, dams, tunnels, and dikes; and protection against attacks on urban water supplies downstream from the treatment plant are all discussed in making the Nation Safer. How much of the long term, imaginative research and development envisioned in Making the Nation Safer has been undertaken by the Department of Homeland Security (DHS)? Not enough. The Science and Technology Directorate of DHS do not have the scope of authority, or the length of vision that the Academies' study urged on Congress. Critics say that it has been difficult for DHS to sustain an expert staff with low enough turn over to build and execute the needed technical strategies. Nor has the Homeland Security Institute been given the necessary scope of independent system-level review of the DHS technical priorities.

Societal Responses to Terrorist Threats

Making the Nation Safer concludes that public fear and confusion are more likely responses to most terrorist attacks than is terror, that is, a level of fear so intense that individuals are rendered incapable of acting rationally. The main dangers are panic and destructive behaviour as a result of the lack of credible and timely public information. Thus, a loss of public confidence in those responsible for protecting the public can also be an attack amplifier. The government faces a number of dilemmas, such as using a color-coded warning system to alert the public to the perceived likelihood of additional terrorist attacks. Some citizens feel that this system itself may needlessly amplify the threat, thus doing terrorists' psychological job for them. An urgent issue to be addressed is for government to train and introduce to the public, well in advance of any attack, a number of trusted and knowledgeable people who are prepared to provide accurate and trustworthy information quickly and authoritatively.

Technical strategies

From the great variety of threats studied by the National Academies' experts, several commonsense conclusions about technical strategy can be extracted:

Repair the weakest links (single-point failures) in vulnerable systems and infrastructures use defenses-in-depth (do not rely only on perimeter defenses or firewalls) use "circuit breakers" to isolate and stabilize failing system elements build security and flexibility into basic system designs where possible design systems for use by typical first responders focus priority attention on the "system of systems" technical challenge to understand and remedy the inherent weaknesses in critical infrastructure that are inherent in their architecture ensure that first responders, including technical teams from critical infrastructure service industries, are properly trained and equipped, and the targets themselves are designed to be more resilient in the face of disaster emphasize the importance of flexibility and agility in responding to disasters that were not anticipated in the system design and personnel training The last point is particularly important. Future attacks are likely to involve multiple complex systems. There are a number of dimensions to the systems engineering challenge of homeland security.

The multiple critical industrial infrastructures are closely coupled. Almost all of the responses to terrorist threats require the concerned action of national agencies, state and local authorities, private companies, and in many cases, friendly nations. The technologies used in counter-terrorism will themselves be coupled, complex systems. An evident example is the notion of complex networks of sensors that are coupled to databases, within which the network output is fused with other information, and from which sensible and useable information for local officials in Emergency Operations Centers must be provided. Thus, setting priorities requires modeling and simulating attack and response, and "red teaming" to test the effectiveness of proposed solutions. Finally, there is a need to build up investments in the social sciences, which will be especially important in devising strategies for countering terrorism. Both the roots of terrorism and its consequences need to be better understood. Social science can also contribute to a sustainable effort, involving multiple levels of government, with minimal economic cost, and where the perceived conflict between security activities and protection of individual freedom can best be informed and adjudicated.

Because major terrorist attacks against civil populations may be separated by considerable intervals of time, there is reason to be concerned that the public will lose interest in the threat, and that none of the organizational or investment needs will be satisfactorily met. For these reasons, the strategy for maximizing civil benefits deserves high-priority attention. There are many obvious examples of how counter terror research and development can create values appreciated by the public and of economic value to firms, such as creation of a more agile vaccine development and production capability, information and communications networks that are more resistant to cyber attack, energy systems more robust in the face of natural disasters and human error, security technologies that are more effective yet more unobtrusive and convenient for the public. Sustainability will be a challenge for those in political power in the United States, for they find themselves compelled to emphasize the public's vulnerability (for example, with the color-coded alert system, which is largely successful in making the public nervous) and at the same time to emphasize that the government's efforts "have the terrorists on the run."

Indeed, we can easily imagine that terrorist organizations such as al Qaeda may deliberately wait long intervals between attacks to decrease the alertness of the target's defenses. Sustainability requires one additional strategic element that is of the highest importance. The compromises to civil liberties that the public will readily accept during a traditional war, which is expected to be of short duration, will not be acceptable in the context of a terrorism threat that knows no end, that offers no victory. Thus, the public must be very alert to the kinds of emergency legislation and exercises of executive authority that may be helpful in the short term, but carry the danger of concentrating too much political power in the incumbent government over an indefinite length of time. There are two kinds of expressions of government authority that must be carefully constrained. One is specific legislation that may deprive individuals of constitutional rights, including rights that are found in the Supreme Court interpretation of the founders' intent. Others are the aggregation of administrative authority in government that permits officials to behave arbitrarily, without proper definitions, process, and remedy. An example is the management of information security. The temptation to create a category of information called "sensitive but unclassified" has already created a great deal of confusion and nervousness in the technical community, since the criteria for defining a security breach seem to be created after the fact in each case.

One solution is to recognize the principle that governmental responsibilities should be assigned to the level of government where the information about a threat is located, where the damage will be inflicted, and where the human resources to deal with it must be mobilized. Under the U.S. Constitution, states have quite adequate police powers to address many terrorist threats, if assisted by federal financial, technical, and intelligence resources. If constraints on civil liberties (still consistent with constitutional protections) are adopted more locally, the trade-off of value and cost is more likely to be politically acceptable and less likely to lead to a loss of power in the central government. The national government's role should be to ensure that the states do not go too far in constraining personal freedoms; it should not be the instrument of abuse of those freedoms. Indeed, the observation cited above, that the open societies that tolerate dissent are most vulnerable, clearly implies that any strategy for protection from terror attack must be designed to protect the right of political dissent, not to suppress it in the search for those who might be sympathetic to terrorist objectives. Technology can play a role here too. By reducing the number of attractive targets, decreasing the likelihood of a successful attack, and increasing the resilience of those targets that are attacked, the need for more extreme abuses of civil liberties can also be reduced.

There are seven major points that I would conclude from this discussion. First, only a far-sighted foreign policy, addressing the roots of terrorism and denying terrorist ideologies a foothold in other societies, can make the United States and its allies safer in the long run. Second, weapons of mass destruction are potentially devastating, but the most probable threats will be fashioned from the economy itself, as was the case on September 11, 2001. Private property and commercial industry is most often the target of terrorist attacks, and may be providing the weapons for their own destruction. Thus, the federal government must devise both positive and negative incentives for private investments in hardening critical infrastructure and urban targets. Third, the protection of critical infrastructure must, to the extent possible, be accomplished through a civilian benefits maximization strategy. Fourth, reducing vulnerabilities in critical infrastructure is a highly complex systems problem; it requires a strategy tested by the most modern systems analytic approaches. Fifth, since most of the science and technology capability of market economy governments lies outside the security agencies, governments must be able to coordinate and fund a national science and technology strategy. Sixth, a degree of cooperation between industry, cities, and government unknown in prior experience is required. In particular, local authorities must have an effective voice in setting the technical agenda for equipment for which they are the customer. Finally, for the protection against terrorism to be sustainable, more than a civilian benefits maximization strategy is required. The negative effects on civil freedoms from increased authority in the central government must be resisted, since the threat of terrorist attack is indefinite and emergency measures may never be relaxed.

9

Suicide Terrorism and Its Menace

Terrorism is a pervasive and often effective form of political violence. Gaining insight into why groups and individuals embrace terrorism, especially suicide operations, is therefore essential to countering it. Specifically, how can we understand the individual and social "psychology of terrorism?" In its simplest expression terrorism is 'instrumental violence' that is, the use of force or violence (i.e., kinetics), by individuals or groups that is directed toward civilian populations and intended to instill fear as a means of coercing individuals or groups to change their political and social positions. Essentially, it is the psychology of fear and kinetics (i.e., violence) that gains terrorism attention and gives it power and influence. Suicide operations are a growing concern worldwide. Daily suicide attacks — in Iraq, Afghanistan, Pakistan, Israel or elsewhere — involving vehicle or person-borne devices reinforce the effectiveness of the tactic.

Military, intelligence, and law enforcement professionals study terrorism in order to discover who are or may become terrorists, in order to detect, identify, target, and eventually neutralize terrorist threats. Yet, many factors and complex behaviours are involved in the creation of a terrorist. The lack of a typical terrorist profile makes it difficult to predict who will become terrorists or detect, identify, and target them once they accept the terrorist mantle. Psychiatrist Jerrold Post observes that there is a broad spectrum of terrorists, terrorist groups, and terrorist organizations, each having a different psychology, motivation, behaviour, and decision heuristics. Post rightly asserts that we should not speak of a terrorist psychology in the singular, but rather of terrorist psychologies in the plural. Thus, terrorists and terrorist groups are best studied by addressing their own unique characteristics and dynamics.

Group mindsets determine how the group and its individual members view the world. Knowing a specific group's mindset enables better assessment of that group's likely targets and operational behaviour under varying circumstances. A group's mindset can be profiled by assessing their transactions (i.e., activities and statements) for specific signatures. The importance of seeing things from the terrorist perspective (i.e., motivations and intentions) cannot be overstated. This technique (i.e., red teaming or seeing things through the mind's eye of the terrorist) has been refined by antiterrorism specialists in Iraq and is called forensic operational red teaming (FORT). The underpinnings of the forensic operational red team are to know your enemy and do it to him before the enemy does it to you.

Sun Tzu in the 6th century B.C. advised leaders to know their enemy and know themselves. Red Teaming is means of gaining a sophisticated, insightful, and practical look into the enemy's thinking, strategy, tactics, and techniques – it is creating a portal into how (from the enemy's perspective) the enemy thinks, operates, and is likely to act and adapt to the tactics being used against him. Without knowing our enemies we cannot think like them to anticipate how they may act or behave in a variety of situations. The premise behind forensic operational red teaming is two folder: (1) Think and act like he, enemy from his perspective (especially when using a low technological approach to defeat high tech systems of conventional forces) to attack and/or adapt to our tactics, techniques, and procedures (2) Deny the "enemy" (be he a suicide bomber or terrorist) his anonymity and ability to blend into the local population using biometrics and forensics.

The goal is to make the suicide bomber, IED maker, terrorist, or insurgent more identifiable by gathering forensic characteristics or markers (i.e. fingerprints, iris scans, DNA, facial recognition features, tool marks, power residues, voice prints, geographical profiling). One area of great interest for red teaming and forensically is why and how people become suicide bombers and/or terrorists.

Terrorism's Psychological Components

People become terrorists in many different ways and for many different reasons. Clark McCauley, a noted social psychologist, simplifies the range of possible explanations for why people become terrorists: they are crazy, they are crazed by hatred or anger, or they are rational within their own perspective: A commonly held view is that terrorists must be mentally disordered, suicidal, or pathological. Yet, research offers little evidence that terrorists do in fact suffer from psychopathology.

Nevertheless, terrorist violence has psychological components that manifest themselves in motives and belief systems, social learning, aggression, or other behaviour markers. Understanding of the circumstances (i.e., the psychology) that cause a person or persons to become terrorists and carry out terrorist acts (i.e., the kinetics) is the goal of forensic terrorist profiling. The forensic psychology of terrorism is an emerging and evolving discipline. Important actors investigated include: motivation, cognitive restructuring, psychopathology, group dynamics, moral disengagement, dehumanization, frustration-aggression theory, and other models.

Clearly, there is no single motive for engaging in terrorism — suicide or otherwise. The motives are multiple and complex expressions of historical, political, economic, social and psychological factors. Understanding terrorism requires a careful consideration of psychosocial dynamics. Group dynamics and social networks are important in understanding terrorist actions and behaviour. Individuals make a commitment to the group; they share a common mindset. Group identity and loyalty trumps other considerations. Terrorists use groups and networks for both logistical and psychological support. Groups afford a sense of belonging, a sense of purpose, perhaps even a sense of identity.

Homicide Bombers

Suicide attacks have appeared throughout the history of the world. Most contemporary researchers mark the 1983 suicide attack on the U.S. embassy in Beirut, as the beginning of a modern era of suicide terrorism. Existing research reveals a marked absence of major psychopathology among "would-be" suicide attackers; that the motivation and dynamics for choosing to engage in a suicide attack differ from those in the clinical phenomenon of suicide; and that there is a rational "strategic logic" for the use of suicide attack campaigns in asymmetric conflict or fourth generation warfare.

As with other terrorists, there is no indication that suicide bombers have psychological disorders or are mentally unbalanced in other ways. In contrast, their personalities are usually quite stable and unremarkable, at least within their own cultural or group context. There is also no single profile of suicide terrorists. For example most, but not all, suicide terrorists are aged between 16 and 28. Most are male, but 15% are female and that proportion is rising. Most come from poor backgrounds and have limited education, but some have university degrees and come from wealthy families.

For example the 9-11 hijackers came from generally middleclass backgrounds, were older, and many had university level education. In an alarming recent example, a 64-year-old Palestinian grandmother blew herself up on a suicide-homicide mission in November 2006. Indeed, the term suicide terrorist or bomber is controversial because the main objective is not suicide but mass homicide carried out by means of self-destruction designed expressly to inflict lethal harm on others. The suicide terrorists who planned and executed the 11 September 2001 attacks would not conceptualize the acts as suicide but instead as acts of martyrdom rationalized and justified as a legitimate struggle in a conflict of national and religious dimensions.

The goal of all terrorism is psychological; its aim is to create fear and psychologically debilitate a targeted civilian population. Given the psychology of terrorism, it is clear that understanding and countering suicide terrorism is a pressing need. Terrorism is usually goal-directed behaviour. Political, social and ideological goals help drive the decisions of terrorists as well as their organizational goals. Profiling suicide terrorists is in many ways analogous to profiling criminals. Criminal profiling describes the processes of inferring distinctive personality characteristics of individuals responsible for committing criminal acts from physical and/or behavioural evidence. Criminal profiling does not provide a discernable profile of all criminals, but does provide insight into violent criminal acts of serial rape and serial sexual homicide. While there is no specific terrorist profile that expresses itself psychologically, there is potential for identifying discernable psychological attributes for suicide terrorists. Such profiles are essential to understanding and countering terrorist threat.

Political fresco

The murals represent two conflicting communities and the resulting clash of cultures, symbols and values. Loyalist and republican communities have developed into segregated units over the past 30 years. Their violent births resembled "ethnic cleansing" in the conflict in the former Yugoslavia. In addition to representing conflict, the murals in both communities express an effort to literally paint a coherent structure out of confusion of civil conflict. This effort underlines the changing context of the contemporary states, whose presence in such areas is greatly circumscribed. This change can be described as deterritorialisation because it undermines the Westphalian division of the political world into clearly defined spatial units with absolute and complete authority within their boundaries. One response can be seen in the non-state actors' attempts to control public space.

Northern Ireland is a political unit that never really fit into the liberal-democratic paradigm and so cannot be understood as a conventional Western political space. The province was created by the British government through the Government of Ireland Act, 1920 following the Irish War of Independence. The legislation territorially separated two Irish communities that have separate definitions of "Irishness". Prior to 1920, no territorial unit in Irish history corresponded to Northern Ireland. In the seventeenth and eighteenth centuries, the entire island was a British colony in which Penal Laws deprived Roman Catholics and Presbyterians of civil equality with members of the Church of Ireland (Anglican). Ireland gained a Westminster-style parliament in the 1780s, but was wholly incorporated into the United Kingdom in 1801. Partition of Ireland into Free State and North followed Unionist resistance to devolution and independence.

Political Fragmentation and Northern Ireland

The effect of partition in Ireland was complex and is still being felt. The impact is evident in various attempts to represent an image of Northern Ireland, where an institutional, governmental representational monopoly was exercised by Protestants from 1922 until 1969. Representing Ireland has been a contentious issue for hundreds of years. After the 1798 Rebellion and Great Famine of the 1840s, visually articulating a sense of Ireland was integral to both nationalism and unionism. The dispute was not over location or existence of Ireland, but rather the meaning and import of imagined community and control of public space. Romantic nationalist painting in the nineteenth century, for example, depicted critical moments in the national mythology, such as marriage of Strongbow to Aoife [The marriage of the Norman Richard Fitzgilbert to Aoife, daughter of Diarmait McMurrough, King of Leinster, in 1170, followed a Norman slaughter of the defeated Irish in Waterford.

After McMurrough lost the kingship of Ireland to Ruaidri, Prince of Connacht, he fled to England and sough the assistance of Henry II. Henry agreed and Diarmait was able to secure the help of Strongbow in exchange for his elder daughter's hand and succession to the kingdom. At the same time, Pope Hadrian IV, an Englishman, granted Henry II the Irish throne at the request of John of Salisbury. Once Strongbow's victory was secure, he offered the throne to Henry. Irish nationalists trace the beginning of English colonization and imperialism in Ireland to this event. - MD] The nationalist artist's subject was part and parcel of "the spirit of the burgeoning cultural nationalism of the mid-nineteenth century" and Celtic imagery represented an imaginary "nation striving to see its Celtic legacy as part of a glorious past awaiting revival". Through painting, the viewer entered a nationalist, de-colonizing and later post-colonial discourse.

The discourse was manifest in political, cultural, social and linguistic nationalism as well as economic pressure on vested interests. Nationalist discourse was met by unionist and later loyalist response [Part of the unionist-loyalist cultural response to Irish nationalism involved the adaptation of the Medieval tradition of religious and artesian processions through the vehicle of the "loyal orders" that appeared in the late eighteenth-century. These processions have long spawned serious problems of public order. For example, a violent riot at Dolly's Brae on July 12, 1849 led to the deaths of 30 Catholics and provoked anti-procession legislation in 1850 in the form of the *Party Procession Act*. Similarly, government forces used buckshot (a nineteenth-century version of plastic bullets) to disperse an Orange demonstration in Dungannon in 1880. The violence and intensity of Orange marches has historically reflected the rising and waning of Irish nationalism.

Irish post-colonialism was written in the island's division into two political entities: republic and British province. Separation of the six northern counties from the rest of Ireland did not remove the region from this discourse since "both unionist and nationalist identities in Ulster remain heavily informed by representations of nineteenth-century ethnic nationalism". Nonetheless, Northern Ireland's distinctiveness lies in its "unagreed" (because non-consensual) character, which eventually led to an undeclared thirty-year civil war. The resulting political formation does not fit into the classic paradigm of a Westphalian state, as both units were supposed to do when founded. This unagreed Ireland is represented by political wall murals in Belfast and elsewhere in the North.

The murals in effect demarcate post-colonial political fragments, entities that are unrecognized in international law and theories of political society and organization, but which can also be detected in Sierra Leone, Bosnia and the Philippines. In all these cases, paramilitaries exercise power and reduce the state to a nominal status. In Belfast, the state is literally bunkered, walled in behind compounds and armoured vehicles. One principal manifestation of deterritorialization in post-colonial political fragments is the lack of interface between civil society and the state. This is expressed as radical lack of consent, an absence of what Rawls calls "the acceptance of the principles of right and justice [that] forges the bonds of civic friendship and establishes the basis of comity amidst the disparities that persist".

Another way to express the character of these fragments is to emphasize the primacy of a sense of place over that of territoriality or political space within them. Northern Ireland is in cease-fire, not at peace. Periodic violence between the two communities stem from their basic disagreement over the form of state that civil society might assume, mutual distrust, and willingness to resort to arms. Richard Kearney argues that the claim of either [British or Irish] national government to "represent" both Ulster communities (British and Irish) as "one and indivisible" is doomed to failure. No matter how it is viewed - as part of a United Kingdom or of an eventual United Ireland - the pluralist character Northern Ireland defies the question of absolute sovereignty with a unitary body. Hence the need (i) to separate the notion of nation from that of state; (ii) to acknowledge the co-existence of different identities in the same society; and (iii) to extend the models of identification beyond unitary sovereignty to include more inclusive and pluralist forms of association.

Reading the postcolonial narrative of loyalism and republicanism in contemporary Northern Ireland must transcend Kearney's pluralism. Because it might very well take 15 to 20 years to create conditions for pluralism (i.e. both parties recognizing that the other side might have a legitimate narrative), a non-linear, non-developmental perspective of post-colonial theory suits societies in which the literal barricades of Belfast streets, built to obstruct and delay the movement of the military, are simultaneously the "random-riot" of memories and unruly associations, a defamiliarisation of modern rationalities through a parody of the modernist and postmodernist device of the list that simultaneously deploys the dislocated temporalities of a (post)colonial culture.

Post-colonial in loyalist and republican representations can be seen through reading wall murals. In general, murals are a response to the sense of disorder and incompleteness in Northern Ireland society. The images aim to provide coherence for and control of public space that is otherwise lacking. In this sense, murals are a public medium with four features. First of all, they are located in specific places. Secondly, they address an unknown body of viewers. Thirdly, mural images are allegorical and moralizing. They are linked to a concept of inherited culture and ennobling reconstruction of a history that was lost. Finally, murals have a volatile relation to public space, debates about governance and visual language. They might frequently be painted over as circumstances change.

Martyrs and Warriors

Loyalist murals began as an expression of control of public space. As continuing controversy over Orange parades illustrate, control of public space is central to loyalism. Control is expressed by the presence of murals, parades, flags, arches and other emblems of loyalist tradition, which lend permanence by altering the physical surroundings [Flags are also central to control of space in Northern Ireland. The number of Ulster Defence Association (UDA) and Ulster Volunteer Force (UVF) flags in loyalist areas represents territorial competitiveness between two paramilitaries. Republican attitudes to flags are quite different, but no less controversial. Sinn Fein ministers Martin McGuinness and Bairbe de Brún refuse to allow Union (i.e., UK) flags to fly over their departments, even on the twenty days designated for hoisting it.

Loyalists, particularly since control over their destiny has gradually slipped out of their hands, earnestly believe that they have, against their wishes, become physically, psychologically and increasingly spiritually detached from their nation. Unlike their Catholic counterparts, who enjoy sympathy throughout Ireland, within the ranks of the political left in Britain and particularly amongst the huge Irish community in America, support for the loyalist cause is minimal and unionists feel friendless, deserted and betrayed, both by the political actions of their governments and by a general public whose apathy and indifference they greatly resent.

In the period after they first appeared, loyalist murals often depicted William of Orange, a conquering Protestant hero seen to have triumphed over treachery (in loyalist terms: Catholicism) and betrayal (supporters of James II) to assert individual rights and liberty as public values. The first murals appeared as the British government prepared to implement home rule, a plan for devolved Irish government that would have ended Protestant domination. In this sense, loyalist wall murals began as a politically and culturally defensive act. After creation of Northern Ireland, murals symbolized control of public space, discourse and power by unionists. Mural imagery subsequently evolved during Northern Ireland's thirty-year civil conflict.

In general, Belfast loyalist murals in June 2000 focused on the themes of martyrs, warriors and history. This apparent thematic narrowness did not prevent a rich variety of representations, images and icons to be incorporated in the paintings. The need for interpretation is complicated by division of the loyalist universe into two distinct variants organized around the Progressive Unionist Party (PUP) and its paramilitary wing, the UVF, and the Ulster Democratic Party (UDP), and its paramilitary wing, the UDA-UFF (Ulster Freedom Fighters). The murals generally express a community that sees itself as under siege, has difficulty in building alliances and poorly communicates its anxieties to the wider world. Loyalists are very much aware that republicans draw much more international attention and support. Today's murals are thus part of a loyalist counter-narrative, a tale of its own self-image.

Given that loyalism and the wider unionist community fragmented in the years since the 1985 Anglo-Irish Agreement, the dual nature of loyalist murals reflect a new reality, a time of political uncertainty when the parties linked to the paramilitary groups have begun to break with traditional unionist rhetoric . . . [and] . . . it was perhaps necessary to offer a reassurance that loyalist interests would be defended and that there would be no sell-out. Both UVF and UFF murals portray martyrs. UVF murals use red-blue-yellow colours, which symbolize an independent Ulster. Red-blue-yellow is juxtaposed to the red-white-blue of the Union Jack, which is found everywhere in Belfast's loyalist neighbourhoods on murals, curbstones, flags and bunting. The theme of warriors is closely associated to martyrdom through figures such as Billy Wright, who was murdered in Maze Prison by members of the republican Irish National Liberation Army (INLA). Other warrior figures on murals ranged from sci-fi figures to Celtic mythological characters such as Cúchulain.

The latter previously figured exclusively on republican murals, but is now integrated into loyalist mythology. Loyalist mural historiography follows two parallel paths. In the first, UVF murals openly identify with paramilitaries. The UVF name was taken from an organization created in 1913 to coordinate paramilitary activities during the Home Rule crisis. Volunteer paramilitaries formed in 1911-12 in Ulster were brought under Ulster Unionist control through the first UVF, which had 90,000 members and was led by retired British military officers. The UVF was revived during the Irish War of Independence and incorporated into the Ulster Special Constabulary, which played a leading role in fighting the IRA in the North until the Royal Ulster Constabulary (RUC) was formed in 1922.

The UVF title was resurrected in 1966 by Belfast loyalists who opposed reforms by then-Northern Ireland PM Terence O'Neill. A ruthless core of members eluded arrest in the 1970s and 1980s. From 1969 until its leaders signed the joint loyalist cease-fire in 1994, the UVF was the main loyalist organization that carried out political and sectarian assassinations. The UVF's main commando groups are the Red Hand Commandos and Protestant Action Force. The second loyalist history on murals is that of the UDA and its paramilitary wing, the UFF. UDA-UFF murals use constitutional symbols and emblems. The UDA was set up in 1971 and active in protests against abolition of the Stormont parliament by the British government. UFF assassinations sometimes targeted republican activists, but often randomly-selected Catholics, in response to IRA actions. The UDA also operated drinking clubs, other businesses and protection rackets and conducted gangster-style activities.

However, it is also associated with a pragmatic approach to the Northern Ireland conflict. In 1975, the UDA attempted to form a coalition with the mainly-Catholic Social Democratic and Labour Party (SDLP), but was blocked by the mainstream Ulster Unionist and Democratic Unionist parties. A combination of extreme violence and political flexibility continues to characterize the UDA, which set up the "Combined Loyalist Paramilitary Command" (CLPC) with the UVF in 1994 and organized the UDP for elections. Urban, working class UDA leaders consistently avoid domination by more conventional politicians, especially Ian Paisley.

Images on UDA murals are more elaborated than UVF ones and constitute an effective "signature". The UDA often uses the Ulster coat-of-arms, a red cross on a white shield, alongside the Ulster Red Hand below a six-pointed star. The motto "Quis Separabit" (Who Shall Separate Us) is also widely used. The actual UDA symbol has a Red

Hand on a blue field under a Crown. The Crown represents the British monarchy, loyalty to which is a distinguishing feature of loyalists. Since neither the PUP nor UDP are represented at Westminster, identification with the Crown makes sense and expresses feelings abandonment by the British government and Westminster parliament that are widespread among Protestants. A clenched red fist and the Scottish flag also appear on UDA murals.

Many loyalist murals honour the dead. Aside from paramilitary "martyrs" many images refer to the Battle of the Somme. If any one event in the great War might be selected as the moment which symbolized the psychological partition of Ulster Unionism from the rest of the island, it was probably the impact of the Battle of the Somme upon the Ulster Unionist psyche, and the Ulster Protestant community generally, coming as it did so soon after the Easter Rising . . . The lesson drawn by many Unionists after the Easter Rising, when they compared their blood sacrifice for King and Country, was that of instinctive Nationalist disloyalty.

The Somme is important because of the role of the 36th (Ulster) Division, which included many original UVF members. In two days of fighting in 1916, the Ulster Division suffered 5000 killed, wounded and missing. Today's loyalists compare themselves to the dead at the Somme in terms of defence of Queen and Country, fighting spirit, and readiness for blood sacrifice. In June 2000, the Somme continues to visually resonate as loyalists come to terms with the impact of the Good Friday Agreement, which mandates power-sharing with Catholics and an end to 80 years of Protestant hegemony in Northern Ireland. The message on the murals is one of defence: compromise does not equal no protection or a sell-out. In addition, honouring the dead signals an end to the conflict, a need to commemorate and acknowledgement that a significant break with the past has occurred. In linking the current situation to the past, loyalist assertion of tradition aim to express permanence.

The first republican murals appeared in 1981, seventy-three years after their loyalist counterparts. Their appearance occurred during the republican hunger strikes in which Bobby Sands died. The murals were part of a republican effort to get their message out to a wide public ["After January 1971 the system of reference upwards [for permission to interview members of the IRA] operated (more or less) as a means to ban interviews with the IRA altogether. Permission had always to be sought and therefore was requested less and less often - and when requested it was more and more frequently refused", Anthony Smith, "Television Coverage of Northern Ireland", in *War and Words: The Northern Ireland Media Reader*.

Doing so had been a problem for the nationalist-republican camp since unionist domination of Northern Ireland meant that "any public manifestation of Catholicism and Irish nationalism could be represented as a threat to the state and therefore dealt with accordingly". In 1980, a sixteen year-old boy was shot dead as he painted republican slogans. The RUC officer who shot him claimed that he thought the brush was a gun and was found not guilty of murder. Republican mural interpretation is considerably simplified by the fact that, aside from occasional INLA graffiti, the IRA-Sinn Féin (SF) has visual hegemony.

There is a certain parallel focus to loyalist murals through themes such as martyrs, warriors and history, but the breadth and depth of imagery on the republican side is much richer. Overall, republican murals aim to commemorate history, celebrate Irish culture and are part of a political campaign. In addition, many republican murals incorporate images of women, as in the case of the well-known mural "Who fears to speak of Easter Week" on

Whiterock Road in Belfast that adds the figure of Countess Markievicz, an important turn-of-the-century nationalist women's leader, alongside the seven leaders of the Easter Rising who signed the Proclamation of Independence.

Aside from the INLA, the only exception to IRA-SF mural narrative in republican Belfast is the Roman Catholic Church, whose portrayal of the Virgin Mary is political in a society whose very origin is linked to militant Protestantism. The Church's murals co-exist with republican murals that address several themes. Commemorative murals mark the deaths of both the 1981 hunger strikers (especially Bobby Sands) and the Gibraltar Three [On March 6, 1988 in Gibraltar, three unarmed IRA members were shot dead by the British SAS at point-blank range. Seán Savage, Daniel McCann and Mairéad Farrell were known republican activists. Farrell served a ten-year jail term and McCann was imprisoned for two years for terrorist activities. The trios were followed around Gibraltar by the MI5, but SAS soldiers in civilian clothes later over surveillance, allegedly intending to arrest them. The SAS claimed that they were spotted, feared a bomb was about to be detonated, and shot the trio.

Several witnesses who saw Savage and Farrell shot claimed they were given no warning. One IRA member was shot 16 times. The IRA trio was not carrying arms and no explosives were later found in their car although it contained electrical equipment used to make bombs. Solidarity murals proclaim IRA support for Catalan nationalists. Symbols of Irish nationalism and republicanism abound in the murals: the phoenix (symbol of the Irish Republican Brotherhood), the starry plough, orange sunburst, the Irish tricolour, lilies and coats-of-arms. The Irish language is used extensively in republican murals to draw together cultural and republican identities. Cease-fire murals are also widespread. A well-known mural says "Time for peace, time to go", showing a white dove carrying a British soldier away from an Irish flag toward a British one. Anti-military themes are also common.

Since the republican community was long marginalized in Northern Ireland and unable to spread its message through conventional media, wall murals developed as a form of mass media as well as the most powerful example of republican visual display. As Jarman notes regarding the murals in general, republican images have an ambiguity due to the fact that their meaning can be interpreted differently. Rather than weakness and confusion, ambiguity gives murals their strength: they are able to speak to a broader public and retain multiple meanings. Multiple meanings moreover co-exist alongside the use of particular images in specific places, which gives the murals an ability to express a sense of place and community. As such murals show the power of political imagery. They illustrate the process of constructing difference, which in turn is used politically to build identities.

In both loyalist and republican communities in Belfast, murals serve to define public space and lend coherence to an otherwise mute physical place. Rolston argues that murals are windows into political worlds. Loyalism and republicanism are not equivalent political practices; their imagery thus has very different origins and purposes. Each political ideology has its themes and traditions and above all separate relationship to the British state. Given that, it is as naive to accept murals as identical cultural artifacts as it is to reject them out of hand

In the context of a globalizing international scene, wall murals also express a transnationalising process of deterritorialization. In this process, even old states such as the UK increasingly find themselves at odds with new, less tangible and less territorial agents that undercut their abilities to exercise "absolute dominion" within their political space. The republican and loyalist postcolonial political fragments in Belfast exemplify these agents, which are situated within two communities and "sign" their presence through murals. Arriving in the Shankill neighborhood in Belfast, I was struck by the rapid appearance of a local loyalist, who seemed to monitor comings and goings. He abruptly raced up in a car, but then engaged my driver, traveling companion and myself in a friendly and casual conversation about murals and the general political climate in Northern Ireland. I rarely encountered symbols of the government of Northern Ireland (government offices, post offices, police officers) in my visit, aside from appearance of two RUC officers in a heavily armoured Land Rover, a rapidly passing British army convoy and several heavily bunkered RUC stations. The state does not control the streets in these areas, its presence is episodic and, one suspects, surgical. Loyalist and republican paramilitary organizations and their political conjoint have taken over. Murals express their re-organization of the political universe.

Socialist Movement Online

The Starry Plough [The term refers to the constellation Ursa Major, the Great Bear or Plough of the heavens. - MD] is the emblem of the Irish Republican Socialist Movement (IRSM). The Starry Plough was used by the Irish Citizen Army (ICA) in 1914 and became its official emblem. The early version, on a background of green bordered by a gilt fringe, flew above the Imperial Hotel in Dublin during the 1916 rising. The IRSM adopted a modified version, with white stars on a blue background, to point to its links with Ireland's struggling class warrior predecessors, militant Irish socialism and, in particular, ICA leader John Connolly. The Starry Plough is seen as a symbol of working class militancy, flag of rebellion, class war and social revolution. The electronic Starry Plough in the title of this paper links this IRSM symbol to its hyper mediated environment on the Web.

All social and political movements base their appeal for support and messages to the public in identitarian terms. Movements use symbols to define the lines of debate and establish boundaries. Boundaries can be moral, as in the case of charivari, which was used in Medieval Europe to shame, taunt and intimidate. Boundaries may also have more abstract purposes and "enclose elements which may, for certain purposes and in certain respects, be considered to be more like each other than they are different". In politics, boundaries have been largely territorial since the seventeenth century. The ways in which these political boundaries have been expressed includes flags, parades and national symbols. This symbolic expression of politics is also reproduced among non-state actors in politics. The IRSM is an example of one such group, which has now introduced its symbolism into an electronic environment.

The Socio-political Context

The context of IRSM information is peculiarly complex given that it straddles two distinct sovereign states, the UK and the Irish Republic. Much of the IRSM focus concerns Northern Ireland and the thirty-year civil conflict known as "The Troubles". This conflict is based in the division between Northern Ireland's 1.69 million inhabitants, who are almost evenly split between Catholics (38.4%) and Protestants (50.6%). The conflict has been exacerbated by economic decline over the past century, although the regional economy has recently experienced significant growth [Manufacturing output is up, and GDP grew by 11.6% in 1990-95. Unemployment is 11.2%, but an improvement from highs of 17% in the 1980s. Once a shipbuilding and linen producing giant, in the 1970s Northern Ireland was a net importer of most goods and exported little. An expanded welfare state and massive growth in security forces due to the Troubles were the region's main economic stand-bys.

Civil conflict and economic decline produced a distinct set of social conditions: at the end of the 1980s, about 40% of the workforce was employed in the public sector, with many working in security-related areas such as policing and prisons. The dual economy was also based in identity-based inequalities. In 1991, Catholic males were over two times more likely to be unemployed than their Protestant peers. Inequalities are also present in terms of occupations. In 1991, 29% of Catholic males were white-collar workers as opposed to 39% of Protestant males. For the last 30 years, Protestant males have been over-represented in security related occupations and services, management and administration and skilled engineering while Catholic males are over-represented in lower skilled and paid manufacturing and construction jobs. The historically disadvantaged Catholic community has made gains in the past 30 years, but its overall socio-economic position is still inferior to most Protestants.

A Catholic middle class has moved beyond serving its own community to positions of authority in the public sector, but still has far to go to achieve proportionate representation in occupations and equal Protestants in the economy. In political terms, the Northern Ireland "statelet" has undergone many mutations. Territorially, it incorporates six of the nine counties from historical province of Ulster. Because it does not incorporate the entire province, the IRSM views it as a political misnomer to call the statelet "Ulster" (as do Protestant loyalists and unionists) and instead refer to the region as Northern Ireland. The political system was founded on principles of representative democracy and individual rights and liberties that are evident in free and contested elections based in universal suffrage.

However, the practical functioning of liberal democracy has not been so clear cut. Political structures have been subject to constant change and protest. From 1921 (the date of partition and creation of the Free State in the south) to

1972, Northern Ireland was governed by a regional parliament at Stormont, a form of Home Rule that, ironically, unionists opposed when they were part of a single Ireland. The Stormont assembly legislated for local affairs and left foreign affairs, trade and taxation, and defence to Britain. Stormont was abolished by the British Parliament in 1972, after years of civil unrest and political violence and the British government took control of Northern Ireland from Westminster in an arrangement called "Direct Rule". From 1974 until the *Good Friday Agreement* was implemented in 1998, the Westminster Parliament had to approve all laws for Northern Ireland and placed local government departments under control of the Secretary of State.

In the 1970s and 1980s, the British government attempted to devise a settlement to re-instate local regional government, but these failed due to unionist intransigence and nationalist boycott. The GFA of April 10, 1998 is the most recent attempt at establishing a constitutional mechanism in the form of community safeguards and a 108-seat assembly proportionately elected by single-transferable-vote. The new assembly has legislative and executive authority over agriculture, economic development, education, the environment, finance and personnel, and health and social services. The Assembly has also set up a number of statutory committees to assist during the transitional period. A nomination process of candidates for the executive is designed to provide equal representation for nationalist-republican and unionist-loyalist parties.

Electoral manipulation has historically been the greatest obstacle to a properly functioning liberal democracy in Northern Ireland. Given long-standing divisions between the Catholic minority and Protestant majority, voting patterns tend to reflect ethnic identity and the electoral system is an important structure through which different identities are expressed. Protestants mostly vote for Unionist parties that seek to maintain the Union with the UK and secure the Protestant identity from assimilation in a united, Catholic Ireland. The evolution of the electoral-party system is thus vitally important for understanding The Troubles. After partition and creation of the Free State in 1921, the Northern Ireland electoral system was based in a proportional representation (PR) system of single transferable vote (STV).

By the mid-1920s, PR facilitated emergence of political parties that threatened the ruling Ulster Unionist Party (UUP). The UUP government "realized that PR had allowed the electorate a measure of choice incommensurate with Unionist Party ambitions" and replaced PR with the British plurality or "first-past-the-post" system. The electoral threat was not only from nationalist and republican organizations, but also marginal Protestant parties that wanted to break ties with Britain and form an Independent Northern Irish State and labour and socialist parties. The change from PR to plurality voting drastically impaired electoral competition: Unionists represented 66% of the population, but controlled 85% of all local authorities by the late 1920s. Plurality voting was maintained until PR was re-introduced was 1973. Predictably, abolition of the plurality system led to increasing fragmentation of the Unionist vote and increased electoral power for the SDLP and Sinn Féin. However, PR was only applied to local election since Direct Rule meant that real political power was held by the Westminster parliament whose elections were still held under the plurality system.

Given the high Catholic birth rate, fear spread in the unionist community that its power would be diminished nationally as well as locally. Manipulation by re-drawing constituency boundaries became common. The highly polarised nature of Northern Ireland was further accentuated by slicing electoral boundaries through communities, creating Catholic minorities where they were the demographic majority. Another barrier to democratic rights and freedoms is the *Prevention of Terrorism Act* (PTA). The PTA was implemented in 1974 in response to the Troubles as a temporary measure in authorities' "fight against terrorism". One section of the PTA allows the authorities to detain suspected terrorists for up to seven days without charge. Critics of the PTA argue this section breaches the European Convention on Human Rights and infringes on citizens' basic civil rights in a liberal democratic state. The PTA also prevents suspected terrorists from entering other parts of the Union, which limits individual freedom of movement.

Threats to freedom of speech also exist in Northern Ireland. Although many papers either implicitly or explicitly express sectarian sentiments, "there are those who suggest that sections of the media have served the interests of the British state by acting as channels for the dissemination of government propaganda". The state has nonetheless placed real limits on freedom of speech. Between 1969 and 1993, about 100 television programmes on the Troubles were banned. In 1988, the British government imposed a ban on all programmes that contained interviews with individuals who were either directly or indirectly linked to illegal paramilitary organi-zations. The ban was not revoked until 1994. In addition, the media has also been affected by self-censorship due to the threat of legal sanctions and restrictions on media production. The parallel context in which the IRSM is active, the Republic of Ireland, presents dramatically different conditions from the North. Ireland has experienced extremely strong economic growth over the past ten years. The growth rate in recent years has been about 8% and unemployment has declined from 18% in 1987 to 8% in 1998. In 1999, the GDP increased by an estimated 9.5% and incomes started to increase for all groups despite inflationary pressures.

The Republic is a parliamentary democracy that has a proportional electoral system. Recent political issues in the

Republic have centered on managing the consequences of growth: for e.g., income inequalities, corruption and new social values. The overall picture is a dramatic transformation of an impoverished, highly religious society on the margins of Western Europe into a dynamic social, economic and cultural formation. Given these developments, the IRSM focus in the Republic is social, not national.

The IRSM incorporates several related organizations: the Irish Republican Socialist Party (IRSP); Irish National Liberation Army (INLA); the British wing of the IRSP; and, the Irish Republican Socialist Committee North American (IRSCNA). The IRSM Website is divided into sections on the organization's history and principles, group statements and communiqués, the IRSM "Honour Roll", the IRSP; IRSCNA; IRSP London, contact information and links. The site is divided up between different kinds of documents. There are approximately 267 texts in all, ranging from less than a page to 10 pages in length. The shortest and most numerous texts are political communiqués and the longest are historical pamphlets. Except for communiqués, which are all dated, all documents are undated and anonymous.

The first group of documents on the site is generally analytical. The analyses pertain largely to the domestic situation in Northern Ireland and especially the Troubles. The IRSM explains the Troubles and proposes ways to resolve the conflict. Its analysis includes theoretical texts on Ireland and the struggle for Irish national liberation as well as historical documents written by Irish republican socialists like James Connolly. The theoretical texts also examine capitalism and economic development from a Marxist-Leninist perspective. Secondly, the site outlines IRSM positions and policies and contrasts them to other nationalist groups. Thirdly, the site contains a number of statements or communiqués that refer to a wide variety of topics. The statements clearly spell out IRSM actions and how they respond to domestic and international current events. Lastly, several sections on the site commemorate members and support political prisoners. These sections list IRSM members killed in action (the group uses the term "assassinated"), and a "prisoner of war" section lists IRSM members who are in prison for subversive activities.

Political Goals and Analysis

The Website addresses a number of conflicts. Above all, it focuses on the conflict over British sovereignty in Northern Ireland, which is called a struggle for national liberation. Secondly, the site focuses on the IRSM struggle against capitalism and its goal of creating a workers' republic in Ireland. Lastly, the site addresses the conflict between the IRSP-INLA and other Republican movements, particularly Sinn Féin (SF) and the Provisional Irish Republican Army (PIRA) as well as the Official Irish Republican Army (OIRA). Both the IRSP and INLA distinguish their republican socialism from the republican nationalism of SF-PIRA. The IRSM aims to secure national liberation of Northern Ireland and establishment of a workers' state on the island. The movement defines its struggle for national liberation so as to distinguish it from mainstream nationalism.

The IRSM sees the latter as a form of chauvinism produced by advanced capitalist states such as Britain, which has an imperial ethos and foreign policy. The IRSM argues that, in contrast, national liberation is a struggle to liberate national territory by expelling an external, imperial power. In this way, the IRSM identifies its struggle with those in the Third World, especially Cuba, Vietnam, Angola, and Algeria. Secondly, the IRSM defines itself as a socialist organization that is committed to armed struggle. This distinguishes it from republican organizations that have abandoned class struggle and define themselves as mainly nationalist, specifically SF-PIRA.

The IRSM alleges that the latter's position conforms to the material interests of the Catholic petty-bourgeoisie. But the IRSM also distinguishes itself from 'reformist' socialism like the Official IRA (now the Workers' Party) out of which it developed. The IRSM says it belongs to the history of 'green' Marxism in Ireland. Green Marxism is based in the writings and activities of James Connolly (The IRSM's "Connollyite Marxism" as well as the legacy of "Green Marxism" in Ireland are found in "What is Irish Republican Socialism?" and "James Connolly and Irish Freedom". Accessed on July 25, 2000), an Irish socialist leader executed for his role in the 1916 Easter Uprising. Connolly located the "prime mover" of the "Irish Question" in British imperialist policies, maintaining that the cause of the conflict were exogenous.

According to this argument, British imperialism seized Irish Catholic land in the North and settled Scottish colonists on the best acreage. British imperialist policy then divided the Protestant and Catholic working classes, following its "divide and conquer" colonial policy. Connolly thought the only way to solve Irish problems was to get rid of the British presence in a national liberation war and establish socialism. The latter two processes were inextricably linked for him. IRSM Green Marxism follows Connolly's theory, arguing that the Troubles are a consequence of British Imperialism ("Irish Republican Socialist Movement-20 years of Struggle" July 25, 2000). The IRSM argues that the British used partition to divide the Irish working class between Catholic Republicanism and Protestant Loyalism. In Northern Ireland, the Unionist parties then manipulated legitimate Protestant working class concerns over civil and religious liberties in a united Ireland and tied its material interests to British imperialism. The Catholic working class, for its part, was duped by conservative republicans into believing its interests are identical to the Catholic middle class.

Given the above analysis, the IRSM views the regimes in Northern Ireland and the Republic as illegitimate. The IRSM sees the North as an imperialist state let set up by a foreign occupation force and, as such, unreformable. The IRSM sees the only solution in reunification with the South and joint transformation into a socialist workers' state. The Irish Republic is seen as an illegitimate "bourgeois class-state" that gave up armed struggle against British imperialism. It moreover aided in persecuting militant republicanism (particularly socialists) and "watered down" its claim to sovereignty over the six counties of Northern Ireland. The Irish Republic is also viewed as a state beholden to the "medieval" interests of the Catholic Church, which further de-legitimizes it in IRSM eyes.

Principles and Policies

As a revolutionary party with Marxist-Leninist principles, the IRSM believes in a dialectical unity of revolutionary theory and revolutionary practice. For the IRSM, revolution means overthrow of the social, political and economic system in all of Ireland and its replacement with an entirely new order based on people's needs and welfare as well as national independence. It sees revolution as a two-phase process that involves: 1) an end to partition and seizure of the state; and, 2) set up of a "dictatorship of the proletariat" and construction of socialism under IRSM leadership. This entails abolition of parliamentary democracy and the party system and their replacement by a system of representation by means of a single revolutionary party. The IRSP revolutionary programme distinguishes between principles as the basis upon which a revolutionary programme is built and policies, which are determined by given historical situations and thus more flexible. Policies are considered a matter of strategy and tactics while principles are seen as goals.

Policies are divided into two groups: 1) power policies; and, 2) reconstruction policies. Power policies are geared towards the first revolutionary phase: the seizure of state power. Reconstruction policies are designed for the second phase: building socialism. The IRSM commitment to armed struggle is understood as a power policy (i.e., not a matter of revolutionary principle) that can be renounced if this is for the movement's good: that is, if it furthers the organization's revolutionary principles. As a political party, the IRSP has formulated a series of positions:

- Britain must renounce claims to sovereignty over Northern Ireland or any part of Ireland;
- dissolution of the Ulster Defence Regiment (UDR), Royal Ulster Constabulary (RUC) and Royal Ulster Constabulary Reserve (RUC Reserve) and withdrawal of British troops from Ireland;
- release of all political prisoners and grant of amnesty;
- British compensation for those who suffered from imperialist violence and exploitation;
- opposition to imperialist control over Ireland's resources and wealth;
- rejection of partition and view of both states as illegitimate;
- convening an All-Ireland Constitutional Conference to develop a democratic and secular constitution;
- armed struggle as an inherent right of the Irish people to achieve self-determination and national liberation ("The Broad Front".).

The IRSP does not only concentrate on revolution, but also on issues concerning daily life in Northern Ireland. The IRSP articulates a point-of-view on a series of issues. The party argues that Britain set up a sectarian state in Northern Ireland and deliberately fostered working class sectarianism and a women's movement that is divided between support for national liberation and pro-imperialist positions. (Accessed on July 25, 2000). It charges that the dominant role of the Church in Irish society strengthens patriarchy by perpetuating patriarchal social values such as those that oppose abortion, divorce, birth control and the entry of women into the workforce. It argues that the power of the Catholic Church over society must be limited.

The group notes that while birth control is legal in Ireland, those who use it are stigmatized and doctors with Catholic values often refuse to provide contraceptives. Women need their husbands' consent to be sterilized, which implies that they belong to men. The IRSP supports easy and unconditional access to birth control. Given that abortion is for the most part illegal in the North and the Republic, the IRSP supports pro-choice movements and legalized abortion. The IRSP also supports the right to divorce, pay equity, free childcare, the fight against healthcare cutbacks, tougher sentences for rapists, an end to strip-searching, and an end to discrimination against lesbians.

The IRSM has released about 129 statements on domestic issues. These statements cover issues such as: Loyalist violence; the peace process; UK troops and the British government; the RUC; prisoners-of-war; the Derry Monument to hunger strikers; domestic calls of solidarity; unionism and parading; and, miscellaneous political statements. Most statements are miscellaneous. They range from commentary on policing policy in Northern Ireland, condemnations of political positions by either British or Irish governments to pay equity and parking. "Revolutionary statements" released for May Day reaffirm the necessity of building socialism and fighting for workers rights. Statements on loyalist violence are frequent. Most either denounce violence or comment on its increase. The peace process is also a frequently addressed. The IRSM campaigned against the GFA and was very critical of the treaty.

The organization called the GFA a failure, declared electoral support for SF, and called for no compromises on arms decommissioning. Yet, the INLA has provisionally renounced armed struggle. The IRSM repeatedly condemns British security forces and the RUC for violence and corruption. Finally, some statements on the Website focus on the actions of unionists, parades, solidarity with the Irish Lesbian and Gay organization, and anniversaries of the armed struggle. Many IRSM communiqués respond to foreign events, which are divided into memorials and/or commemorations (African Liberation Day, Kurdish New Year and International Women's Day), calls for solidarity (Solidarity for Kurdish Struggles and liberation in South Africa) and condemnations (Actions condemned include: arrest of anti-NATO protesters in Italy, imprisonment of Mumia Abu-Jamal, the war in Kosovo, Kurdish leader Abdullah Ocalan's "abduction" and death sentence, arrest of Puerto Rican activists, Third World debt, the Pope's comments on Pinochet, sanction against Libyan sanctions, US extradition of IRSP POWs, and British acts of international terrorism. The organization also calls for dissolution of NATO).

INLA communiqués largely concern the armed struggle. While most commemorate volunteers who died for the cause, others take responsibility for attacks on military targets, deny responsibility for assassination of particular loyalists and concern cease-fires. The final component of the Website is links that cover a wide range of movements and organizations. The Electronic Starry Plough is a case in point in the shift from territorial politics to a system of multiple and overlapping interests, meanings and authorities. However, it is unlikely that politics will be radically transformed to serve individual input or create community by the Internet alone. At first, radio and television were also thought to herald new individualism and new communities. Their eventual impact, a greatly enhanced role for interest groups, was not foreseen when the technologies were first introduced.

To have impact through the Internet, a group must either attract a broad public or mobilize a particular constituency.

Irish republicanism has a long history of successfully doing just this, largely due to the deterritorializing impact of events such as nineteenth century famine, which eventually produced an affluent and sympathetic Irish American relay to the republican movement. The Internet's capacity to integrate groups outside the mainstream provides opportunities for such groups to spread their message. Manuel Castells concurs when he states electronic politics will have "profound consequences on the characteristics, organization, and goals of political processes, political actors, and political institutions.

Electronic activists such as the IRSM now benefit from a fragmented public, eroding national boundaries, increased cynicism about governments, and awareness of transnational issues such as the environment and human rights. However, these conditions might be not signal long-term social transformation. Internet access is rapidly growing, but inaccessible to most of the world's population. The issue is what its impact will be within the privileged areas of the globe. Electronic activism also requires time, energy, and mental effort to sort, filter, interpret, and utilize information and so it is not clear "whether, on balance, communications have served to empower citizens or states". In effect, global communications mean that we have to rethink how we understand information and question our view of it as a resource rather than as something created.

Electronic activism changes the conditions of sovereignty. Few insurgents and radical groups want to abolish states. Indeed the IRSM amply illustrates a group that wants to transform a state rather than reject state-based politics. States will certainly retain their capacities to wage war and make peace as well as remain the central goal of many political movements and critical international actors. Electronic activism might then unsettle specific governments and substantiate a new global bipolarity between universal instrumentalism and specific identities or just as easily be subsumed by other, as yet unanticipated, organizing principles. The IRSM shows how information and communication are central to political conflict: the will to deliver a message. However, this shifting narrative depends on a social context, without which it might disappear without physical trace.

10

Extreme Violence and Terrorist Motivations

Misconstruing the underlying causes of Islamist rage or overacting to Islamist violence may only intensify militancy, not temperate it." For policy-makers, understanding the source or cause of discontent serves as the best hope to remedy the ills that lie beneath what some refer to as "sacred" terrorism or religious terrorism. Yet a basic question is what would extremists hope to achieve by resorting to such violent acts? Is terrorism ever rational? Can terrorism be deterred? All too often, our analysis of extremist motives begins with our reaction to the terrorist act itself. However, for certain extremist organizations, channeling efforts to identify and isolate the root cause for such events requires a deeper understanding of the intricacies that foment such profound actions, specifically suicide terrorism and the use of a weapon of mass destruction. In a recent review by Jeff Goodwin of Jessica Stern's Terror in the Name of God, he stated that few studies probe deeply into the cause of terrorism and, as a result, "it remains a mystery. A contributing factor is that social movement scholars with very few exceptions have said little about terrorism.

Nor have they paid sustained attention to the more general question of how movement organizations make strategic choices, of which terrorism is one." To resolve group level problems we need to view it from a group level or movement level perspective. It is at that point that we can start crafting more tailored solutions to counter the extremist threat. The central theme of this essay is to examine the rational behind terrorist use of weapons of mass destruction. Here, I compare Aum Shinrikyo and al Qaeda to analyze to what extent their actions were the result of strategic choice or group behaviour. In brief, Aum Shinrikyo's decision to attack civilians on a Japanese subway reflects an organization in a desperate fight for survival. According to Martha Crenshaw's organizational perspective, "terrorist actions often appear inconsistent, erratic, and unpredictable" and terrorist acts occur as a result of internal group dynamics.

The group's ultimate decision to strike a Tokyo subway system was as much an attack on Japan's political culture as it was an act by a desperate group. In contrast, al Qaeda's methodical planning and extensive preparation reflects an instrumental approach where the act of terrorism is that of strategic choice founded on the basis of collective values. According to Crenshaw, such an organization ultimately fails when the group is unable to reach its political objectives or when the cost of conducting such terrorist acts exceeds any foreseeable benefits.

Today, evolving before us is the fear of continued acts of "megaterrorism" such as the use of a weapon of mass destruction (WMD). Authors such as Graham Allison, Bruce Hoffman, Walter Laqueur, and others have written about the prospects of such actions. In fact, Thomas Schelling in 1979 wrote that "Sometime in the 1980s an organization that is not a national government may acquire a few nuclear weapons.... By 'organization' I mean a political movement, a government in exile, a separatist or secessionist party, a military rebellion, adventurers from the underground or the underworld, or even some group of people merely bent on showing that it can be done." Through his description, Schelling argues that distinctions exist between terrorist groups. If terrorist groups are distinctive in their motives, it would stand to reason that in order to deter or influence such organizations, one must also be able to isolate and differentiate the group's goals and objectives from their rhetoric.

For example, in comparing the Japanese terrorist cult Aum Shinrikyo to al Qaeda, we find distinctions in orientation and ideology, yet both are often characterized by the use of religious extremism to serve ideological objectives. Before the events of 9/11, Aum Shinrikyo unleashed fears of extreme terror with the release of sarin gas in a Japanese subway in 1995. Led by a religious mystic, Shoko Asahara, followers of the movement had come to believe that "Armageddon will come at the end of this century and...only a merciful, godly race will survive. The leader of this race will emerge in Japan." Asahara, characterized as charismatic, highly ambitious individual, methodically built a cult that, at its peak, reached 40,000 members world-wide with an estimated 30,000 followers in Russia and other areas to include Australia, Sri Lanka, and the United States.

The group capitalized on millennial visions and apocalyptic predictions to frame their group's doctrine which was deeply influenced by the works of Nostradamus; his work serves as a cornerstone of the group's teachings. Aum's followers actively recruited students and professionals in the fields of medicine, science, computers, engineering, and other technical areas. Asahara's charisma and message seemed to have a great appeal to many who felt alienated by the industrialized, secular, and conformist aspects of Japanese society. At its peak, it is estimated that Aum Shinrikyo's worth was as much as $1.5 billion. With such great financial resources, Aum Shinrikyo invested capital to support high-tech, state-of-the-art laboratories and funded its own research circumventing restrictions normally associated with larger corporate research laboratories.

In addition to collecting monies through donations, tithing, and sales of religious materials, Aum conducted seminars and courses in the cult's teachings charging hundreds to tens of thousands of dollars to participate in these sessions. In fact, Aum Shinrikyo diversified its enterprises by running a chain of restaurants in Tokyo as well as owning a computer manufacturing firm that assembled and sold computers in Japan with parts imported from Taiwan. Other more surreptitious practices included the manufacturing of illegal drugs that was supported by the Japanese mafia (the Yakuza) with a marketing agreement. Further, Aum engaged in a practice referred to as "green mail" where Aum would extort community leaders by threatening to establish a "branch" office or school within their local community.

By engaging in such practices, the cult succeeded in gaining leverage through extortion, coercion, theft, and murder as a form of fund-raising for the cult. Asahara and his closet followers planned to defend themselves against the coming Armageddon by creating a formidable arsenal that would enable Aum Shinrikyo to survive and become the most powerful group in the world. Despite high expectations and several attempts at local elections, Asahara and other leaders failed to gain a seat in the Japanese parliament. The result seemed to have radicalized the core leaders even more resulting from unmet expectations and the group's goals in changing Japanese political culture. He would later preach that it was "the duty of Aum members to hasten Armageddon" and subsequent efforts to attack the Japanese legislature also were indicative of Aum's disappointments with the democratic system.

While the group's most notorious act involved the release of sarin gas, Aum attempted to acquire various types of other weapons to include biological, nuclear, and radiological material. The cult's close relationship with followers in Russia positioned Aum Shinrikyo to leverage its vast wealth, contacts with Russian security forces, and dealers in the black-market yet failed to acquire weapons-grade fissile material. Aum remained open to all alternatives but ultimately chose to pursue the chemical option and made several attempts with limited results between 1990 through 1995 leading up to the attack of the Japanese subway in Tokyo. Asahara and his core leaders would soon discover that days prior to the subway attack, local authorities and law enforcement personnel had plans to conduct police raids against cult facilities and offices. By March 20, 1995, Aum's leaders believed that the only strategy that remained was a pre-emptive attack to strike fear as a last act in order to ensure the group's survival. Despite having limited success in its previous efforts with chemical agents, Aum had believed that a successful attack would have sufficient psychological impact as to allow the group to exist. In the end, what remains clear is that Aum displayed a great deal of resolve in its effort to employ tactics that would cause mass- casualties.

The perceived response by Japanese authorities compels Asahara and his inner circle to go further underground. From Aum's perspective, this act improved the cult's chances for survival while reducing the likelihood of death or capture, particularly among the group's leaders. Going underground isolates the movement from the outside world limiting the opportunity to add new recruits or re-replenish losses. Additionally, this action has the added effect of further radicalizing the group's tactics and ideology. As a result, terrorist behaviour begins to reflect the internal dynamics of the organization rather than achieving a specific strategic objective. The group begins to develop a tight identity, social connections, and interpersonal bonds that a sense of cohesion. It intensifies the groups resolve to move towards more violent activity.

The organization's decision-making begins to reflect the group's internal dynamics and group think eliminates decision within the leadership's inner core. Loyalty to the peer group takes on a more profound meaning and an important motive as activists shift towards a deepening commitment to the cause. Survival is at stake and the group becomes more willing to use extreme violence to counter any threat to its existence. Within the context of Aum's value system, the cult's actions appear logical. Aum felt cornered and that their last option for its survival was to strike back with its weapon.

Despite previous failures, the group had committed itself to developing and using chemical toxins as their primary instrument of extreme violence. As a self-legitimizing organization, Aum had rejected Japanese society and believed it had no other option but to confront authority. Its survival was at stake. One can argue that Aum sought an indirect approach to counter society's overwhelming preponderance of military and law enforcement forces by resorting to indirect methods. In failing to reach its goal of achieving political power through legitimate means, the group's leadership decided that a pre-emptive strike was their best and only option.

Al-Qaeda

Similarly, one can draw parallels between Osama bin Laden and the development of anti system frames used by al Qaeda to provide ethical justification for violence against civilians. For example, on February 23, 1998, Osama bin Laden released his Jihad Against the Jews and Crusaders, where he states his three major grievances with the United States; first, the occupation of "the lands of Islam in the holiest places, the Arabian peninsula"; the second, "the crusader-Zionist alliance": the third, "to fragment all the (Arab) states of the region such as Iraq, Saudi Arabia, Egypt, and Sudan into paper statelets and through their disunion and weakness to guarantee Israel's survival and the continuation of the brutal crusade occupation of the peninsula." Released by the World Islamic Front, this fatwa "became the manifesto of the full-fledged global Salafi jihad" allowing the jihad to carry "the fight to the 'far enemy.'"

By tapping into a view supported by a broad public, bin Laden attempts to draw support from among the greater Muslim community. His message strives to appeal to a wider global audience and rally a Muslim population of over one billion people to al Qaeda's cause. His effort is intended to reduce the psychological cost of participating in a radical cause or terrorist organization. In an article by della Porta, the author states that "The ideology of the terrorist organizations offered (1) a justification of political violence, including murder; (2) an image of the external world that masked the failures of the armed struggle; and (3) a positive evaluation of the role of individual action." Similar to Aum, al Qaeda has drawn from those sympathetic to al-Qaeda's cause. Bin Laden has leveraged common cultural frames and religious ones to serve as part of the group's strategic ideological objectives.

Therefore, as with Aum Shinrikyo, one must distinguish and separate between religious and ideological factors that shape the group's short-term and long- term objectives. Unlike Aum, however, al Qaeda's influence has extended to groups with known or alleged connections to al Qaeda including the Jemaah Islamiyah in Indonesia, Malaysia, and Singapore; Abu Sayyaf in the Philippines, al-Gama'a al-Islamiyya in Egypt; Harakat ul-Maujahidin in Pakistan; the Islamic Movement of Uzbekistan in Central Asia; Jaish-e-Mohammed in India and Pakistan; and, al-Jihad in Egypt. But the distinction between al Qaeda and its regional surrogate groups differ in that al Qaeda possesses a global view whereas the concerns by these various groups are more local. Likewise, these local groups have gone to considerable lengths to justify their support to the local population and would be less inclined towards resorting to mass violence. While they may agree that an attack on the

United States is justified, a similar response locally would be counterproductive to the group's cause.

Yet, to the extent that these corollary groups support al Qaeda directly or through more passive means, knowledge and understanding of the overall network is critical to determining the groups' vulnerabilities and potential opportunities to influence, deny, degrade, or disrupt threats of extreme violence. Arguably, in the case of a group like al Qaeda, the framing of such religious zeal serves a useful purpose to promote the group's ideological objectives as well as justifying the use of collective violence. According to Hafez, "Muslims rebel because they encounter an ill-fated combination of political and institutional exclusion, on the one hand, and reactive and indiscriminate repression on the other. When states do not provide their Islamist opposition movements opportunities for institutional participation, and employ repression indiscriminately against these movements after a period of prior mobilization, Islamist will most probably rebel."

Hafez describes how radical Islamists organize themselves and demand strict ideological and behavioural adherence of each of their members. In a similar way, Aum used threat, fear, murder, and intimidation to mitigate dissention within the group. This radicalized view, however, further isolates the organization from the rest of society. The increased radicalization produces a "spiral of encapsulation" that gradually isolates Islamists rebels from the broader movement. Such extremism increases moral justification for its cause while inducing a separation from the greater society. To be successful "Organizers of violence must align their tactics with cultural norms, symbols, and ethics that give moral meaning to acts of violence. Culture provides a "tool kit" of concepts, myths, and symbols from which militant organizations could selectively draw to construct strategies of action."

However, if a society places a premium on such sacrifice,

cultural framing can succeed in intensifying and reinforcing extreme use of violence such as suicide terrorism. Thus, martyrdom and suicide terror becomes the weapon of choice for producing mass violence. Academics would argue that mass terror, like suicide terrorism, serves a strategic purpose and is considered a coercive tool by terrorist organizations. While nation-states apply the threat of economic sanctions and conventional firepower as a means of coercion, terrorists increasingly use suicide terror as the instrument of choice. Unlike Aum Shinrikyo, al Qaeda used a technologically conservative weapon combined with variants on a familiar tactic of hijacking, bombing, and martyrdom as suicide terror. Yet, like Aum, al Qaeda expressed a strong interest and effort in acquiring weapons of mass destruction. Long before Bin Laden's 2003 fatwa, "the global jihadist network have made their desire for nuclear weapons for use against the United States and explicit, by both word and deed. Bin Laden has called the acquisition of weapons of mass destruction (WMD) a 'religious duty.'"

Ayman al Zawahiri, leader of the Egyptian Islamic Jihad (EIJ) expands bin Laden's views by stating that the objective of the global jihad against the United States and its allies is to: 1. To inflict maximum casualties against the opponent; 2. To concentrate on the method of martyrdom operations as the most successful way of inflicting damage against the opponent and the least costly to the Mujahedin in terms of casualties; 3. Targets as well as the type and method of weapons used must be chosen to have an impact on the structure of the enemy; 4. To reiterate that focusing on the domestic enemy alone will not be feasible at this stage. As reported in The New York Times, bin Laden's group, like Aum, sought to build a nuclear-yield weapon. After a few attempts, bin Laden's organization fell victim to scams by vendors in an effort to acquire weapons-grade material. The inability to acquire the necessary fissile material is likely to have convinced al Qaeda planners to shift its focus to chemical agents as a possible weapon of choice.

However, as demonstrated by the multiple failed attempts by Aum, successfully executing a chemical attack is not a simple task. In a conversation with Dr. David Rapport, he stated that he believes the use of chemical weapons is less likely due to the historical difficulty in weaponising and delivering a chemical attack. As al Qaeda training videos surfaced in August 2002, the public at large became convinced of the group's motivation, desire, and intent to using chemical and biological toxins if given the opportunity. In the wake of 9/11, the idea never seemed more plausible, yet al Qaeda displayed a very pragmatic approach in resorting to a strategy that seemed tried and true. To al Qaeda, history had shown that suicide terrorism is a highly effective asymmetric weapon that could yield results. In a recent article, Robert Pape proffers five key observations on how terrorist organizations have assessed the effectiveness of suicide attacks and the limits of their coercive ability.

First, he states that suicide terrorism is strategic. He asserts that the majority of suicide attacks occur as part of an organized group's activities in support of a broader strategic framework to support a particular goal. Second, the suicide terrorism is geared to forcing democracies to give ground on nationalistic causes. Third, he states that "during the past twenty years, suicide terrorism has been steadily rising because terrorists have learned that it pays." Suicide terrorists sought to compel American and French military forces to abandon Lebanon in 1983, Israeli forces to leave Lebanon in 1985, Israeli forces to quit the Gaza Strip and the West Bank in 1994 and 1995. Following this logic, the Madrid Bombings which occurred three days before a nationwide general election, resulted in the death of 192 civilians.

The dramatic events had an immediate impact on the Spanish elections and subsequent withdrawal of Spain's troops in Iraq. Published reports would later reveal the al

Qaeda had identified Spain as a key target in their overall strategic plan. The belief was that Spain was "very vulnerable to attacks, primarily because public opposition to the war is total, and the government is virtually alone on this issue." Pape believes that "although moderate suicide terrorism led to moderate concessions, these more ambitious suicide terrorist campaigns are not likely to achieve still greater gains and may well fail completely." States may choose to abandon or concede short-term goals in lieu of any major concessions. Decisions that would have long term implications such as compromising the state's overall security, significant loss of territory, or economic deprivation would be unlikely. Secondly, the "most promising way to contain suicide terrorism is to reduce terrorists' confidence in their ability to carry out such attacks on the target society."

In essence, terrorists resort to suicide terrorism because on some level it works. As a strategy, martyrdom and mass violence gives hope to the extremist cause and the historical precedence is indicative that at some level, success can be achieved through the use of extremist violence. By focusing solely on the prevention of a similar attack, we do so at the expense of understanding the root cause and motives that led to the violent attack in the first place. Concentrating our energies as to why and how organizations resort to extremism requires an analysis of how and why groups employ terrorism.

Strategic Choice

Martha Crenshaw emphasizes the importance of analyzing how terrorist groups behave as a key process in developing effective policy recommendations. She develops two approaches to better understand terrorism and its consequences. The first approach argues that terrorism represents a strategic choice from a set of possible alternatives by a political actor. Behaving on a set of collective values, an organization may choose terrorism to achieve radical political and social change. This instrumental approach is viewed as a response to government behaviour and actions. The corresponding view is that as cost for conducting such activity increases or as the reward for such actions decreases, violence will be less likely to occur. The instrumental perspective takes a basic rational approach of cost/benefit analysis in choosing terrorism. The second approach emphasizes the internal organizational process within a particular group or across similar groups who have common objectives.

The emphasis is on the internal dynamics of a group where leaders offer incentives to individuals or control their actions to discourage defection of dissent within the organization and foster intense loyalty. In effect, the actions of this type of group may not correspond to the organization's stated political objectives and more reflective of an erratic organization displaying unpredictable behaviour showing more of a struggle of survival rather than activity that supports ideological objectives. Such a group would be more inclined to change internal incentives towards individuals in response to perceived threats from external pressures applied to the organization. How then would this apply to the Aum Shinrikyo and al Qaeda? We shall first compare the similarities of both organizations. Drawing from these conclusions, we begin to see the contrast between the organizations.

While Aum expresses political change as their ultimate desire, its decision-making reflects more of an organizational survivalist construct in achieving its ends. Unlike al Qaeda, Aum becomes focused in using a weapon of terror to achieve its objectives. This obsessive fixation continues despite numerous experimental attempts and failures. Aum's leaders appear almost unconstrained by their own ego and driven to validate its extensive investment in research and equipment by using chemical weapons. In contrast, al Qaeda abandons its effort only after repeated attempts failed to achieve desired outcomes leading the group to instead modify known capabilities, bombing, and hijacking, with the intent to improve their chances of success. In keeping with a more instrumental approach, al Qaeda maintains its focus on accomplishing its operational objective despite the specific tactical means of doing so.

Although al Qaeda had the wealth, resources, and contacts necessary for such a venture its leaders decided to pursue other alternatives to achieve the desired effect. However, what both examples show is that despite wealth and connections problems still exist in pursuing weapons of mass destruction. A second key observation is the difference in how each organization frames its cause. Al Qaeda leveraged existing sentiments and feelings shared among a large majority of the Muslim world. The leadership within al Qaeda drew upon widely shared beliefs that roots of the Muslim world's problem lies with the continuing influence of the West in Islamic affairs.

His message had a broad appeal because it resonates with existing cultural, religious, and societal beliefs. Al Qaeda's leaders hijacked existing beliefs to satisfy ideological objectives. In contrast, Aum's belief core is wholly manufactured, synthetic in its origins. First, while Asahara dabbled in the practices of Hinduism, its belief structure was pieced together from various religious and non-religious beliefs, such as the writing of Nostradamus. Second, unlike life in a predominantly Islamic culture, Aum Shinrikyo's teachings were not necessarily reinforced by everyday surroundings, societal contacts, and interactions. Unless a follower of Aum lived on one of its communities, individuals were susceptible to external influences. To some degree, this constraint contributed to need for suppressing dissention within the group.

The likelihood of terrorist use of weapons of mass destruction in the post-9/11 era remains unclear. However, the scale of attack on 9/11 suggests that despite the technical challenges, groups will continue to expend efforts in possessing a capacity to cause extreme violence whether through conventional or unconventional means. As Dr. McAdam suggests, more effort and dialogue between academic and government communities is necessary to understand the role of extremism and source of contention behind groups that may spawn from social movements. This would help policy-makers identify and distinguish groups who approach terrorism from an organizational or instrumental perspective. Pressures applied to a group dominated by internal dynamics would compel the organization to implode by isolating the particular individual goals versus political ideology. This is best exemplified in the discussion of Aum Shinrikyo above.

Within the context of Aum's value system, the cult's actions appeared logical. Their rejection of Japanese society is best illustrated in their response to pending raids by Japanese authorities. In lieu of achieve political power through legitimate means, the group ultimately sought to achieve its objective through extreme violence. In contrast, a group choosing terrorism among other alternatives will calculate actions based on perceived benefits and costs. This approach would suggest that presenting a set of different alternatives as substitutes or increasing costs to the degree that any benefits gained by terrorist in using extreme violence would not be sufficient to achieving political objectives. In the case of al Qaeda, the pursuit of weapons of mass destruction was simply a part of the range of options available for instrumental purposes. Aum's obsession with WMD technology combined with the permissive environment of Japanese legal system enabled Asahara's followers to pursue WMD technology despite numerous failed experiments.

Today, changes in the legal system and law enforcement techniques would make the duplication of Aum's extensive

WMD apparatus more difficult. In other words, the changes adopted by Japan's legal system and experience gained from Asahara and his cult have raised the cost of pursuing such tactics, thus mitigating any desire to replicate Aum's program in Japan. In light of 9/11 and for groups who follow al Qaeda, an attack using chemical, biological, radiological, and nuclear weapons has yet to be seen. The potential is undeniable. Technical challenges will remain an issue in the short-run which will make conventional weapons applied in an asymmetric approach a primary means to cause mass disruption. As a result, the long-term goal should be continued emphasis on enforcing constraints and controls on the proliferation of sensitive materials to include commercially available fissile matter and not solely weapons-grade material. Experts contend that a radiological dispersal device (RDD) or "dirty bomb", a combination of both conventional explosives with low grade radiological material, is a greater threat than a nuclear weapon.

However, future terrorist groups may examine both cases a draw from them the next most probable course of action. For example, where Aum failed to hire the expertise necessary for a nuclear weapon's program, would an instrumentalist group like al Qaeda stand a better chance of recruiting Islamic extremists with the requisite skills? Secondly, some argue that Islamist groups like al Qaeda are on their way out. If this is the case, what would preclude a group from following Aum Shinrikyo's model of resorting to extreme violence with the use of a more catastrophic weapon? In either case, the goal should be eliminating a terrorist's hope for success, shoring up defenses, and deterring the proliferation of WMD technology. Eliminate the means and we reduce the likelihood osf a mass attack. Likewise, by understanding the problem we increase the probability of mitigating potential extremist growth while reducing the seeds of future threats.

One Terrorism

The events on 11 September 2001 (henceforth 9/11) served as a wake-up call to the world that transnational terrorism poses grave risks. The four simultaneous hijackings on 9/11 represent watershed terrorist incidents for a number of reasons. First, the deaths associated with 9/11 were unprecedented: the human toll was equal to the number of deaths from transnational terrorism from the start of 1988 through the end of 2000. Second, the losses associated with 9/11 topped $80 billion and caused insurance companies to end automatic coverage of terrorist-induced losses. Since 9/11, many companies have been unable to afford terrorism insurance. Third, 9/11 showed that ordinary objects can be turned into deadly weapons with catastrophic consequences. Despite the huge carnage of 9/11, the death toll could have been much higher had the planes struck the towers at a lower floor. Fourth, 9/11 underscored the objectives of today's fundamentalist terrorists to seek maximum casualties and to induce widespread fear, unlike the predominantly left-wing terrorist campaigns of the 1970s and 1980s that sought to win over a constituency.

Fifth, 9/11 mobilized a huge reallocation of resources to homeland security – since 2002, the US Department of Homeland Security (DHS) budget has grown by over 60% to $36.2 billion for the fiscal year 2004 (DHS, 2003). In fiscal year 2005, the DHS budget grew another 10% to $40.2 billion (DHS, 2004). A little over 60% of DHS's budget goes to defending against terrorism on US soil. This expenditure is small compared to proactive measures taken in fighting the "war on terror," including the invasion against the Taliban and al-Qaida in Afghanistan on 7 October 2001. Still other proactive spending involves improving intelligence, tracking terrorist assets, and fostering cooperative linkages with other countries. Sixth, protective actions taken by rich developed countries have transferred some attacks against these countries' interests to poorer countries – for example, post-9/11 attacks in Egypt, Indonesia, Morocco, Kenya, Saudi Arabia, and Turkey.

The events of 9/11 heightened anxiety worldwide and resulted in trade-offs in terms of trading reduced freedom for greater security; society had not been willing to surrender as much freedom prior to 9/11. Society lost innocence on that fateful day that it will never regain. The threat of catastrophic terrorist events – though their probability is low – is etched indelibly in everyone's mind. The Madrid train bombings on 11 March 2004 have made Europe more aware that large-scale terrorist events can occur on European soil. The anxiety that terrorists seek to create is amplified by people's proclivity to overreact to low-probability but ghastly events.

The study of terrorism has been an active field of research in international relations since the early 1970s and the start of the modern era of transnational terrorism (that is, terrorism with international implications or genesis). Of course, the interest in the study of terrorism grew greatly after 9/11, with many new courses being taught at the undergraduate level worldwide. Subscriptions to the two field journals – *Terrorism and Political Violence* and *Studies in Conflict & Terrorism* (formerly *Terrorism*) – that publish scholarly articles increased following 9/11. General journals in the social sciences are now more willing to publish articles on terrorism. Grant opportunities to study terrorism have also increased greatly through DHS, government agencies, and private foundations. These opportunities can now be found not only in the United States but worldwide. Scholarly conferences on terrorism have also grown in number in the last few years.

The purpose of this book is to present a widely accessible political economy approach that combines economic methods and political analysis. Where possible, we apply theoretical and statistical tools so that the reader can understand why governments and terrorists take certain actions even when, on occasion, these actions may be against their interests. Often, we are able to explain behaviour that appears counterintuitive once the underlying *strategic* interactions among agents (for example, among targeted governments) are taken into account. Throughout the book, we provide insights that run counter to conventional wisdom but that are supported by the data. Our reliance on statistical analysis means that we do *not* eyeball the data in order to draw conclusions that may not hold up to statistical scrutiny. Our approach relies on statistical inference, which is less apt to change tomorrow as new terrorist groups with new objectives and modes of action come on the scene.

Our intention is to offer a fresh approach that can inform not only students but also researchers, practitioners (for example, insurers), policymakers, and others interested in an up-to-date treatment of the political economy of terrorism. Terrorism is the premeditated use or threat to use violence by individuals or sub national groups in order to obtain a political or social objective through the intimidation of a large audience beyond that of the immediate victims. Two essential ingredients characterize any modern definition of terrorism: the presence or threat of violence and a political/social motive. Without violence or its threat, terrorists cannot make a political decision maker respond to their demands. Moreover, in the absence of a political/social motive, a violent act is a crime rather than an act of terrorism.

Terrorists broaden their audience beyond their immediate victims by making their actions appear to be random, so that everyone feels anxiety. In contrast to a drive-by shooting on a city street, terrorist acts are not random but well-planned and often well-executed attacks where the terrorists account for risks and associated costs as well as possible gains. In addition to violence and a political motive, a minimalist definition hinges on three additional factors: the victim, the perpetrator, and the audience. Of these three, the most controversial is the identity of the *victim*. Is an attack against a passive military target or a peacekeeper a terrorist act? The Israelis include an assault against a passive military target as a terrorist attack, whereas other countries may not if the military person is part of an occupying force. Virtually all definitions consider terrorist attacks against civilians as terrorism. The data set *International Terrorism: Attributes of Terrorist Events* (ITERATE) includes terrorist actions against peacekeepers, but not against an occupying army, as acts of terrorism.

While not as contentious as the victim, the *perpetrator* also presents some controversy. If a state or government uses terror tactics against its own citizens (for example, Stalin's reign of terror), is this terrorism? We apply the convention to call such actions *state terror* but not terrorism. In our definition, the perpetrators are individuals or sub national groups but not the state itself. States can, however, support these sub national terrorist groups through safe havens, funding, weapons, intelligence, training, or other means. When a state assists a terrorist group, the resulting terrorist act is known as *state-sponsored terrorism*. Libya is accused of state sponsoring the downing of Pan Am flight 103 over Lockerbie, Scotland, on 21 December 1988, and agreed in 2003 to compensate the victims' families. The US Department of State branded number of nations – Cuba, Iran, Libya, North Korea, Sudan, and Syria – as state sponsors of terrorism.

Finally, the *audience* refers to the group that the terrorist act is intended to intimidate. For example, a terrorist bomb aboard a commuter train is meant to cause anxiety in the public at large, because such bombs can be placed in any train or public place. The audience thus extends beyond the immediate victims of the attack. On 9/11, al-Qaida's audience was everyone on the planet, not just the unfortunate victims associated with the four hijackings and their aftermath. Why do terrorists seek such a wide audience? Terrorists want to circumvent the normal political channels/procedures and create political change through threats and violence. By intimidating a target population, terrorists intend that this population will apply pressure on political decision makers to concede to their demands. From a rational calculus viewpoint, political decision makers must weigh the expected costs of conceding, including possible counter grievances from other groups, against the anticipated costs of future attacks.

If the latter costs exceed those of conceding, then a besieged government should rationally give in to the demands of the terrorists. Suicide attacks have gained prominence since 1983, because they raise the target audience's anxiety and, in so doing, greatly increase the government's anticipated costs from future attacks. This follows because a suicide attack kills on average thirteen people, while a typical terrorist incident kills less than one person. Thus, governments have more readily given in to *modest* demands following suicide campaigns – for example, Hezbollah's car bombing of the US Marine barracks in Lebanon on 23 October 1983 resulted in the US withdrawal from Lebanon, whereas the October 1994–August 1995 Hamas suicide campaign against Israel led to the partial Israeli withdrawal from the West Bank. Concessions also encourage more terrorism as the government loses its reputation for toughness – these reputation costs must also be weighed against the gains of giving in (e.g., released hostages or an end to attacks). Terrorist tactics are more effective in liberal democracies, where governments are expected to protect lives and property. Understandably, suicide campaigns have been almost exclusively associated with liberal democracies.

To show how definitions may vary, we investigate a few official ones, starting with that of the US Department of State, for which "terrorism means premeditated, politically motivated violence perpetrated against noncombatant targets by sub national groups or clandestine agents, usually intended to influence an audience". An interesting feature of this definition is the characterization of the victims as "noncombatants," meaning civilians and unarmed or off-duty military personnel. Accordingly, a bomb planted under a US soldier's private vehicle in Germany is an act of terrorism. This nicely illustrates how the designation of a victim can be quite controversial. The State Department's definition is silent about whether a threat is a terrorist act.

The US Department of Defense (DoD) defines terrorism as "the unlawful use or threatened use of force or violence against individuals or property to coerce or intimidate governments or societies, often to achieve political, religious, or ideological objectives". Three contrasts between the DoD's and the State Department's definition are worth highlighting. First, the *threat* of violence is now included. Second, the noncombatant distinction is dropped, so that the roadside bombing of a US convoy in Iraq would be terrorism. Third, religious and ideological motives are explicitly identified. Even two departments of the same government cannot fully agree on the definition. Nevertheless, these definitions identify the same five minimalist ingredients – violence, political motivation, perpetrator, victim, and audience. The definitional problem lies in precisely identifying these ingredients. Slightly different definitions of terrorism also characterize those of the Federal Bureau of Investigation (FBI), the Defense Intelligence Agency, and the Vice President's Task Force on Terrorism of 1986.

The political nature of defining terrorism comes into focus when the official UN definition is examined: "terrorism is the act of destroying or injuring civilian lives or the act of destroying or damaging civilian or government property without the expressly chartered permission of a specific government, this by individuals or groups acting independently...in the attempt to effect some political goal" (emphasis added). A difficulty with this definition is that it may not brand a state-sponsored skyjacking or bombing as an act of terrorism if it is sanctioned by a specific government – for example, Iran's action to maintain the takeover of the US embassy in Tehran on 4 November 1979 for 444 days. Loopholes such as this arise when so many nations have to agree on a definition and governments do not want to tie their own hands in the future. Since 9/11, the United Nations has ignored its official definition and taken a more pragmatic approach, branding violent acts perpetrated by sub national groups for political purposes as terrorism. This new pragmatic definition agrees closely with our definition.

Another definitional issue concerns distinguishing terrorism from warfare. In its classic sense, war targets combatants with weapons that are highly discriminating in order to limit collateral damage on civilians. Unlike war, terrorism targets noncombatants in a relatively indiscriminate manner, as 9/11 or the downing of Pan Am flight 103 illustrates. Unfortunately, the fire bombings of Dresden and Tokyo during World War II blur the wartime distinction about noncombatants and discriminating attack. For our purposes, we distinguish warfare and terrorism in this standard way despite some issues of this kind. The Dresden and Tokyo bombings were not terrorist attacks, because they were perpetrated by governments, not sub national groups, during a declared war. Definitions are essential when putting together data to examine propositions, trends, and other aspects of terrorism. A well-defined notion is needed so that events can be classified as terrorism for empirical purposes. To this end, we rely on our definition, which takes a middle ground with respect to other definitions and comes close to the US Department of State's definition and the pragmatic UN definition following 9/11.

Transnational Terrorism

Another essential distinction is between domestic and transnational terrorism. Domestic terrorism is homegrown and has consequences for just the host country, its institutions, citizens, property, and policies. In a domestic incident, the perpetrators, victims, and audience are all from the host country. In addressing domestic terrorism, a country can be self-reliant if it possesses sufficient resources. Antiterrorist policies need not involve other countries insofar as neither the terrorist acts nor the government's responses need impose costs or confer benefits on foreign interests. Domestic terrorist campaigns result in a country taking antiterrorist measures to limit the threat. Most terrorist events directed against the United States do not occur on its soil. The kidnapping in January 2002 and subsequent murder of reporter Daniel Pearl in Pakistan; the destruction of the Al Khobar Towers housing US airmen in June 1996 near Dhahran, Saudi Arabia; and the bombing of the US embassies in Kenya and Tanzania in August 1998 are three gruesome examples of transnational terrorism.

Terrorism is transnational when an incident in one country involves perpetrators, victims, institutions, governments, or citizens of another country. If an incident begins in one country but terminates in another, then it is a transnational terrorist event, as is the case for a hijacking of a plane in country *A* that is made to fly to country *B*. An attack against a multilateral organization is a transnational incident owing to its multi country impact, as in the case of the suicide car bombing of the UN headquarters in Baghdad on 19 August 2003. The toppling of the World Trade Center towers was a transnational incident because victims were from ninety different countries, the mission had been planned abroad, the terrorists were foreigners, and the implications of the event (for example, financial repercussions) were global.

With transnational terrorism, countries' policies are interdependent. Efforts by the European countries to secure their borders and ports of entry may merely shift attacks aimed at their people and property abroad, where borders are more porous. US actions that deny al-Qaida safe havens or that destroy its training camps limit the network's effectiveness against all potential targets, thereby conferring a benefit on other countries. Intelligence on a common transnational terrorist threat that is gathered by one nation can benefit other potential target countries. As such, transnational terrorism raises the need for countries to coordinate antiterrorist policies, a need that countries had resisted until 9/11. Even now, this coordination can be much improved.

Other Aspects of Terrorism

The motives of terrorists may vary among groups. Traditionally, many terrorists are motivated by ethno-nationalistic goals to establish a homeland for an oppressed ethnic group. The Tamils in Sri Lanka fall into this category, as did the Sudanese People Liberation Army's (SPLA's) struggle against the Muslim majority in the north of Sudan. The Palestinians are also applying terrorism as a way to gain a state. Terrorism may also be motivated by nihilism, left-wing ideology, religious suppression, intolerance, social injustice, or issue-specific goals. In recent years, some groups have resorted to terrorism to establish a fundamentalist-based regime. For example, Harakat ul-Jihad-I-Islami/Bangladesh wants to establish Islamic rule in Bangladesh; Al-Jihad (also known as the Egyptian Islamic Jihad) wishes to set up an Islamic state in Egypt; and Jemaah Islamiyah intends to create a pan-Islamic state out of Indonesia, Malaysia, Singapore, the southern Philippines, and southern Thailand. Many other rationales – for example, publicizing an alleged genocide, a millennium movement, and animal protection – have motivated terrorists' violence against innocent victims.

Terrorists employ varied modes of attack to create an atmosphere of fear and vulnerability. Hostage missions are logistically complex and risky, and include kidnappings, barricade and hostage taking (that is, the takeover of a building and the securing of hostages), skyjackings, and the takeover of non-aerial means of transportation. Ransoms from kidnappings have been used by some terrorist groups as a revenue source to support operations. This is especially true of some Latin American terrorists who have kidnapped business executives for ransom. Bombings can take many forms, including explosive, letter, and incendiary bombs. Bombings are by far the favorite tactic of terrorists, accounting for about half of all terrorist incidents. Assassinations are politically motivated murders. Threats are promises of future action, while hoaxes are false claims of past actions (for example, falsely claiming that a bomb is aboard a plane). Suicide attacks can involve a car, lone terrorist carrying explosives, or some other delivery device (for example, a donkey cart). Other terrorist modes of attack involve armed attacks (including sniping and shootouts with authorities) or sabotage.

Table: *Some Terrorist Tactics*

Terrorist Operations

- Hostage missions (e.g., skyjacking, kidnapping, and barricade and hostage taking)
- Bombings· Assassinations
- Threats and hoaxes
- Suicide attacks
- Armed attacks
- Sabotage
- Nuclear-related weapon attacks
- Chemical or biological attacks

Other Actions

- Bank robberies
- Propaganda

- Legitimate efforts to gain political recognition

Since the 20 March 1995 sarin attack on the Tokyo subway by Aum Shinrikyo, the growing worry has been that terrorists will resort to weapons of mass destruction (WMD) in the form of a nuclear weapon, a radiological ("dirty") bomb, a chemical weapon, or a biological weapon. The dirty bomb consists of a conventional bomb that disperses radioactive material, which contaminates an area for years to come and causes delayed deaths. Other terrorist actions involve bank robberies or criminal acts to finance operations. In some cases, terrorists also spread propaganda and use legitimate political actions to induce change. For example, Hamas, Hezbollah, the Irish Republican Army, and Euskadi ta Askatasuna (ETA) have political wings that promote the group's viewpoint.

Terrorists must allocate resources between terrorist attacks and legitimate means for achieving political goals. Ironically, actions by the authorities to limit protest may close off legitimate avenues of dissent and push terrorists into engaging in more attacks. Even among attack modes, terrorists must weigh expected costs and expected benefits from different actions in order to pick the best combination for their campaigns.

11

Political Approach to the Study of Terrorism

The primary contributors to the study of terrorism during the last thirty-five years have been the political scientists, who have enlightened us on terrorist campaigns, groups, tactics, motives, finances, state support, and trends. Much of their analysis has been comparative – for example, when researchers distinguish among terrorist groups or countries harboring terrorists. The comparative approach has taught us much about what is common and what is different among terrorist groups. For instance, political scientists have characterized many of the European terrorist organizations coming out of the antiwar protests of the late 1960s as "fighting communist organizations" with a Marxist-Leninist ideology, an ant capitalist orientation, a desire to limit casualties, and a need for an external constituency. Over the last few decades, political scientists have identified the changing nature of terrorism – for example, the rise of state sponsorship in the early 1980s and the more recent increase in fundamentalist-based terrorism.

Political scientists have also analyzed the effectiveness of antiterrorist policies, but typically without applying statistical inference – Brophy-Baermann and Conybeare is an important early exception. Since 9/11, political scientists have been more interested in empirical analyses of terrorism. Until recently, political scientists rarely relied on rational-actor models of terrorist behaviour – for example, Bueno de Mesquita applied such models. An advantage of the political science approach has been its eclectic, multidisciplinary viewpoint encompassing historical, sociological, and psychological studies. Historical studies identify common features among terrorist campaigns and indicate how the nature of terrorist tactics and campaigns has evolved over time. Sociological analyses examine norms and social structure within terrorist organizations.

In recent psychological studies, researchers have identified internal and external variables associated with the escalation of violence in terrorist events. Factors that induce an individual to become a suicide bomber include both sociological – the approval of a group – and psychological considerations. Other psychological studies indicate the personality traits of different types of terrorists, including those who use the internet to coordinate attacks.

Economic methodology has much to offer to the study of terrorism because it adds theoretical models and empirical analyses that have not been prominent. The application of economic methods to the study of terrorism started with Landes (1978), who applied the economics of crime and punishment to the study of hijackings in the United States. His study derived an "offense function," which relates the number of hijackings to policy variables – for example, probability of apprehension, presence of sky marshals, probability of conviction, and average length of sentence – that can be controlled by the authorities. Landes then estimated this offense function using data from past US hijackings to ascertain the marginal impact that each variable had on the number of hijackings.

For example, Landes quantified the immediate and large influence that the installation of metal detectors at US airports in January 1973 had on the number of hijackings. In a scientific tradition, Landes first built a theoretical behavioural model of terrorists that he later tested using the data. Over the next twenty-five years, other economists and political scientists have followed his methodology. After 9/11, many economists have turned their attention to examining terrorism insurance, antiterrorism policy evaluation, terrorist-imposed risks, and economic impacts of terrorism.

Observations Regarding Changing Views on Terror

Since the 11 September 2001 incidents in the United States of America (US) and the escalation of terror attacks in Iraq, numerous articles and comments have addressed these issues, described by some as the 'new terrorism'. Others argue that some of the basic trends had, however, existed previously, and were now only receiving more attention or becoming more pronounced. The aim of this article is to explore number of these issues, particularly those pertaining to an apparently changed perception or view of the phenomenon of terror. These include changes regarding certain components of the standard definitions of terror, with specific reference to motives and certain forms and targets of terror; the continued relevance of an overall political motive; the continued relevance of the so-called 'national liberation movement' designation; the broadening of the scope of non-combatants targeted by terror attacks; and the distinction between transnational, international and domestic terror. For purposes of this and given the scope of issues addressed, it is obviously not intended to provide an extensive analysis of each of these issues, but rather to provide an overview of changed perceptions in each case.

New Perceptions or New Trends

Although this article is about seemingly new perceptions regarding terrorism, and not about new trends in terrorism, it is argued that even the latter seems to be at least partially based on perceptions and some disregard of history. In this regard, the main trends associated with the 'new terrorism' after the events of 11 September 2001, are that terrorists now operate transnational and in loosely organised networks; that they are largely motivated by religious extremism; that they aim at mass casualties and specifically attempt to obtain weapons of mass destruction; and that targeting is indiscriminate and not selective. However, it has been pointed out that continuity between the 'old' and the 'new' terrorism exists to the degree that the distinction between the two is open to serious questioning. Terrorism can only be described as 'new' if historical research clearly shows that it has not occurred previously, or if a new historical interpretation is provided. While it is clear that the selection of targets and the increasing tendency towards political-religious motivations do represent certain changing trends in terrorism, continuities exist and caution has been expressed regarding generalisations about trends in terrorism based on particular attacks such as the World Trade Centre bombing.

The Political Objective of Terror and Related Motives

In keeping with the standard definition of terror, Wilkinson states that terrorism is "the systematic use of coercive intimidation, usually to service political ends". Innocent civilians are often killed or injured in terror attacks. The US Code defines terrorism as meaning "premeditated, politically motivated violence perpetrated against noncombatant targets by sub-national groups or clandestine agents". This significantly does not include either domestic or international terror committed directly by the agents of the state itself, although certain countries continue to be designated as 'state sponsors' of terrorism by the US State Department. In this regard it has been suggested that the term 'terror' refers to a state's use of it, while 'terrorism' refers to substate use, the latter also being known as factional terror.

The US National Counterterrorism Center (NCTC) also emphasises the existence of an overall political motive underlying terrorism, referring to incidents as being "politically motivated, potentially including religious, philosophical, or culturally symbolic motivations" with ordinary criminal activity, genocide and tribal violence excluded. It seems to be clear that the overall political motive or purpose is viewed as one of the main characteristics of terrorism in these definitions, and those other more specific motives such as religion, would then complement the political motive. Wilkinson, for instance, refers to 'religio-political' terrorists, apparently to distinguish this from a 'purely' religious phenomenon, and states that what at first sight seems to be such a phenomenon, is in fact largely about political control and socio-economic demands.

The above view is reinforced by Duyvesteyn who states that while religion has played a role in terrorist targeting, these represent clear political positions and political targets. The so-called 'new terrorism' is therefore both political and religious, and aims and motivations overlap. Various United Nations (UN) resolutions have been adopted, especially since 2001 where the issue of motives has been addressed. UN Security Council Resolution 1377 of 2001, *inter alia* states that the UN "(r)eaffirms it unequivocal condemnation of all acts, methods and practices of terrorism as criminal and unjustifiable, regardless of their motivation, in all their forms and manifestations, wherever and by whomever committed".

During 2003, the UN General Assembly adopted a resolution similarly addressing the issue of motives, formulated as follows: "criminal acts intended or calculated to provoke a state of terror in the general public, a group of persons or particular persons for political purposes are in any circumstances unjustifiable, whatever the considerations of a political, philosophical, ideological, racial, ethnic, religious or any other nature that may be invoked to justify them". In the latter resolution, it seems that political motives are placed on par with other motives, although an overall 'political purpose' is required. One explanation may be that there may be different political motives, hence the repetition. Some would also argue that ideological motives are inherently political.

In some instances, reference to the primary or overall political motive is absent in national anti-terrorism legislation, and political motives are seen as one of a range of possible motives. The South African Protection of Constitutional Democracy Against Terrorist and Related Activities Act, 2004 (Act No 22 of 2004), defines terrorist activity as "(a) any act committed in or outside the Republic, which (i) involves the systematic, repeated or arbitrary use of violence by any means or method". It then continues to list specific acts such as exposing the public to any toxic chemical, destruction of or substantial damage to any property or natural resource whether public or private, serious interference with banking or financial systems etc, and which is intended to threaten the unity or territorial integrity of the Republic; intimidating or causing feelings of insecurity within the public; or unduly compelling, intimidating, forcing, coercing or inducing or causing a person, a government, the general public or a segment of the public to do or to abstain from doing a certain act, or to adopt or abandon a certain standpoint. The qualification added to the above acts is that they are "committed, directly or indirectly, in whole or in part, for the purpose of the advancement of an individual or collective political, religious, ideological or philosophical motive, objective cause or undertaking".

In addition to the above, the so-called 'Convention offences' such as those related to hijacking, destruction or the endangering of the safety of fixed platforms; hijacking of aircraft; and hijacking of a ship or the endangering of maritime navigation are also included in the legislation. In this regard, as in the case of hoaxes involving, for instance, noxious substances or explosives, even purely criminal motives underlying these actions may constitute an offence. Although the latter is in accordance with international practice regarding so-called 'Convention offences', the separation of an overall political motive from other motives in the basic definition of terror (and indeed to include it as one of a range of motives), obviously confuses certain acts of a purely criminal nature (and which are sometimes called 'criminal terror', with terrorism proper.

The qualification that the acts for instance threaten the unity and territorial integrity of South Africa, could of course in certain circumstances be viewed as implying a primary political motive, but "causing feelings of insecurity among the public", may just as well be the result of 'criminal terror'. It may be argued that in certain instances, acts of 'criminal terror' justify being dealt with under terrorism legislation (as in the case of the 'Convention offences'), but a too wide view, not directly linked to an underlying or overall political motive, can result in situations where the underlying causes are not addressed in attempts to counter terror, but only manifestations; elevating certain criminal acts to the level of political acts; and where crime is seen as the result of political grievances and a redress of past inequalities, and not, for instance, as an act of revenge or greed inspired by personal motives.

On the other hand, it has also been argued that the link between terrorism and politically-motivated behaviour may exclude certain acts that are deemed to be terrorist in nature but with a criminal motive. As previously stated, this problem can, however, partially be overcome by specifying certain acts which would be viewed as terrorism, even if the motive appeared to be purely criminal.

The South African legislation seems to lean heavily on the Organisation of African Unity (OAU) Convention on the Prevention and Combating of Terrorism, which uses the exact wording to include political motives underlying terror, as one of a range of motives not constituting a justifiable defence against a terrorist act.

Both the South African legislation and the OAU Convention (supplemented by the African Union—AU—Protocol of 2004), retain the concept of so-called 'national liberation movements'. The OAU Convention stipulates in this regard that "the struggle waged by peoples in accordance with the principles of international law for their liberation or self-determination, including armed struggle against colonialism, occupation, aggression and domination by foreign forces shall not be considered as terrorist acts".

The South African legislation, however, adds the qualification that it is especially the principles of international humanitarian law that have to be adhered to in such instances. In this regard, the South African Chief State Law Adviser responded to concerns regarding the seeming exception made in the case of 'national liberation movements', by stating that acts for self-determination would have to be done in accordance with international law and international humanitarian law in order not to constitute acts of terrorism.

While UN resolutions on terrorism contained similar provisions during, for instance, the 1970s and 1980s (to accommodate organisations such as the Palestine Liberation Organisation—PLO), these have been omitted in more recent resolutions. The UN Secretary-General's Report of the High-Level Panel on Threats, Challenges and Charges referred to the right to resist foreign occupation, but stressed that this does not justify the targeting and killing of civilians and non-combatants. In this regard, reference was also made to the Geneva Convention and Protocols to the Convention. In practice, the foregoing provisions are largely symbolical. The principle of self-determination in international law is at any rate still surrounded by uncertainty. What it does, however, confirm, is that being a member of a 'national liberation movement', and does not condone acts of terror. This is also in accordance with the principle that no motivation of any nature justifies an act of terror.

Targeting of civilians or the death or injury of civilians which could be foreseen as a result of an act of terror, have been a standard component of definitions of terror. In this regard, the US State Department has, however, stated that "(t)he term 'non-combatant' which is referred to but not defined in 22 USC 26 56f(d)(2), is interpreted to mean, in addition to civilians, military personnel (whether or not armed or on duty) who are not deployed in a war zone or a war-like setting". The US NCTC goes further, stating that non-combatants included civilians and police, as well as "military assets outside war zones or war-like settings", in addition to including combatants who are in a non-combatant status. The traditional definition of terrorism, specifically in the US, has also been questioned due to contemporary developments. The criterion of 'violence' in the US definition tends, for instance, not to cover the disabling of a national infrastructure caused by sabotage in the form of a computer virus.

A further issue relates to sabotage, and whether this equals an act of terrorism. Wilkinson states in this regard that although acts of sabotage may at times cause the loss of life, it is not terrorism as the loss of life was not intended by those responsible for the incident. In practice, though, this distinction is not maintained in UN resolutions, or by the US State Department in its annual survey of international terrorist incidents. Neither is this the case in, for instance, the South African anti-terror legislation. It, however, remains true, as Wilkinson states, that terrorism is primarily about fear or publicity in this regard ('armed propaganda'), and that sabotage is more often combined with guerrilla warfare.

It has been stated that effective international countermeasures to international terrorism have been hindered by the lack of agreement on a definition of terrorism. In this regard, it has even been argued that terrorism be viewed as the "peacetime equivalent of war crimes" (for instance deliberate attacks on civilians and the taking of hostages). This would then, however, result in attacks on military installations in non-war situations, for example, being excluded. Particularly linked to the above issue is, however, also the problem of over-broadening the concept of terrorism.

During May 2005, the following comment regarding the US Justice Department view, for instance, was made: "Newly released documents show that the U.S. Justice Department has greatly broadened how it defines and counts terrorism-related cases, a move that helped justify the department's call for more funding and greater powers. However, the scant information provided about those cases has watchdog groups and members of Congress crying foul".

In the case of the United Kingdom (UK) it has been stated with reference to the use of 'control orders' (such as curfews and electronic tagging) issued by the Home Secretary under the Prevention of Terrorism Act of 2005, that "the Act relies on an extremely broad definition of terrorism, opening the door for the widespread use of control orders". In the case of certain African countries, fears have also been expressed that new anti-terrorism laws may be used to suppress legitimate dissent.

Transnational, International and Domestic Terror

The majority of definitions seem to continue to distinguish between international and domestic terror as one of the primary typologies, but the concept of 'transnational' terror seems to have increasingly developed as a third category. This is partially seen as a new trend in terrorism, and partially as a new perception. In addition to international terror, which is defined in the US Code as "terrorism involving citizens or the territory of more than one country", transnational terrorism has been described as referring to terrorists who operate internationally with the express long term aim of global revolution or of establishing a revolutionary supranational world order. It has also been used to refer to cooperation between various groups of individuals in different countries. The terms international and transnational are, however, often used as synonyms.

The US State Department argues that there is no statutory guidance regarding the definition of transnational terror, and that current 'transnational' terrorism is based on decentralised local groups loosely affiliated or inspired by the Islamist ideology espoused by al-Qaida. In this sense a specific act of terrorism could be domestic and not international, but still viewed as 'transnational'. It has, however, been argued that the current concept of 'new terrorism' being essentially transnational (not bound by national ties, and loosely organised networks) is in fact not so new. 'Traditional' terrorists also operated transnationally (for example, joint training facilities for various organisations previously in Libya), and in certain cases also established networks instead of hierarchically-based organisations.

What could perhaps be argued is that the concept of a 'global jihadist' movement specifically characterises transnational terrorism as opposed to more traditional terrorism. On the other hand, it could be argued that traditional Marxist-inspired movements had the same goal, although perhaps not the appeal of al-Qaida, as a focus point. As far as the distinction between international and domestic terrorism is concerned, many acts of domestic terrorism have international consequences, and in some cases domestic groups targeting national targets only, receive some form of international support. Nevertheless, the distinction remains important. It is international terrorism that draws most attention and tends to be more spectacular. Also, while these incidents can to some extent be quantified, the same cannot be done in the case of domestic terror with anything approximating correctness.

The UN, while pledging to prevent, combat and eliminate terrorism in all its forms and manifestations, seemingly continues to focus on international terrorism. The problem of a distinction between 'political violence' and 'terrorism' also occurs in respect of domestic terrorism, although this is also the case regarding international terrorist incidents. The US Department of State Country Reports on Terrorism, 2004, for instance states that "terrorist acts are part of a larger phenomenon of politically inspired violence, and at times the line between the two can become difficult to draw". It is added that the report includes terrorist acts as well as other violent incidents which do not necessarily constitute international terrorism.

On the occasion of the release of the above document, the interim Director of the US NCTC, John Brennan, also stated with regard to the distinction between domestic and international terrorism, that the distinction could hinge on the presence of only one foreign national at the target. The example of two Chechen suicide bombers blowing up two Aeroflot flights in 2004, one containing only Russian citizens and the other an Israeli national, was mentioned as a case in point. The former is classified as domestic terror, the latter as international terror. In Brennan's view, the statutory classification of international terrorism is therefore somewhat problematic in the above types of incidents. He concluded that "our intent is to capture any incident where a non-combatant is targeted or indiscriminately attacked and the attack is politically motivated".

That this may be an overly ambitious undertaking, especially since it seems to include all acts of domestic terrorism as well, leaves little doubt. Even as far as international terrorist incidents are concerned, only 'significant' incidents have been recorded by the US so far. These include incidents involving kidnapping, killing or wounding of non-combatants (unless injuries were minor). Other incidents regarded as 'significant' were those resulting in physical or economic damage of approximately US$10,000 or more. The NCTC has also questioned the traditional definition of international terrorism as defined in the US Code, stating that it was appropriate for state-sponsored terrorism, but not for transnational terrorism.

As stated in the introduction, the concept of the 'new terrorism' has mainly focused on inherent characteristics or trends in terror, such as the increase in terrorism inspired by religion; the use of, and search for more devastating weapons; and increased indiscriminate targeting. Regardless of whether the above trends are in fact new or not, international and national perceptions of terrorism seem to have also undergone certain changes. The broadening of the definition of terrorism in certain cases, and a more severe stance on terrorism (particularly by the UN), are some features of this changing perception. While this demonstrates the intent to deal firmly with terrorism, regardless of motives or causes, the inherent risk in for instance an over-broad view of what constitutes terrorism, lies in the fact that a 'war' on terror may readily promote actions against legitimate reformist elements, especially in certain African countries.

Also, although motives or causes are no justification for acts of terror, overlooking underlying grievances (to the extent that they can be addressed), treats the symptoms only. In the case of South African anti-terror legislation, for instance, and following lobbying from amongst others trade unions, the final draft of legislation included a provision that acts in pursuance of any advocacy protest, dissent or industrial action and which does not intend the harm contemplated in the definition of terrorism in the legislation, shall not be regarded as a terrorist activity.

Security and Ambiguity

Academic discussions of "terrorism" begin by explaining that a universally accepted definition of the term still eludes scholars and government officials. Sharryn Aiken has suggested that the words "terrorist" and "terrorism" are nearly meaningless as a legal category. The U.S. District Court for the District of Columbia deplored "the lack of any precise definition of the term 'terrorism' as a major hurdle in determining when illegal, sanction able terrorist activity had occurred". One survey of leading researchers uncovered 109 different definitions and also so many exist that a mere compilation of these would form a fair-sized book.

The term "terrorism" first emerged to describe a period of the French Revolution, the Reign of Terror, in which the Jacobins unleashed a campaign of repression that resulted in thousands of people being tortured, imprisoned, and guillotined. In this context, T. H. Mitchell states that "terrorism was perceived as an unspeakable crime - the product of moral depravity and madness". Hence, terrorism was coined to indicate a state's brutal treatment of its citizens. During the course of the nineteenth and twentieth centuries, however, the term became increasingly politicized.

This politicization reveals the power of semantics in demarcating the moral and ethical parameters of a conflict. For some, the definition of terrorism includes both state and non-state participants, but excludes acts motivated by revenge. For others, the definition encompasses only "sub national groups or non-state entities". A poignant illustration of the murky nature of the term rests in the fact that the U.S. State Department, U.S. Department of Defense, and the Federal Bureau of Investigation (FBI) all employ different definitions. The primacy of the U.S. State Department in international affairs has caused its definition to gain widespread acceptance: "premeditated, politically motivated violence perpetrated against noncombatant targets by sub national groups or clandestine agents, usually intended to influence an audience"

Equally important, the definitional ambiguity of terrorism is intensified by the rhetorical power of the word "terrorist," which causes governments to apply the term according to political preferences. No country wants to admit to terrorist actions or support of terrorist groups, yet many states, including the U.S., have been involved with or have lent support to groups considered by other countries to be terrorists. At the heart of the matter is that one person's terrorist is another person's freedom fighter. J. Zulaika and W. Douglas ask, "What can we make of the fact that terrorism has become such a shifty category that yesterday's terrorists are today's Nobel Peace Prize winners?" Likewise, Zulaika and Douglas argue that the use of terrorism as a conceptual category, in lieu of a universally accepted definition, must be seen for what it is: a highly charged political position embedded in the particularity of a given cultural, social, and tactical context.

Despite debate over the definition, core characteristics of the term are agreed upon within the literature. These include the use of threat and/or violence, the existence of political motive, the selection of targets who are representative of a target category, the aim of terrorizing, the goal of modifying behaviour, the use of extreme or unusual methods, and the use of terrorism as an act of communication.

Methods of Counterterrorism

Just as attempts to define terrorism generate political controversy, the debate over the necessity and appropriate reach for antiterrorist legislation in the U.S. stems from disagreement over what constitutes terrorism and when it exists. There are just as many ways to prevent terrorism and to bring known terrorists to justice as there are motivations behind terrorist acts. Possible state responses to terrorism include political and diplomatic measures, economic measures, overt military action, covert military action (e.g., intelligence operations), and law enforcement.

Retired U.S. Army Major General William Nash voices concern that the U.S. is viewed by the world as represented by a military force rather than as a democratic, free-market, rule-of-law nation. He also intimates that national security in the 21st century is far more political, economic, and social in nature, and the security aspects are more nonmilitary, than ever before. The tenacity and longevity of groups such as the Basque Fatherland and Liberty (ETA), Irish Republican Army (IRA), and Revolutionary Armed Forces of Colombia (FARC) are reminders that military-backed counterterrorism alone is not likely to eliminate the threat. Conversely, progress on the political front can go a long way in reducing violence.

The growing gap between the world's haves and have-nots exacerbates the problem of terrorism. For example, in Pakistan and to some extent Afghanistan, the bulk of the people who enter *madrissas* (religious seminaries) that provide military training for terrorists are from a disadvantaged class; parents find it convenient to send their children there because they know the children will be housed, fed, clothed, and educated. Victims of the modern world view Osama bin Laden as a combination of avenging angel and Robin Hood. It has been said, "Terrorism is the half thinking man's conditioned reflex to sustained oppression and lack of personal empowerment" (Qadir 333). Countering terrorist activities with military operations will not be successful without addressing global economic inequality and peacekeeping itself is an issue of post-conflict development ("Reinventing War" 43).

Nevertheless, Strobe Talbott, former deputy Secretary of State, points out that the September 11th suicide pilots, for the most part, did not come from the worlds desperate and aggrieved. He states that their fanaticism, like bin Laden's, was nurtured in privilege and in individual madness (Talbott 75). If this is the case, then is military reaction the solution? In order for the U.S. to deploy military forces in response to a terrorist act, six criteria need to be met: a relatively immediate, positive perpetrator identification; perpetrator repetition; direct targeting of a U.S. citizen working in an official U.S. government-related capacity; the *fait accompli* nature of the incident - i.e., already accomplished and irreversible in nature; flagrant anti-U.S. perpetrator behaviour; and political and military vulnerability of the perpetrator (Malvesti 100).

U.S. Senator Richard Selby, vice chairman of the Senate Intelligence Committee, blamed the September 11th tragedy on inadequate intelligence funding, a dearth of Arabic-speaking agents, and insufficient international intelligence-sharing and cross-border cooperation (Sprinzak 72). John Deutch, former head of the Central Intelligence Agency (CIA) and Jeffrey H. Smith explain that the model of U.S. intelligence was created in a different era for solving a different problem. The National Security Act of 1947 produced the CIA, which was envisioned to deal with enemy states during the Cold War.

The result was a collection of organizations based on distinctions of domestic vs foreign threats, law enforcement vs national security, and peacetime vs. wartime. The FBI is responsible for the former, while the intelligence community, including the CIA and others, is responsible for the latter. This fragmented approach makes it possible for one intelligence agency to have information before a terrorist attack, but to be unable to share and synthesize in time to avert the attack (Deutch 64). Terrorist attacks pose a unique challenge to states in that they are both a law enforcement and a national security issue, simultaneously a criminal act and an act of war. The Posse Comitatus Act of 1878 prohibits the U.S. military from engaging in civilian law enforcement activities, and many argue that military training for local police and firefighters to handle (weapons of mass destruction) terrorist incidents falls into this category. Two dominant models have been developed to address this dilemma in Israel.

The war model regards terrorism as an act of revolutionary warfare, whereas the criminal justice model regards it as a criminal act. The war model places the response to terrorism in the hands of the military, encouraging the armed forces to use all its power to quash terrorist action. The criminal justice model accords the police with the responsibility to respond to terrorism, and its actions are naturally restrained by the states criminal legal system.

If the purpose of terrorism is to terrorize, that of antiterrorism is to terrorize more (Qadir 333). In many ways, counterterrorist efforts must be viewed on balance because they often involve fundamental alterations to civil liberties, policies toward ethnic minorities, international relations, and the economic system. Prudence must be exercised to avoid using counterterrorism as a blanket justification for victimizing innocent people (Aiken 127), and C. B. Keely and S. S. Russell urge the use of caution to prevent the perpetrators from winning by making "us" like "them". A struggle between civil liberties and the vulnerability to terrorism often develops during the genesis of counterterrorist measures. This clash is seen in the debate over passenger profiling, roving wiretaps, surveillance, tracking systems, and immigration.

Policymakers entertain proposals to erode *posse comitatus*; repeal assassination and torture prohibitions; use criminal informants; introduce military courts, indefinite detention, and identity cards; and widen powers of information gathering (Donohue 48). The more aggressive the selected model of counter terror, the more likely be that democratic foundations will be sacrificed during the process. Paul Wilkinson writes that the primary objective of counterterrorism should be the protection and maintenance of the rule of law and liberal democracy (*Terrorism and the Liberal State,* 1986), but arguments in favor of secret evidence and classified deportation proceedings speak not of an open, liberal, democratic society, but of one cloaked in secrecy (Donohue 48). One must also consider the words penned by Thomas Jefferson: "A society that will trade a little liberty for a little order will deserve neither and will lose both".

Incursions into civil liberties via stringent counter-terrorist law also risk alienating ethnic minorities within the U.S., and subjecting them to disproportionate and degrading security checks and procedures, which marginalize them even more. For example, the perception of Arabs as terrorists in the U.S. has come to dominate the public imagination. Larry B. Stammer and Somini Sengupta eloquently describe the common perception: "Words and images run together like watercolors on a child's easel - Arabs, mosque, terrorist, Muslims, extremists - making it hard to tell where one began and the other left off". This almost reflexive association became ingrained during the Iranian hostage crisis in 1979 and the Persian Gulf War in 1991. Complicating matters for Arabs in the U.S. is that a number of overseas organizations that sponsor terrorists also fund religious and charitable projects; Hamas operates orphanages, old-age homes, hospitals, women's clinics, religious colleges, sports clubs, kindergartens, vocational schools, and even a match-making service.

In addition to the sacrifice of civil liberties and the mistreatment of ethnic minorities, U.S. counterterrorist actions can have a profound influence on enemies as well as allies abroad. The Organization of the Islamic Conference's declarations regarding the September 11th attacks condemned the violence as being opposed to the tolerant message of Islam; reaffirmed the need to hold an international conference on rejecting terrorism in international relations; suggested that the focus on the U.S. should not cause the international community to ignore state-sponsored terrorism in Israel; and expressed concern over the death of innocent civilians in Afghanistan, territorial integrity of Afghanistan, and targeting of any other Islamic or Arab state under the pretext of fighting terrorism. Though the attacks on September 11th reduced the priority of developing a national missile defense (NMD) or theater missile defense (TMD), it is widely believed that the creation of a NMD/TMD will trigger a new arms race, especially with Russia and China, and strain relations with Europe. In terms of deterrence, its effectiveness in the post-Cold War era remains to be seen.

Modern societies such as the U.S. face a cruel paradox: Fast-paced technological and economic innovations may deliver unrivaled prosperity, but they also render rich nations vulnerable to crippling, unanticipated attacks. The total cost of the September 11th attack in lost economic growth and decreased equity value around the world could equal $1 trillion, and the cost of the attack was probably a few hundred thousand dollars, so the economic multiplier is close to a million fold. Possible changes that would reduce U.S. economic vulnerability to terrorism include greater use of decentralized, local energy production and alternative energy sources (e.g., small-scale solar power); increased autonomy of local food production networks; and increased supplies of raw materials and parts so that firms can continue production when these inputs are interrupted. These changes would decrease economic efficiency, but the extra security of more stable production networks could far outweigh the costs.

Though it would be easy to introduce this last paragraph with "in conclusion," it would be premature to do so. In closing, the intent of this work is to provide a glance at the meaning and politicization of the term "terrorism," to explicate the different means of countering terrorism, and to probe the implications of counterterrorist efforts. With U.S. military operations in Afghanistan, ostensibly to fight a war on terrorism, as well as renewed violence between Israelis and Palestinians, where each side alleges terrorism by the other, the definitions of terrorism and the methods of counterterrorism take on even greater importance in the quest for peace. Much work needs to be done before terrorism is concluded.

renounced armed struggle. The IRSM repeatedly condemns British security forces and the RUC for violence and corruption. Finally, some statements on the Website report on the actions of unionists, parades and unity with the Irish Lesbian and Gay organization, and commemorations of the armed struggle. Many IRSM communiques respond to foreign events, which are divided into [illegible] and/or commemorations (African Liberation Day, Kurdish New Year and International Women's Day), calls for solidarity (Solidarity for Kurdish Struggles and Liberation of South Africa) and condemnations (Actions condemned include arrest of anti-NATO protesters in Italy, imprisonment of Mumia Abu-Jamal, the war in Kosovo, Kurdish leader Abdullah Ocalan's "abduction" and death sentence, arrest of Puerto Rican activists, Third World debt, the Pope's comments on Pinochet, sanction against Libyan sanctions, US extradition of IRSP POWs, and British acts of international terrorism. The organization also calls for dissolution of NATO).

INLA communiqués largely concern the armed struggle. While most commemorate volunteers who died for the cause, others take responsibility for attacks on military targets, deny responsibility for assassination of particular loyalists and concern ceasefires. The final component of the Website is links that cover a wide range of movements and organizations. The Electronic Starry Plough is a case in point in the shift from territorial politics to a system of multiple and overlapping interests, meanings and authorities. However, it is unlikely that politics will be radically transformed to serve individual input or create community by the Internet alone. At first, radio and television were also thought to herald new individualism and new communities. Their eventual impact, a greatly enhanced role for interest groups, was not foreseen when the technologies were first introduced.

To have impact through the Internet a group must either attract a broad public or mobilize a particular constituency.

12

Suicide Bombers' Motivation

"Mankind's common instinct for reality has always held the world to be essentially a theatre for heroism. In heroism, we feel, life's supreme mystery is hidden. We tolerate no one who has no capacity whatever for it in any direction. On the other hand, no matter what a man's frailties otherwise may be, if he be willing to risk death, and still more if he suffer it heroically, in the service he has chosen, the fact consecrates him forever."

The motivations underlying suicide terrorism are of major interest to terrorism researchers, possibly for two underlying reasons. One reason is epistemic, and it stems from curiosity about a bizarre phenomenon: The readiness of seemingly unexceptional human beings not only to massively murder innocents, but also to sacrifice their life in the process, contrary to the basic human instinct of physical survival. The second reason is pragmatic. Understanding terrorists' motivation may be a pre-condition for altering it, hence it offers a potentially important tool for counterterrorism.

Major recent analyses devoted considerable attention to terrorists' motivations. They differed, however, in the kind and variety of motives identified as relevant to suicide terrorism. Some authors emphasized a singular motivation; others listed a potpourri of motives. For instance, Sageman's

(2004) work on terrorist networks emphasized the quest for emotional and social support by Muslims in European Diasporas who feel rejected by, and alienated from the local societies. Pape (2005) highlighted resistance to foreign occupation as a main motivating force. Spekhard & Akhmedova (2005) assigned this role to personal loss and trauma. And Nasra Hassan's (2001) concluded that Hamas terrorists' main motivation concerned entering "Paradise being in the presence of Allah... meeting the prophet Muhammad" and reaping the rewards of participating in a Holy war.

In contrast to an emphasis on a single crucial motivation (quest for social support, coping with trauma, martyrdom), Bloom (2005), listed diverse motivations for suicide terrorism, including honor, dedication to the leader, social status, personal significance, pain and personal loss, group pressure, humiliation and injustice, vengeance, or feminism (i.e., convincing society of women's contribution). In a similar vein, Ricolfi suggested that "the motivational drive to engage in suicide missions is likely to be found in a cocktail of feelings, which include desire for revenge, resentment, and a sense of obligation towards the victims, as revealed in the...video recorded pronouncements"

A reasonable step in dealing with such heterogeneity might be to reduce it by classifying the varied motives identified so far into fewer, more general, motivational categories. Several authors have hinted at such a classification typically based on a partition between ideological reasons, and personal causes for becoming a suicide terrorist. In these terms, alienated individuals' quest for social and emotional support may be assumed to stem from their personal experience. So do the pain, trauma, and redemption of lost honor, often listed as motives. In contrast, liberation of one's land or carrying out God's will pertain to ideological factors that transcend individual actors' life circumstances.

By ideology one usually means a belief system centered on some social or collective ideal (e.g., based on the values of justice, fairness, or inalienable rights). Ideology's motivating power resides in identifying a discrepancy from an ideal state, and offering a means of removing the discrepancy through action. A terrorism justifying ideology identifies a culprit (the enemy) presumed responsible for the discrepancy and portrays violence against that culprit (e.g., jihad) as an effective method for moving toward the ideal state.

Beside ideological reasons and personal causes, a third motivational category likely involved in suicidal attacks involves a sense of social duty and obligation whether internalized or induced by peer pressure. This is apparent in data on the Japanese Kamikaze pilots (e.g., Ohnuki-Tierney, 2006) but it is also relevant to present day suicidal terrorism. Classification of terrorist motives into ideological, personal, and social is helpful, yet insufficient. It is descriptive rather than analytic and it stops short of explicating the underlying dynamics of suicide terrorism. Several questions remain. For instance, is either of these motive categories unique to terrorism, or could they foster alternative activities in alternative circumstances? The answer seems obvious. Alienation, pain and trauma could foster numerous nonviolent activities. The same holds for ideological objectives and social pressures. As concerns ideological objectives, Mahatma Ghandi's ideological commitments identified non-violence as supreme means for the pursuit of freedom from foreign rule and were adopted by Martin Luther King in reference to the civil rights movement in the U.S. Similarly, social pressures and a sense of duty and obligation, represent psychological mechanisms of influence capable of inducing any kind of commitment not necessarily a commitment to violence. So, the question is what precise role these motives play in terrorism, and under what circumstances might they instigate it.

It is also of interest to ask whether all three motivational categories constitute authentic terrorism-driving forces and if not which is, and which isn't. Different authors varied in their position on this issue. Some regarded personal circumstance factors as the true explanations of terrorists' behaviour and viewed their ideological statements as post hoc justifications. As Spekhard and Akhmedova put it "The political statements of the individuals involved in terrorism appear less of a driving force for their participation than as a means of justifying their actions..." Similarly, Sageman agreed with Dambruoso that, "[the jihadists motivation] is not religious, it is psychological and personal."

Other authors put greater faith in terrorists' idealism. Pape (2005) in particular noted that "egoistic and anomic motives are insufficient. Altruistic motives, either alone or in conjunction with others, play an important role". Too, Gunaratna argued that "what actually motivates Al Qaeda is not power, wealth or fame but an ideological belief in their struggles". Atran observed that terrorists "...are motivated not by personal comfort or immediate gain but rather by religious or ideological conviction and zeal" and that "debriefings with captured Al Qaeda operatives at Guantanamo, and with Jemmah Islamiyah prisoners in Singapore suggest that recruitment to these organizations is more ideologically driven than grievance-driven". Yet other authors proposed a differentiation whereby some individuals carry out terrorist acts for ideological reasons (such as commitment to a cause or an ideology), whereas others do so because of personal crises. In short, recent analyses of terrorists' motivations enumerate a broad variety of possible motives and include heterogeneity of positions and perspectives on this issue. These differences among scholars require sorting out.

By synthesizing a widely dispersed literature, it seeks to uncover a deep motivational structure that may afford a common understanding of numerous disparate instances of this phenomenon, and suggest how the various motive-categories identified thus far may functionally relate to each other. As a preview of what is to come, we first introduce the concept of "significance quest" as an overarching motive propelling suicidal terrorism. We then explore the implications of this motivational notion, and review empirical evidence relevant to those implications. We finally explore the ramifications of our analysis for counter-terrorism, and discuss strategies for minimizing suicidal terrorism at levels of military strategy, foreign policy, immigration programs and educational initiatives.

The Quest for Significance

The quest for personal significance has been hailed by psychological theorists as a major motivational force in human behaviour. In this vein, Victor Frankl wrote "that fundamental characteristic of the human reality [which he came to term] its self transcendent quality [denotes the fact that] being human always relates and points to something other than itself... [Person] is oriented toward the world out there. [She or he] is actualizing himself to the extent that he is forgetting himself by giving himself...through serving a cause higher than himself. [According to Frankl then] self-transcendence is the essence of human existence."

Abraham Maslow's influential theory of motivation identifies self-esteem and self actualization concerns as top level human strivings of obvious affinity to Frankl's "search for meaning" notion. In Maslow's terms, "the business of self actualization" can best be carried out via commitment to an important job", that is, to a transcendental cause of recognized societal significance. Recent analyses of human motivation have implied that in the human species the biological need for physical survival is intimately linked to the quest for personal meaning and significance. The reason is assumed to stem from humans' awareness of their own mortality, and the implied threat of personal insignificance;

the nightmare of ending up as "a speck of insignificant dust in an uncaring universe". It is this awareness that motivates people to "do well" in culturally prescribed ways, and be "good" members of society.

A supreme "goodness" in this sense is the readiness to sacrifice oneself for the group in an hour of need (typically, in case of a severe perceived threat to the group's survival). Putting the group first is highly valued and rewarded by the promise of immortality. The group remembers its heroes and martyrs; symbolically then, their lives go on in the group's collective memory. Also, through the act of sacrifice one's personal identity is meshed with that of the group (Post et al., 2004); so that the group's continued existence becomes inseparable from one's own. As Elster noted "a common denominator [of motivations for suicidal terrorism] is a desire to transcend death by living on in the grateful or admiring memory of others..."From a yet different perspective, personal sacrifice may serve the individual's gene pool and/or value system shared by one's kin. Hence, suicidal terrorism may be powered by evolutionary forces.

Finally, in the jihadist ideology at least Shahadat (martyrdom) does not signify an end of individual existence, but rather immortality in highly pleasurable circumstances. For male shaheeds it entails the promise of paradise, and the allure of wedding numerous (seventy two) virgins of incomparable beauty. Paradise is also promised to female shaheeds. It is believed to entail removal of the strict restrictions on their sexual relations, the possibility of having liaisons with past Muslim heroes, becoming one of the seventy two virgins, bestowal of great beauty irrespective of one's worldly physical appearance, the opportunity to meet Allah and the prophet Muhammad, and liberation from the grave's pains for 70 members of one's family.

Crenshaw summarizes it: "Clearly the act is not just about dying and killing. The expectation of gaining status and respect as a martyr for the cause is important, so that individual action is linked to anticipation of both popular approval and collective political success...Sacrifice for the cause is both personally redemptive and a mark of honor, a way of becoming a hero and part of an exalted elite. It [contrasts sharply with] is an otherwise insignificant or disappointing life."

Paradoxically then, whether reflecting symbolic immortality and a place in the group's collective memory, or concrete immortality as denizens of paradise, the willingness to die in an act of suicidal terrorism may be motivated by the desire to live forever.

Quest Unique to Suicidal Terrorism

Is the significance quest assumed to underlie suicidal terrorism unique to this particular phenomenon? Obviously not. As noted by motivational theorists such as Frankl, Becker or Maslow the quest for significant existence constitutes a fundamental human striving, accounting for a broad preponderance of human activities. We behave in accordance with the dictates of our culture and its norms. The adolescent culture tells the teenager what counts as "cool" and what activities are "trendy" and likely to gain the peers' approval. The norms of aesthetics and morality suggest to members of a community what is valued and respected in their culture, hence what constitutes a "good life," that confers significance on one's existence. At moments of crisis, however, an opportunity may present itself for an enormous significance gain, unimaginable in ordinary circumstances; such opportunity may be often coupled with the potential for considerable significance loss in case one had failed to respond to the challenge.

On this analysis, the underlying motivation for suicide terrorism involves the coupling of a quest for significance with a crisis situation, involving a perceived threat to one's group, and a terrorism justifying ideology whereby a suicide attack is portrayed as an act of heroic sacrifice (martyrdom) lending one's existence and demise an aura of supreme glory. As Gambetta put it "All suicide missions belong to a family of actions in which people go to the extremes of self-sacrifice in the belief that by doing so they will best further the interests of a group or the cause they care about and identify with." This raises the question of motivational commonalities and differences between suicidal and non suicidal brands of terrorism. To start with a commonality, endorsement of a terrorism-justifying ideology may well underlie the activities of non-suicidal participants in the terrorist enterprise, operators of improvised explosive devices (the IEDs), and other personnel carrying out the logistic, financial, supply, or transportation tasks of a terrorist organization.

A major difference between suicidal and no suicidal terrorists seems to reside in the specific role one assigns oneself within the common ideological context. Thus, whereas many may agree that the goal of the terrorist organization is worthy, and that terrorism constitutes an effective and morally warranted means to that goal, only some may adopt the act of suicidal terrorism as their personal assignment. Because of the extremity of the act, and its exclusivity (that is, incompatibility with alternative, socially sanctioned, objectives) it will likely require a conjunction of psychological forces of supreme magnitude (particularly intense significance quest, particularly powerful social pressures, and a particularly engulfing presence of a suicide-prompting rhetoric). In this sense then, the motivations involved in suicidal and no suicidal types of terrorism may differ in degree rather than in kind.

Simply put, suicidal terrorism confers upon one greater prestige and represents a more auspicious opportunity for significance gain. For instance, in the case of Liberation Tigers of Tamil Eelam (LTTE) even though all member of the organization are required to commit suicide when captured, the "Black Tigers, the LTTE suicide unit.. are considered elite". As Ricolfi put it in reference to Palestinian suicide bombers: "A martyr is not an anonymous militant who caries out a mission, and whose name may remain unknown. A martyr is a volunteer who has been selected, who leaves a last will and testament..., and who will be remembered by his fellow countrymen through photographs, posters, murals, and plaques exhibited in public places...While a militant may die anonymously, and thus sacrifice himself twice, a martyr pays 'only' with his life but obtains fame and recognition in return.

The symbolic calculation may explain why certain people may prefer to choose martyrdom directly over militancy of a more traditional kind." In summary, suicidal terrorism represents an extreme case of significance quest, an opportunity to catapult oneself to the pinnacle of cultural veneration by an act of supreme sacrifice for an ideologically touted cause. Our analysis has several testable implications. If reminders of one's own mortality convey one's potential insignificance then such reminders should augment the quest for significance as defined by one's cultural norms and accepted ideological frames. In some cases, such norms and ideologies may identify the suicide mission against one's groups' enemies as a most honorable act, lending one a sense of immense veneration and significance.

In this connection Holmes had the following to say concerning the likely motivational "rationality" of the 9/11 attackers: "The future hijackers...were surely encouraged to draw the logical conclusion that it be better to make their deaths meaningful rather than meaningless, to exit life with flags flying, on a combat mission, for their community's honor, rather than as insignificant observers sitting on the sidelines." If our analysis is valid, adoption of cultural causes that lend one a sense of personal significance should reduce death-anxiety. Furthermore, perceived loss of significance through events other than mortality reminders should fuel efforts at significance restoration. Finally, a threat of potential loss of significance should instigate preventive actions designed to fend it off. Taken as a body, these implications identify a deeper motivational theme, of significance quest, that ties together the categories of personal circumstances, ideological reasons, and social pressures involved in suicidal terrorism. This theme is consistent with empirical data of various kinds. We review them next.

Terror Management Research

Much recent psychological research supports the idea that reminders of one's own mortality motivate individuals to embrace their group's culture and ideals. By now this prediction was corroborated in hundreds of psychological experiments carried out in numerous world locations. In one well known study, it was found that when research participants were reminded of their mortality they recommended a more severe sentence for a prostitute, representing a deviant from cultural norms. Yet other work found that exposing Italians to death reminders increased their bias in favor of Italy (their in-group), and the perception that Italy was cohesive and united. As Castano and Dechesne recently summarized it, "Becoming part of collective entities [allows] individuals to extend their selves in space and time [and hence] to overcome the inherent limitations of their individual identity inextricably linked to a perishable body."

Recent research by Pyszczynski and colleagues looked at the effect of mortality salience on Iranian students and their respective support for martyrdom (terrorism). When Iranian students answered questions about an aversive topic (unrelated to death), they evaluated a fellow student who opposed martyrdom attacks against the United States more favorably then a student who supported martyrdom attacks. However, the reverse was found when Iranian students answered questions about their own death. In this instance, they rated more highly the student who supported martyrdom then one who opposed it.

Mortality reminders can come in the form of personal trauma occasioned by the loss of a loved one. Spekhard & Akhmedova carried out an extensive study of Chechen suicide terrorists via interviews with their family members and close associates and with hostages who spoke with the terrorists during the three days siege in Moscow's Dubrovka Theater. As can be seen, all of the interviewees mentioned traumatic events that appeared to alter the course of the fallen terrorists' lives. Indeed, the authors concluded: "when we looked for the primary motivation in our sample of terrorists we would have to say that it was trauma in every case". Of particular interest, Spekhard and Akhmedova observed that their subjects sought out ideological inspiration in response to their personal trauma. Specifically, "In the interviews concerning the accomplished suicide terrorists eighty-two percent (28/34) were secular Muslims prior to their experiences of trauma.

Of these twenty-seven had no prior relationship to fundamental militant groups but sought out the Wahhabists radical groups in direct reaction to the traumas they had endured knowing full well of the groups' beliefs and terrorist practices." It appears then that personal trauma, feelings of alienation, and disenfranchisement, etc., may spur a quest for meaning that in cases of a severe inter group conflict may be afforded by a terrorism-justifying ideology. Terror management research demonstrates a link between overcoming death anxiety and commitment to cultural causes. In turn, commitment to cultural causes may attenuate death anxiety. In other words, if death reminders cause anxiety because of the insignificance threat (the "speck of dust" prospect) they convey, and if embracement of cultural causes restores one's sense of significance then embracement of cultural causes should attenuate death anxiety.

In support of this possibility, Durlak found a significant negative correlation (r=-.68; p<.001) between purpose in life defined in terms of commitment to cultural objectives and measured by Crumbaugh PIL test (Purpose in Life) and fear of death. Illustrating the reverse effect, Mikulincer, Florian, Birnbaum, & Malishkevich, showed that depriving people from a sense of belonging increases death related cognitions. Arndt, Greenberg, Solomon, Pyszczynski, and Simon first reminded half of their participants about death and assessed their reactions to pro and anti-US essays. Findings showed increases in death thoughts accessibility after the reminder of death. Importantly, accessibility of death thoughts declined after participants were given the opportunity to derogate the critic by giving a negative evaluation, in this sense defending the cultural norm.

The link between a sense of "oneness" with the group, and the attenuation of death anxiety (possibly instilling the readiness to sacrifice oneself for the collective) appears to have been intuitively understood by leaders whose causes required from their followers acts of supreme self denial. In this vein, Mao Tse Tung asserted "All men must die, but death can vary in its significance… To die for the people is heavier than Mount Tai, but to work for the fascists and die for the exploiters and oppressors is lighter than a feather..."

Overcoming death-anxiety through commitment to ideological objectives plays a significant part in the indoctrination of contemporary suicide terrorists. One failed suicide terrorist interviewed by Nasra Hassan was asked "How did you feel when you heard that you'd been selected for martyrdom?" He answered: "It's as if a very high, impenetrable wall separated you from Paradise or Hell," he said. "by pressing the detonator, you can immediately open the door to Paradise – it is the shortest path to Heaven." Another failed suicide terrorist recounted: "I spent a month in a mosque. I learned how important it is to be a shaheed. It is the loftiest objective. It's the biggest and most holy thing you can do. And then you receive all the rewards in Paradise..."

Explicit statements by failed suicide terrorists, or farewell videos left by "successful" ones, contain ample evidence for ideological arguments. We examined over three hundred clips from the MEMRI (Middle East Media Research Institute) TV database (from late 2004 to the present). The MEMRI's TV monitoring center that oversees every major Arab channel focusing on political, cultural, religious, and social developments and debates in the Arab and Muslim world and in Iran. Its data base contains a large number of video clips from farewell tapes of suicide terrorists, interviews with captured terrorists, failed suicide terrorists who were captured and imprisoned and those who escaped from prison. It additionally includes interviews with the Mothers (Father in one case) of successful suicide terrorists.

We had four coders independently go through clips in two pertinent categories of from late 2004 to the present, namely "Jihad and Terrorism" and "Suicide (Martyrdom) Operation". All clips taken from interviews with individual terrorists, the family members of successful suicide terrorists, and those from suicide terrorists' farewell videos were selected for analysis. Out of the three hundred clips we examined we identified 58 such video clips. We then analyzed them in terms of the motives they implied for carrying our suicide missions and engaging in terrorist attacks. The researches used a set of keywords to identify and group the motives into the two general categories: ideological/collectivistic and personal. For the category of ideological/collectivistic motives we used the key words: martyr, Jihad, Allah, heaven, role model, pride, honor, love of country, defense/fight for (one's people/country/community/homeland), wedding (to the black eyed virgin of the paradise), support of one's brethren (e.g., Iraqi brethren), fighting infidels (e.g., Americans), occupation (of) homeland, sacred, etc.

We broadened our search by analyzing several recent tapes featured on the website of the Palestine Media Watch (PMW). The PMW is an organization established in 1996 to gain an understanding of Palestinian society through the monitoring of the Palestinian Arabic language media and schoolbooks. It describes and comments on the Palestinian culture and society from numerous perspectives, including studies carried out on youth summer camps, analyses of poetry, schoolbooks, religious ideology, crossword puzzles etc. In September, 2006 this website featured six farewell tapes of recent suicide terrorists. Of these, five mentioned religion as the reason for their fateful decision, represented in terms such as 'Allah,' 'Qu'ran,' 'Prophet,' 'purify,' 'jihad,' or 'martyrdom'. Four mentioned the rewards for martyrdom related to reaching 'Paradise' and wedding the 'Maidens of Paradise'. Two mentioned nationalism, including language about 'liberating occupied Palestinian land', and one mentioned collectivistic revenge for ills inflicted on the Palestinians by the Israelis.

The PMW website also featured 9 recent interviews with Mothers of successful suicide attackers. All nine mentioned religion, expressed in language about 'Allah', 'Shahada', etc. One mentioned nationalism (fighting for the 'homeland'). Three mentioned 'pride and honor' accorded the terrorists and their families by the community, and three out of the nine mentioned Paradise and its Maidens. Again then, the statements by suicide bombers' and their parents suggest that the motivation underlying their acts was ideologically based.

Oliver & Steinberg in a recent work discuss the video titled "The Giants of Al Qassam Imlaq" and recorded by three Hamas soldiers prior to a planned suicide mission. Ideological statements pervade their statements as well. For instance, the first of the three Giants Mahir Abu Surur stated that the martyr's mission was to "present our spirits and make our blood cheap for the sake of Allah and out of love for this homeland and for the sake of the freedom and honor of this people in order that Palestine remain Islamic, and Hamas remain a torch lighting the road of all the perplexed and all the tormented and the oppressed, and Palestine be liberated".

Authentic or manufactured ideologies? One might wonder whether the farewell videos left by would be suicide terrorists or their parents reflected these individuals' genuine beliefs, or whether their statements were prepackaged, and "put in the speakers' mouths" by the terrorists' organizational launchers. But even if the latter were the case (i.e., if the statements were in fact pre-manufactured) it doesn't mean that the statements' substance wasn't authentically embraced by their deliverers. Three psychological arguments militate against such a conclusion: (1) It is unlikely that one would go so far as to sacrifice one's own life for something one didn't actually believe, (2) the sheer act of making such statements, and rehearsing them may well produce the well known "saying is believing effect" in which the communicator ends up believing a statement he or she was induced to recite, particularly if the communication was addressed to a respected audience, and (3) It is generally conceded that such tapes are typically used as effective recruitment devices; if so, they are likely to be believable to candidates for suicidal missions. Furthermore, their contents, if anything, are likely to be embraced more firmly in temporal nearness to the mission, when social and personal pressures to fully commit to the mission mounted.

To summarize, (1) mortality salience may prompt individuals to strengthen their commitment to collectivistic (cultural) causes embodied in prevalent ideologies, (2) in numerous instances personal losses and traumas (arguably representing real life inductions of "mortality salience") may lead individuals to embrace ideological causes (Spekhard and Akhmedova) and (3) in the preponderance of cases suicide terrorists' stated reasons for their actions were in fact ideological. These data are consistent with the possibility that mortality salience represents a significance loss prompting an attempt at significance restoration via an embarkation on a culturally revered act (self sacrifice for a collective cause) identified as such in a prevalent ideological frame.

It is important to note that reminders of one's own mortality constitute merely one among several cues to insignificance. Other cues to insignificance may stem from one's current life circumstances. Feelings of isolation and disenfranchisement by Muslim youth in European Diasporas (Sageman) could be of this ilk. So could social shame and ostracism to which one might be subjected by failing to live up to the norms of one's society.

For instance, Wafa Idris, the first female suicide terrorist in Palestine, was infertile, and wanted to show the community that she still had her pride (Pedahzur). Shifa Adnan Al-Qudsi a twenty-six-year-old from Tulkarm who was arrested before she was able to complete her suicidal mission suffered a social stigma because of her divorce (Pedahzur, 2004, p. 139). Ayat Al Akhras, was socially shunned because she has been rumored to have had extramarital sex (Pedahzur). A sixteen-year-old boy from Nablus who detonated an explosives belt when approached by Israeli police on 16 June 2002 was said to have been infected with the HIV virus etc.. In all these cases, and many others, a sense of personal loss of significance as a consequence of deviating from normative injunctions of a highly traditional society may well have introduced a strong quest for significance restoration believed to be served by sacrificing oneself for a cause.

Relative Deprivation

Often a perceived loss of significance pertains to a sense

of injustice dealt to a group with which one strongly identifies, hence constituting a principal aspect of one's social identity. Indeed, a major motivational analysis of terrorism and political violence (Gurr,) is based on the concept of relative deprivation. This notion refers to the experience of being denied something to which one feels entitled. Political scientists and sociologists invoked the relative deprivation of a social class or sector as an important underlying factor in social movements that in extreme cases may inspire violence expressed in rioting, terrorism and civil wars (Gurr). According to this view, social movements may arise when people feel deprived of what in their eyes constitutes their 'fair share' (Rose, 1982). From the present perspective, "relative deprivation" need not be real or objective, but rather represent a subjective feeling of injustice and a sense of collective grievance.

The emphasis on the experience of relative deprivation and its pertinence to terrorism casts an important light on the findings that poverty, poor education, or political oppression as defined by some absolute standards may not appear to constitute root causes of terrorism and that well-known perpetrators of suicidal terrorism (e.g., Muhammad Atta and his 9/11 co-conspirators) were neither destitute nor poorly educated. Yet there are good reasons to believe they may have felt that either they themselves or their group had less than they deserved, were denied their national (Pape,) or religious (Hafez, 2007) rights or were discriminated against relative to other denizens of their host countries (Sageman).

The psychological relevance of relative deprivation to the notion of significance loss is straightforward. A disparity between what one has and what one feels entitled to may readily induce a sense of disrespect and disparagement on part of the actor(s) deemed responsible for such derision. Should it be allowed to stand, such a humiliation may betoken an acceptance of one's inferiority and hence a profound sense of significance loss relative to what seemed right and just.

Adoption of Collectivistic Goals

Where individuals perceive their group to confront enemies who deprive it of its entitlements— adoption of collectivistic goals, touted in an accessible ideology, may motivate the support for terrorism. Such goals relate to removal of the apparent discrepancy between the group's current outcomes and what it subjectively deserves. In an electronic survey recently conducted in 12 Arab countries, in Pakistan and Indonesia we found that the endorsement of individualistic objectives such as education, professional success and raising a family was associated with significantly lower support for attacks on Americans (whether military personnel or civilians) than endorsement of transcendental goals such as defending one's nation or one's religion. Adoption of collectivistic goals may reflect the motivation to remove the group's state of relative deprivation and in this sense it may represent a significance quest via militancy and terrorism.

The quest for significance doesn't necessarily require acute reminders of insignificance (mortality salience), or the personal experience of significance loss. The notion of relative deprivation pertains to a subjective experience or a belief that one's group's just deserts have been unfairly denied. It thus defines an opportunity for significance gain, inculcated early in the socialization process, or "bred in the bone". Recently, the Egyptian daily Ruz al Yusuf (of August 18, 2006) has published a report about the Hezbollah Shi'te youth movement "Imam al-Mahdi Scouts." These children range in age from 8-16, number in the tens of thousands, and are indoctrinated with the ideology of radical Iranian Islam. According to Ruz al Yusuf the objective is "to train high caliber Islamic generation of children who would be willing to sacrifice themselves for the sake of Allah (awlad istishhadiyyun). Psychologically then, the adoption of ideological goals can represent a quest for significance gain anchored in a shared reality deliberately engineered by an organization.

It is also of interest to suggest that as individuals' baseline level of felt significance increased a "just noticeable" increment in felt significance (marginal utility) would require a successful attack of a correspondingly higher level of importance. For instance, assuming that Osama bin Laden's baseline level of subjective significance is relatively high, one would expect his selected targets of attacks to be proportionately high in significance as well (as assessed in terms of their symbolic value to the targeted population). In this vein, Sprinzak (2001) discussed the "megalomaniacal hyperterrorists" whose sense of personal grandeur may drive them to undertake particularly spectacular acts of devastation. In his words, "They perceive themselves in historical terms and dream of individually devastating the hated system." For example, in 1995 "Ramzi Yousef ...openly discussed his dream of seeing of the World Trade Center towers fall into the other, causing 250,000 casualties. While hiding in the Philippines.. he planned to destroy 12 U.S. air craft in midair. Yousef also entertained ideas about using chemical weapons on a large scale."

Consistent with these notions are recent data reported by Benmelech and Berreby . These investigators find that in the Palestinian context older and better educated individuals are assigned more important missions (indexed by the size of the population centers attacked and the civilian (vs. military) nature of the targets) than younger and less educated individuals. Specifically, age of the suicide bomber is significantly associated with the attack being carried out in a big city, and education of the suicide bomber is significantly associated with the attack being carried out against a civilian (vs. a military) target.

Whereas Benmelech and Berrebi interpret these findings in terms of a rational choice model whereby organizations assign abler operatives to more important targets it is also plausible that the abler (older, better educated) operatives are more likely to volunteer for missions commensurate with their ability, promising to bestow upon the actors the appropriate degree of felt and reflected significance. Indeed, as Benmelech and Berrebi note "on the supply side terrorism may offer greater benefits for those with more education"

Suicidal Attack as the Prevention of Significance Loss

At times, preventing a significance loss could constitute a powerful motivating force in suicidal terrorism. Relevant here is Ohnuki-Tierney's recent analysis of World War II Japanese Kamikaze pilots' letters and personal diaries. It appears that many of them highly valued life and were reluctant to die, but were actually pressured into "volunteering." Their sense of shame, had they refused the mission, as well as honor and solidarity with fallen comrades made it psychologically unacceptable for them to avoid their tragic assignment.

Hayashi Ichizo, a tokkotai pilot (Kamikaze) who died on his mission on February 22, 1945, wrote in a letter to his mother two days before his final flight "I find it so hard to leave you behind... I want to be held in your arms and sleep. [Yet] All men born in Japan are destined to die fighting for the country. You have done a splendid job raising me to become a honorable man..." (Ohnuki-Tierney)

The notion of significance-quest affords an integration of seemingly disparate motivational contexts of suicidal terrorism involving: personal traumas, ideological reasons, and social pressures. In different ways these may relate to the constant human yearning for significance (Frankl,) arguably born of awareness of our temporality. Personal traumas, and frustrations, represent a significance loss, motivating the quest for significance restoration. Often, however, it is beyond the power of the individual to restore her or his lost sense of personal significance. It is impossible to bring back to life the loved ones lost to enemy violence. Neither is it easy to undo the deeds that brought ostracism from one's community, nor to convince members of an indigenous majority to accept a minority immigrant as equal.

Where the direct restoration of one's lost sense of personal significance seems impossible the individual may seek to do so indirectly through alternative means, including an identification with a collective loss (or one's group's relative deprivation) that affords a clear path to renewed significance via participation in militancy and terrorism. Thus, through a kind of "collectivistic shift" individual powerlessness may be overcome by an empowering collectivistic ideology in which name terrorist acts are carried out.

Commenting on Palestinian suicide bombers, Hafez noted in this vein that "Hamas deliberately framed suicide attacks in terms of a culture of martyrdom that was previously unfamiliar to Palestinian society. [Consequently] Palestinians came to venerate martyrdom because of a 'confluence of perceived threats and a sense of victimization." In more general terms, adoption of ideologically based means (terrorism in this instance) may constitute a substitute vehicle for significance restoration, if individual means for doing so were thwarted. The ideologies elucidate what a significance gain according to one's group, consist of, and afford a way of preventing a significance loss involving adherence to these ideological dictates.

At times of a severe danger to one's group, an ideology may call for the ultimate sacrifice from its members, to be repaid by the group's veneration. Promoting one's sense of significance or preventing its loss thus seems to constitute the common motivational denominator in numerous instances of suicidal terrorism. This analysis is supported by a variety of data referred to earlier including the prevalence of ideological narratives in suicide bombers' farewell video-clips, audio recordings, interviews and other materials (Hafez, 2007), by findings that personal traumas seemed to prompt an embracement of such narratives, and by a psychological analysis and supportive data identifying the quest for personal meaning and significance as a major motivating force in human affairs.

Beyond the "fatal cocktail" model. Our analysis goes beyond what "journalist Barbara Victor called the 'fatal cocktail': religious doctrine that promises eternal life, deprivation that offers no hope, nationalism, and the hardships of living under a military occupation". Though personal hardships, humiliation and hopelessness may well instill a sense of significance loss and prompt the quest for significance restoration, they are neither sufficient nor necessary for motivating suicidal terrorism. Instead, such terrorism may arise from a perceived opportunity for an immense significance gain that offers a rare opportunity for "stardom" to individuals (e.g. Mohammad Atta and the 9/11/01 attackers, or the perpetrators of the 7/7/05 attack on the London transit system were neither particularly hopeless, destitute, or oppressed). Finally, suicidal attacks may arise from the desire to avert a future significance loss, as amply illustrated by the Kamikaze case of World War II.

The mainstay of our conception is the significance bestowing ideology that portrays suicidal terrorism as a way of acquiring immense personal importance. It is embracement of such an ideology, and adoption of the personal goals that it implies (i.e. the commission of a suicidal attacks) that seem crucial in explaining suicidal terrorism. From a psychological perspective, such ideology need not be of any particular kind. It could be religious, ethno-nationalist (as the LTTE case clearly demonstrates), or socialist as long as it portrayed given activities as means to the end of significance.

In turn, the adoption of a terrorism justifying ideology, as the adoption of any belief system may be facilitated either by motivational factors such as (a) dire personal circumstances, (b) great personal ambition (Sprinzak's notion of megalomania), or by cognitive factors comprising (c) compelling arguments by revered "epistemic authorities" (d) community consensus and a shared reality in support of given ends and means (such as suicidal terrorism), or by both. Thus, rather than explaining suicidal terrorism by a "fatal mix" of factors our analysis distinguishes between the crucial motivational nucleus of the phenomenon, the suicide advocating ideology, and motivational and cognitive variables that may drive individuals to subscribe to it, and enact its exhortations.

The Process of Motivational Induction

Though our main concern in this paper is with motivational substance, concerning the kind of goals which may prompt individuals to embark on suicidal terrorism, it may be well to briefly comment on the process whereby such goals are formed in the first place. As already noted, the goal that inspires an act of suicidal (or other types of) terrorism may be part and parcel of an ideological framing that portray it as a worthy objective carrying an aura of immense significance (of martyrdom or heroism). To be adopted by individuals as a basis for self sacrifice such framing needs to be (1) accessible in individuals' environment, (2) persuadable in light of their prior values and assumptions.

The role of exposure to terrorism-justifying ideologies as a contributing factor in terrorism is implied by numerous analyses of terrorists' life-trajectories. For instance, Weinberg & Eubank in commenting on the role of women in Italian terrorist organizations of the 1970s and 1980s point out that 27 percent "of the female terrorists were related by family to other terrorists," and that "the process which brought about ...participation of women was more likely to have been mediated through family ties than through prior experiences in ...political organizations.." Thus, family connections (to siblings, or husbands) and other close relationships (e.g. with boyfriends) may have rendered terrorism justifying ideologies accessible to those individuals.

Sageman's analysis of terrorist networks similarly implies the critical importance of exposure to jihadist ideology through social ties to individuals' who espouse it (referred to as "hubs" of the network). Exposure to terrorism justifying ideologies may take place in radical madrassas and mosques and to be facilitated via messages and blogs on the internet promoting self recruitment into terrorism.

Accessibility of terrorist ideology is a mere necessary condition for serving as a basis for individuals' actions. In addition, the ideological framing that advocates terrorism needs to be credible to the individual. In turn, credibility may depend on the degree to which such framing is consistent with individuals' prior premises and assumptions, on the degree to which it is endorsed by charismatic leaders (like Bin Laden, Al Zawahiri, or Al Zarqawi) and on the degree to which it constitutes part and parcel of the group's shared world view and its lore. In this vein, , Sageman observed that "Cliques... define a certain social reality for the ever more intimate friends"), presumably a shared reality wherein the right goal to adopt is that of launching a terrorist operation.

In summary then, the quest for significance (its restoration, gain, or the prevention of its loss) may lead to terrorism via the adoption of a terrorism touting ideology that identifies the performance of terrorist attacks as a noble goal for the individual to pursue. Adoption, in turn, requires that the ideology be accessible in the individuals' environment and be rendered persuasive through its consistency with the individuals' values and perspectives, its endorsement by credible "epistemic authorities" and charismatic leaders (Kruglanski), and it being widely shared within one's referent community.

Though generally consistent with prior data, the present analysis poses a number of questions for further, more specific, research. Thus, it would seem important to ascertain whether the presently postulated "collectivistic shift" occurs automatically in response to individualistic frustrations, or is particularly likely where one's group membership is made salient. It would also seem of interest to inquire whether the type of group to which one belongs moderates the tendency to shift to collectivistic goals in response to one's sense of significance loss. For instance, it might be the case that groups characterized by considerable cohesion, and hence considerable potential for collective action might be more likely to prompt a collectivistic shift than groups characterized by a heterogeneity of opinions and torn by internal strife. One could inquire whether the "collectivistic shift" may be more likely for individuals under a heightened need for cognitive closure known for their proclivity for group centrism. It would also seem of interest to investigate whether the propensity for a "collectivistic shift" is particularly likely where the group's degree of perceived relative deprivation is particularly striking or where the actions geared toward deprivation removal (e.g. militancy, terrorism) are particularly clear cut and well defined. The evolutionary versus acquired nature of the "collectivistic shift" could be also profitably explored in further psychological research.

A different direction of research could address the kind of circumstances that induce a sense of significance loss and how these vary across different dimensions. For instance, individuals whose social reality represents a "culture of honor" might experience a greater degree of significance loss upon a humiliating experience than ones who have been socialized in a different culture. In this connection, research by Cohen, Nisbett, Bowdle and Schwarz showed that southern White males (vs. their Northern counterparts) exhibited significantly stronger reactions to an insult by a confederate. They were more likely to think that their masculine reputation was challenged, they showed a greater rise in cortisol levels attesting to stress, and they were more primed for aggression on physiological, cognitive, and behavioural levels.

More generally speaking, cultures differ in the importance they assign to honor. So called shame cultures (e.g., the Arab, or the Japanese cultures) assign to it considerably greater importance than do so called guilt cultures (the Jewish or the Protestant cultures) hence it seems plausible that members of the former cultures would experience a more profound significance loss upon humiliation than members of the latter cultures. Differences in the value assigned to honor are likely to obtain for individuals within cultures as well. In this vein, Fischer, Rodriguez, van Vlanen, & Manstead find gender differences within cultures, the men being more likely to subscribe to a "culture of honor" than the women. More generally, it seems plausible that the experience of significance loss will be partially determined by individuals' hierarchy of values and the degree to which a given occurrence threatened a value at placed high in that hierarchy.

For instance, cultures or individuals for whom human life represents a supreme value, might experience a more profound sense of significance loss upon an encounter with death, than cultures or individuals for whom human life represents less of a moral concern, or for whom death is less negatively valenced. These possibilities could be profitably probed in further research. As implied above, we regard suicidal terrorism as merely one (albeit an extreme) form of terrorist-violence employed in the service of an ideological cause. In this sense, implications of our motivational analysis for counterterrorism are meant to apply broadly to both suicidal and non suicidal terrorist tactics. But what might such implications consist of? First off, dealing with terrorists' motivation appears of key importance.

Without undermining motivation, reducing terrorist's ability to launch a given terrorist tactic may often have a temporary effect, lasting until the terrorists discovered a way to restore their constrained ability, or found a new terrorist tactic free from prior limitations. For instance, building a fence to prevent infiltrations of a territory by terrorist operatives may prompt them to opt for the use of rockets circumventing that particular obstacle (as in the example of Hezbollah, and Hamas recent missile attacks on Israeli targets). In empirical work relevant to these notions Brophy-Baermann & Conybeare used quarterly data on terrorist attacks on Israel during the period January 1968 to December 1989 (selected from the data bases ITERATE 2 and ITERATE 3) to look at the effects of Israeli retaliations policy on the incidence of subsequent terrorist attacks. Based on a time-series intervention model, the authors concluded that a retaliation of an unexpectedly large magnitude, disrupting and hence reducing the terrorists' ability to operate, may cause a temporary dip in terrorist activity. Yet, the terrorists' may adjust their expectations and prepare for the retaliatory actions, so if the terrorists' motivation for attacks persists, "Retaliation has no long term deterrent effect".

Granting its pivotal importance, how may the terrorists' motivation is addressed in counterterrorism campaigns? The centrality of ideological warrants for suicidal terrorism, suggest the possibility of undermining them through credible communication efforts. As Post put it in reference to Islamist terrorism "This will require active leadership by moderate Muslim clerics and...political leaders countering the extremists in their midst." Recently, Rohan Gunaratna has launched just such an effort aimed at members of the Jamaah Islamiyah and the Moro Islamic Liberation Front detained in Singapore prisons. So did the Saudi Interior Ministry in the past two years. The Saudi effort has included two large-scale projects, one involving an outreach to Saudi security prisoners (carried out by a team of Muslim clerics and jurists [ulama and fuqaha] as well as psychiatrists and psychologists,5 the second involving an online dialogue with extremists, supported by the Saudi Ministry of Religious Endowments and Islamic Affairs. 6 This effort too relied on assistance from psychological and sociological experts. Though the success of the Saudi, and other similar efforts needs careful evaluation, they represent a potentially important first step in an attempt to counter the extremist ideology through the use of "epistemic authorities" credible to the relevant audiences.

But communicative attempts may fall on deaf ears if not accompanied by a reduction in potential recruits' readiness to buy into terrorism-justifying ideologies. This may require an alleviation of significance loss prompting circumstances that instill the motivation to accept suicide (and other) missions as means to desirable ends. Some such circumstances may be highly idiosyncratic and personal (e.g. infractions by an individual with respect to norms of her or his community). Yet other circumstances may be widespread and amenable to general policy initiatives. On the military level, this may mean the minimization of violent responses to terrorist attacks, especially as regards the use of excessive (disproportionate) force likely to cause massive "collateral" damage, likely to and push over the brink those who may have suffered or witnessed the consequences of such violence. In a recent monograph on lessons of the Israel-Hezbollah war Anthony Cordesman stated that the "US needs to give avoiding unnecessary civilian casualties and collateral damage the same priority as directly destroying the enemy."

On the political level, it may require foreign policy undertakings, immigration programs, and educational campaigns aimed to reduce the alienation and embitterment of Diaspora youths and enhance their sense of acceptance by their host societies. Creation of positive intergroup contact (e.g. in the European Diasporas) (Victoroff,) effective anti-discrimination policies (arguably including affirmative action programs), and strong anti-discrimination norms may reduce intergroup tensions and the readiness of disaffected youth to regain their lost sense of significance by making the leap to terrorism. As Kepel recently remarked "The most important battle in the war for Muslim minds during the next decade will be fought not in Palestine or Iraq but in these communities on the outskirts of London, Paris, and other European cities, where Islam is already a growing part of the West."

Tradeoffs and Paradoxes

The present analysis highlights the considerable complexities that coherent counterterrorism policies must confront. Many counterterrorist moves are of a "double edged" variety involving trade offs that need to be carefully considered in reference to a specific set of circumstances. Take the notion that a terrorism-justifying ideology portrays terrorism as an effective tool advancing the perpetrators' group to the ideal state that constitutes its goal. A seemingly straightforward counter move designed to disabuse the group members of these beliefs is a resolute military campaign targeting the terrorists and their leaders. Yet such campaign is also risking humiliating the terrorists and their sympathizers, and inflicting "collateral damage" claiming the lives of uninvolved bystanders. These may inflame the anger of terrorist supporters and potentially boost recruitment to the terrorist stock.

A recent empirical analysis suggests that 'targeted hits' by the Israeli forces actually did just that, presumably due to the Palestinians' motivation to revenge the fallen comrades. Whereas 'targeted hits' do hurt (a repeated demand by Palestinian negotiators was that the Israelis desist from employing this tactic) and may arguably undermine the belief that terrorism is effective (due to the organizational disruptions that the elimination of leaders may create), they concomitantly increase the appeal of terrorism by inflating the intensity of the emotional goal it may serve.

Tough counterterrorism policies including a capital punishment for terrorist activities may on the one hand deter some individuals, yet also create the conditions for martyrdom representing a particularly auspicious opportunity for significance gain. One of the leaders of the Narodnaya Volya, a 19th century terrorist organization in Tsarist Russia actually implied as much in stating "...For me that contrast between a radiant future for the people and our own sad fate was extremely influential… If not for the persecution, I'm not at all certain that I would have become a socialist at that time".

For another example, consider the question whether state actors should be negotiating with terrorists. Though it is generally conceded that negotiating with terrorists may have the ill effect of reinforcing terrorism, it may have other consequences as well that are important to consider, and that may compensate in part for negotiations' deleterious effects. Thus, by negotiating with terrorists one may be able to offer alternative means to their stated goals, potentially more effective and less costly to the perpetrators than terrorism. Furthermore, paradoxically, negotiating with terrorists may restore their sense of significance and assuage their feelings of humiliation, hence reducing the psychological force behind the adoption of a terrorism justifying ideology.

A final paradox has to do with the broad base of community support that terrorist activity typically requires. A strong base in community support defines a shared reality wherein the terrorism justifying ideology is embedded. The broader the support base, the more coherent the social contract endorsing a given strategy of action such as terrorism, hence the more powerful the injunction to pursue that strategy. But a broad consensus might be difficult to sustain for an extreme activity that requires the sacrifice of other objectives (of economic, political and social nature) likely to exist in any large community. Again then, effective counterterrorism policies may need to consider the broader context and steer a careful course wherein the "stick" administered to the terrorists is appropriately balanced by a "carrot" offered the larger community in form of supporting their alternative strivings with which terrorism may be incompatible.

Recent analyses of the motivations for suicidal terrorism have identified a broad variety of motives having to do with potential perpetrators' (1) personal traumas and frustrations, (2) ideological reasons, and (3) social pressures to which they may be subjected. In the present paper we introduced the notion of significance-quest as an integrative concept tying these motivational categories together: Personal traumas and frustrations could encourage a "collectivistic switch" to a terrorism justifying ideologies because the latter may afford a means for restoring the lost significance occasioned by various unsettling events. Besides, terrorism justifying ideologies may afford a relatively simple means of substantial significance gain, and attainment of a hero or a martyr status in the eyes of one's community. Thus, whereas prior authors juxtaposed personal traumas and frustrations to ideological motivations, and/or viewed suicidal violence due to social pressures (e.g. as in the Kamikaze case) as distinct from both, we offer a general model grounded in the psychology of human needs that views all three motivational categories as functionally fitting within an overarching framework of human quest for personal significance. Our analysis is consistent with prior data and it offers implications for discouraging terrorism via communication initiatives designed to undermine its significance-lending warrants, as well as via policies designed to reduce potential recruits' sense of significance-loss, affecting their readiness to embrace such warrants.

The Motivations and Methods of the Terrorist

The underlying causes and motivations of terrorism can be studied at three levels: individual, national or group and international.

- **Individual**

At the individual level, human traits and certain psychological drives may motivate people to resort to terrorism. Some simply see madness as the cause for recourse to terrorism. Others developed the theory of frustration-aggression. The discrepancy between demand and fulfillment drives the individual to aggression, which may be expressed in physical violence to the extreme of terrorism. Some terrorists are just criminals. One of the theories put forward by psychiatrists and criminologists to explain why so many German women were involved in urban guerrilla activities is that it provides them with a form of liberation. Because they are from good homes and are well educated, they consider themselves superior to men and want to display that superiority in action.

There are those who join to find their identities by becoming part of the group. They commit acts to feel accepted. Because of the need to belong to the group, they seldom resign or compromise their involvement. Some joined for money, some for therapy, and some for excitement. Others were attracted by the combination of excitement and the possibility of drugs and sexual indulgence. Culturally motivated terrorists are willing to do anything to defend their language, religion, group membership or native homeland especially if the rewards are high in this world or the next. Sometimes, the families of these terrorists are held hostages to ensure their commitment to the cause.

Rev Michael Bray defended the need to kill and if necessary to die over the issue of abortion. According to him, there has been a great cosmic war going on - the confrontation between the good and evil - one that goes unseen largely because the enemy has imposed its control. His view is that Americans have a disregard for human life and a penchant to kill. These religious struggles can be perceived as a defence of basic identity and dignity and losing the struggle would be unthinkable. When the struggle cannot be won in real time or in real terms, it is elevated to the cosmic plane through terrorism, where it will be in "God's hands". In spiritualizing violence, religion has given terrorism power. Suicide bombers see themselves as religious sacrifices and hope to be richly rewarded in heaven.

Leaders of terrorist groups are usually politically minded. Some leaders have even made the successful transition from terrorism to political leadership while keeping their terrorist organizations intact, for example, Yasser Arafat. These leaders usually received better than average educations and often come from prosperous families. They have the conviction that they can impose their beliefs on others. They use the philosophers to provide them with a persuasive rationalization for their actions. Some come under the influence of political thinkers who preach that violence is essential to make the world a better place for the masses. Eakman characterized Osama Bin Laden's relationship with his chief mentor, former psychiatrist Ayman al Zawahiri as: "It would not be the first time psychiatrists had served as manipulators, systematically feeding their hatreds, stroking their egos, and stripping their consciences, until eventually even the most barbaric act may appear plausible and rational in the name of some twisted cause."

It takes a community of support and in many cases, a large organizational network for an act of terrorism to succeed. It also requires an enormous amount of moral presumption for the perpetrators of these acts to justify the brutal attack on another life, especially the life of someone

one scarcely knows and against whom one bears no personal enmity. It requires social acknowledgement, and the stamp of approval from a legitimising ideology or authority one respects. Because of the moral, ideological and organisational support necessary for such acts, most of them come as collective decisions.

- **National or Group Level**

At the national or group level, specific conditions of the state and of the social system may provoke people to terrorism. Relative deprivation of basic needs that occurs on the individual level can be a factor in uniting a group of people. Hardship may be a cause of terrorism, along with urban growth, and "moral explosion". The existence of a tradition of violence (as in Latin America) is usually conceived as a catalysing factor of terrorism as well as a reaction to it. Huntington postulated that young males are the perpetrators of violence in all societies; their overabundance in Muslim societies is one of the causes for the rise in the number of Islamic terrorists.

Terrorism often becomes a useful tool in the tolerant liberal states, which are vulnerable to it. Severe repression, or under-reaction, implying incompetence on behalf of the reacting government may both attract and encourage further terrorism. The evolution of the modern political terrorism is historically parallel to the development of the liberal state. Terrorism evolved at the same rate as liberal ideas were expanding. First there is anarchist terrorism that is associated with the concept of the "propaganda of the deed". This advocates the propagation of the anarchist message among the masses by terrifying governments and people, so as to bring about a revolutionary atmosphere of socio-political insecurity. Among the ideologies of revolution, Maoism provides a basis for a great deal of justification for terrorism. Maoism has had a great influence on Western New-Leftists as well as modern anarchist terrorism and, especially, on terrorists of the Third World.

Trotsky once said: "Terror can be very efficient against a reactionary class which does not want to leave the scene of operations."

Nationalist, ethnical-separatist aspirations and revolutionary movements compose the next category. Of these organizations, the Irish Republican Army (IRA), the Euzkadi Ta Askatasuna (ETA, Spain), etc, all make use of the terrorist method. The Israelis succeeded in setting up their own state through the use of the terror weapon. Indeed the Israeli Prime Minister, Menachem Begin, was once leader of Irgun Zvi Leumi who blew up King David Hotel in Jerusalem, killing 89 military and civilian personnel. The Palestinians can also be considered as "territorial terrorists". To them, Palestine means the whole of Palestine, and they want to recover that land from Israeli possession and to control it themselves. There is also the revolutionary terrorist seeking to change the socio-political scene (Japanese Red Army, Red Brigades, fascist movements in Italy, Turkey, etc).

Rarely if ever is religion the major cause of war, but it is often a critical factor. Faith serves to legitimate, motivate and increase intensities, whether promoting or protesting war. Religions routinely legitimize violence and contribute to it through their theologies, rituals and organizations. From earliest wars of conquest to colonial wars and contemporary ethnic conflicts, religion is at the core of war making. Many religious terrorist groups are labeled as fundamentalists. However, not everyone who takes his religion seriously is a fundamentalist. These fundamentalists or "religious warriors" are not motivated by religious sensibilities; rather, they exploit religious fervor for their own irreligious ends. A fundamentalist believes that circumstances require him to act politically and probably violently to fulfill his religious obligations. Many fundamentalists are often well-educated people. Yet they feel strongly that Western society erred grievously when they replaced God, religion and divine law with human reason and secular political principles as the basis for the legal and social order.

Jewish, Christian or Muslim fundamentalists are selective in choosing certain scriptures or theological teachings from the past and insisting that true believers "fight to the death" (literally and figuratively) to protect these "fundamentals". Their pattern of thought is absolutist (the truth we proclaim is perfect, complete and irreformable); inerrantist (free from any kind of error); and dualist (we are children of light while others are children of darkness). Fundamentalists also believe that they are living in a special time in history, perhaps in the last days. In the final days, when these believers find themselves in direct combat with the enemy, they retrieve teachings that justify violent action in defence of the faith.

The initial motivations for groups to resort to terrorism may be simple. However, later rationalisation may blur their motives. Some Palestinian groups, for example, have developed a commitment to world revolution almost as total as their devotion to the recovery of their homeland. The past support of the Soviet Union for almost any group that could embarrass the West, whatever that group's political alignment, blurred the picture even more. Nowhere could there be more confusion than in the welter of reasons the Provisional IRA gives for its campaign of terror: national, political, social and religious causes mixed together provide them with their rationalisation.

- **International Level**

At the international level, confusion within the global system facilitates the development of terrorism. As a cheaper type of warfare involving few clearly definable risks or international responsibility, it has become more convenient for states to have recourse to the services of individual terrorists, supported by various groups and conversely, for groups to resort to terrorism as a result of the support they receive. These transnational terrorist groups do not act on behalf of any particular state; membership and resources are drawn from supporters in more than one state; and the area of operations, including targeting, transcends state borders. Examples of such groups are those that provide fighters for religiously motivated wars around the world (such as the Balkans and Chechnya) and those targeting certain countries (such as US and Israel).

According to the *RAND Chronicle of International Terrorism*, the US headed the list of countries whose citizens and property were most frequently attacked since 1968. There are many reasons for this. In its role as trading partner and political ally, the US has a vested interest in shoring up stability of regimes around the world. It is a common refrain among America's critics in the Middle East that the US props up objectionable local leaders out of selfish interests. For example, to protect its access to oil the US supports repressive princes in the Persian Gulf states. This also puts her as a defender and promoter of secular governments, raising strong objections by religious opponents. Others viewed the US as meddling in their domestic affairs according to her own interests. Carlos Marighella wrote in his handbook of guerrilla warfare: "Kidnapping American personalities who live in Brazil, or who have come to visit here, is a most powerful form of protest against the penetration of US imperialism into our country."

America is so comfortable with its own brand of capitalism and consumer culture that it cannot fathom just how revolutionary these forces can be.[33] Americans tend to believe that their institutions and values democracy, individual rights, the rule of law and prosperity based on economic freedom appeal to all cultures. Furthermore, the US's success as the sole global superpower may encourage animosity and resentment more than admiration, including contempt for US culture as a threatening export especially in the form of alcohol and sexy movies. For example, the commercial success of Hollywood films is often judged as a political or cultural threat, from Paris to Kabul.

Unfortunately the US also fails to realize that its culture of individualism clashes with some of the collective customs of these countries.

The impact of globalisation (of which the US is the leader) is perceived by some states as cultural encirclement, or a new form of dependency and colonialism. Fundamentalist movements of a religious, ethnic, or communal nature strive on these feelings. According to Osama bin Laden, there is a holy war between Islam and America. His hatred stemmed from American foreign policy in the Middle East. He believes that the US military presence in Saudi Arabia defiles Muslim holy land. He is offended by continued sanctions against Iraq, Syria, Sudan, Libya and Iran. He also objects to America's substantial support of Israel. He blames the US for the killing of Bosnian Muslims by Christian Serbs because of a UN arms embargo against Bosnia until 1994. The symbolic attacks on the World Trade Centre (economic), Pentagon (military) and the failed attempt on the White House (political) can be seen as a defiant act by the terrorists to tell the world what the US has been doing to them. Although Osama's motivations may appear to be religiously motivated, other factors such as political (e.g. US foreign policy and repressive governments in the Middle East), cultural (e.g. individualism and American values), and economic (e.g. globalisation) play important roles.

Strategy, Tactics and Weapons

The strategy for terrorists encompasses the following: First, the act must be horrifying, striking at innocent lives that have nothing to do with the cause the terrorists are espousing; second, it provokes uncertainty and is directed against the society as a whole and does not distinguish civilians and military targets; third, it depends and uses the mass media to communicate and publicise its acts and motives. The use of violence is obligatory in order to induce fear and chaos and it is aimed at the people and the institutions of the established order. Violence provides the glue that binds terrorists together into a unity of purpose even for those who are violently opposed to one another. They also aim to make themselves into heroes and so persuade opponents and neutrals that the terrorists' cause is righteous and their actions are justified. Their strategy is to make the other party appear in the wrong or be guilty of brutality. In religiously motivated terrorism, "Satanization" has been used to de-legitimise an opponent.

Terrorists today are better organized, more professional and better equipped. They are prepared to take greater operational risks, including death. Their delivery methods include suitcases, commercial vehicles or couriers, public transportation systems, private vehicles in land, sea and air. The most devastating asymmetric attacks on civilians in North America, Europe and Japan to date have not relied on military platforms for delivery. They make use of complex terrain, novel tactics and technology (hit and run tactics, fighting in large urban areas where the identification of attacks is hindered by large numbers of civilian bystanders and where counter attacks carry the risk of further civilian casualties). While the US is talking on the synergistic nature of remote fires, precision engagement, battlefield awareness and information dominance, the asymmetric actor will see the synergistic nature of terror, deceit, brutality and unpredictability. The terrorists have the following weapons at their disposal: the mass media, technology, psychology and drugs, and sabotage.

- **The Mass Media**

An important variable in determining the scope of success of a terrorist assault is the mass media. Since terrorism is a violent method aimed at the psychological effect of the deed, the mass media, which occupies a determinant position in the formation of public opinion, becomes a useful tool for any terrorist act. Terrorism enjoys high ratings among the world's TV viewers and terrorists revel in massive exposure. One of the best examples of the use of publicity by urban guerrillas was the Olympic Games massacre at Munich in 1972; they had made the rest of the world aware of the Palestinian cause. Although not a direct cause of terrorism, the media, nonetheless, serve as an accelerator for the spread of the phenomenon and as a factor in the choice of tactics. Without the assistance of the modern mass media, terrorism would probably be significantly reduced. The effect of the mass media on terrorism depends very much on the tone of the media discouraging or encouraging it.

The mass media is a perfect tool for terrorists, providing their services free of charge. It sometimes assists the terrorist's long-term objectives by supporting terrorism, specific terrorist causes and acts, and by opposing government, police or the judiciary. Often the media tends to focus on the background of poor oppressed groups, defining their recourse to terrorism as "freedom fighting" or "guerrilla warfare." This provides an important service in building up the terrorist image and legitimising the terrorist's method. Moreover, there is wide media coverage of detained or freed hostages testifying to the human treatment received from the terrorists. This too, is a precious and conscious component of terrorist strategy. Some careless media may divulge plans of suppression that the terrorists can use to their advantage.

The contribution of the mass media to the production of violence is a well-known theme of sociological and psychological research. It also encourages the rapid appearance of numerous terrorist groups. Irresponsible media coverage may encourage the adoption of terrorist tactics by common criminals. Exaggerated and widespread mass media coverage of terrorism has destructive effects on the social order i.e., the sensitivity of the moral judgement of the terrorist act is blunted and may prompt the terrorist to resort to even more spectacular acts to re-stimulate the public demand for expanded media coverage. Moreover, repeated false information may transform into "subjective truth".

- **Technology**

The developments in technology enable a single terrorist to be extremely destructive. For example, the advent of the jumbo jet has provided the terrorist with the ideal target. Once terrorists are able to threaten the flight crew, they have virtually achieved victory. Not only can the terrorists blow everybody in the aircraft to pieces, they may use the jet as a weapon to target densely populated areas. Weapons of mass destruction (WMD) such as biological, chemical and radiological agents make the killing of thousands of people relatively easy and are thus considered by many to be the most serious terrorism threat. They inflict mass casualties, cause terror and degrade morale. It is also possible for some of these weapons to be produced by individuals, a factor which increases the scope of the potential threat.

- **Psychology and Drugs**

Terrorists also use psychological warfare to support the achievement of objectives. They create fear, flood the market with an addictive or lethal drug, or create chaos through organized crimes that would weaken the country. They could also focus their attacks on politically influential sectors of the populace such as high-level officials, parents (by attacking children) and entertainment elite and celebrities.

Psychiatry or psychiatric treatments have also been employed to facilitate the execution of totalitarian and terrorist objectives. The Japanese *kamikaze* pilots in World War II used psychiatric drugs called amphetamines to get charged up. In the 1980s, such pills were provided for suicide bombers in the Middle East and they underwent "psychological indoctrination" intended to motivate them to move past the "point of no return". Around the world, some 250,000 children, some as young as seven, have been used for armed combat. The Human Rights Watch reported in 1999 "child combatants armed with pistols, rifles and machetes actively participated in killings and massacres, [and] severed the arms of other children. Often under the influence of drugs, they were known and feared for their impetuosity, lack of control and brutality."

- **Sabotage**

These attacks include destroying railroad stations, airports, loading areas, destroying high-value aircraft with short-range standoff weapons and damaging communications or intelligence facilities. Incendiary devices may also be used. Economic disruption is another tactic including attacks on means of production, the produce itself and on commercial infrastructure. Other forms of attack focused on the environment include attacks on chemical plants, power stations and waste-disposal sites in order to cause massive and dangerous pollution; destroying oil pipelines; poisoning water supplies; sinking oil tankers off the coasts; or spreading highly contagious diseases to crops or livestock as an adjunct to biological warfare. Food agents such as salmonella, foot-and-mouth disease and mad-cow disease can set off waves of poisonings.

Terrorism will continue to flourish. As long as extremists believe that violence is the only way to achieve their political aims, terrorism will continue on a greater or lesser level depending on passion engendered by their causes and the success of counter-terrorist forces. The Taliban regime in Afghanistan may be destroyed, but there will be more Talibans and new Osamas.

The "an eye for an eye" approach to terrorism usually fails especially if governments themselves resort to terrorist tactics. Any response to the perpetration of violent acts in the form of retaliation will enhance the credibility of the terrorists within their own community. The terrorism war can only be won by winning hearts and minds as well. This can only be achieved by correcting the historical mistakes made by those who unwittingly promote terrorism (repressive governments and international politicians), by being more sensitive to different cultures and religions and by ensuring future foreign policies of the major players in global politics will not create more terrorism. The recent US withdrawal from the 1972 Anti-Ballistic Missile (ABM) Treaty could unleash a new nuclear weapons build up, perhaps making it easier for terrorists to obtain radiological materials. Secularism, democracy, and modernization take time to develop, especially when seen in the context of individualism, possible moral degeneration and religious corruption.

It is the author's sincere hope that through understanding the mind of the terrorist, responses to terrorism will not produce more terror and anti-terrorism and counter-terrorism measures can be more effective.

Bibliography

Acquaviva, Mike. *Terrorism: Special Studies*. Bethesda, MD: University Publications of America, 1989.

Addicott, Jeffrey F. *Winning the War on Terror: Legal and Policy Lessons From the Past*. Tucson, AZ: Lawyers & Judges Publishing Company, 2003.

Ahmad, Eqbal. *Terrorism: Theirs and Ours*. Open Media Pamphlet Series. New York: Seven Stories Press, 2001.

Alexander, Dean C. *Business Confronts Terrorism: Risks and Responses*. Madison, WI: University of Wisconsin Press, 2004.

Alexander, John B. *Winning the War: Advanced Weapons, Strategies and Concepts for the Post-9/11 World*. New York: St. Martin's Press, 2003.

Alexander, Yonah. *Abu Nidal: The Splinter Festers*. Washington, DC: New World Communication, 1986.

Alexander, Yonah. *Combating Terrorism: Strategies of Ten Countries*. Ann Arbor, MI: University of Michigan Press, 2002.

Alexander, Yonah. *Control of Terrorism: International Documents*. New York: Crane Russak, 1979.

Alexander, Yonah. *Governmental Responses to Terrorism*. Hero Terrorism Series. Fairfax, VA: Hero Books, 1987.

Alexander, Yonah. *International Terrorism: National, Regional and Global Perspectives*. New York: AMS Press, 1976.

Alexander, Yonah. *Legislative Responses to Terrorism*. International Studies on Terrorism; Boston, MA: M. Nijhoff, 1986.

Alexander, Yonah. *Political Terrorism and Business: The Threat and Response*. New York: Praeger, 1979.

Alexander, Yonah. *Political Terrorism and Energy: The Threat and Response*. New York: Praeger, 1982.

Alexander, Yonah. *State Sponsored Terrorism*. Washington, DC: Center for Contemporary Studies, 1986.

Alexander, Yonah. *Terrorism and the Law*. Ardsley, NY: Transnational Publishers, 2001.

Alexander, Yonah. *Terrorism: Theory and Practice*. Boulder, CO: Westview Press, 1979.

Alterman, Jon B. *How Terrorism Ends*. Washington, DC: United States Institute of Peace, 1999.

American Foreign Policy Council, *Confronting Terrorism Financing*. Lanham, MD: University Press of America, 2005.

Anderson, Mark. *Campaign Against Terror*. Videocassette (VHS). Frontline. Alexandria, VA: PBS Video, 2004.

Anderson, Sean. *Historical Dictionary of Terrorism*. 2nd ed., Historical Dictionaries of Religions, Philosophies, and Movements, No. 4. Lanham, MD: Scarecrow Press, 2002.

Ansari, Masud. *International Terrorism: Its Causes and How to Control It*. Washington, DC: Mas-Press, 1988.

Anti-Defamation League, *ADL Paramilitary Training Statute: A Response to Extremism*. ADL Law Report. New York: ADL, 1986.

Anti-Defamation League, *ADL Paramilitary Training Statute: Implementation*. ADL Law Report, Fall 1983, Vol. 8, no. 2. New York: ADL, 1983.

Anti-Defamation League, *Extremism on the Right: A Handbook*. New York: Anti-Defamation League, 1988.

Anti-Defamation League, *Terrorism: Domestic and International Challenges*. New York: ADL, 1994.

Apikyan, Samuel. *Countering Nuclear and Radiological Terrorism*. Brussels, Belgium: Springer, 2006.

Ascher, Michael S. *Countering Agricultural Bioterrorism*. "Committee on Biological Threats to Agricultural Plants and Animals". Washington, DC: National Academies Press, 2003.

Asthana, N. C. *Terrorism, Insurgencies, and Counterinsurgency Operations*. Jaipur, India: Pointer Publishers, 2001.

Barnhart, Stephen R. *International Terrorism and Political Violence*. Victoria, B.C., Canada: Trafford, 2002.

Bassiouni, M. Cherif, ed. *International Terrorism and Political Crimes: Proceedings of the Third Conference on Terrorism and Political Crimes*. Springfield, IL: C.C. Thomas, 1974.

Das, Dilip. *Meeting the Challenges of Global Terrorism: Prevention, Control, and Recovery*. Lanham, MD: Rowman & Littlefield, 2003.

Davies, Barry. *Terrorism: Inside a World Phenomenon*. London: Virgin Books, 2003.

Dewar, Michael. *Weapons and Equipment of Counter-Terrorism*. 2nd ed. New York: Sterling, 1995.

Dobson, Christopher. *Terrorists: Their Weapons, Leaders and Tactics*. Rev. ed. New York: Facts on File, 1982.

Dobson, Christopher. *War Without End: the Terrorists, an Intelligence Dossier*. London: Harrap, 1986.

Elagab, Omer Yousif. *International Law Documents Relating to Terrorism*. London: Cavendish Press, 1995.

Evans, Alona. *Legal Aspects of International Terrorism*. Washington, DC: Lexington Books, 1978.

Gearty, Conner. *Terrorism*. London: Phoenix, 1997.

Ghosh, Tushar K. *Science and Technology of Terrorism and Counterterrorism*. New York: Dekker, 2002.

Han, Henry H., editor. *Terrorism & Political Violence: Limits & Possibilities of Legal Control*. Terrorism (Oceana Publications, inc.) ; 2nd series. New York: Oceana, 1993.

Howard, Russell D. *Defeating Terrorism: Shaping the New Security Environment*. Guilford, CT: McGraw-Hill, 2004.

Howard, Russell D. *Terrorism and Counterterrorism: Understanding the New Security Environment, Readings & Interpretations*. Guilford, CT: McGraw-Hill, 2002.

Howitt, Arnold. *Countering Terrorism: Dimensions of Preparedness*. Cambridge, MA: MIT Press, 2003.

Lutz, James M. *Global Terrorism*. New York: Routledge, 2004.

MacDonald, Donald. *Parliaments Against Terrorism*. Ottawa, Canada: Library of Parliament, 1986.

Mockaitis, Thomas R. *Grand Strategy in the War Against Terrorism*. Portland, OR: Frank Cass, 2003.

Moghaddam, Fathali. *Understanding Terrorism: Psychosocial Roots, Consequences, and Interventions*. Washington, DC: American Psychological Association, 2003.

Norton, Augustus R. *Understanding the Nuclear Terrorism Problem*. Gaithersburg, MD: International Association of Chiefs of Police, 1979.

O'Day, Alan. *Weapons of Mass Destruction and Terrorism*. The international library of essays in terrorism. Burlington, VT: Ashgate, 2005.

Ontiveros, Suzanne. *Global Terrorism: A Historical Bibliography*. Santa Barbara, CA: ABC-CLIO, 1986.

Onwudiwe, Ihekwoaba D. *Globalization of Terrorism*. Burlington, VT: Ashgate, 2001.

Poland, James M. *Understanding Terrorism: Groups, Strategies, and Responses*. Second Edition. Upper Saddle River, NJ: Pearson, 2004.

Schmid, Alex P. and Jongman, Albert J. *Political*

Terrorism: A New Guide to Actors, Authors, Concepts, Data Bases, Theories, & Literature. New Brunswick, NJ: Transaction, 2005.

Steven, Graeme C. S. and Gunaratna, Rohan. *Counter-terrorism: A Reference Handbook*. Santa Barbara, CA: ABC-CLIO, 2004.

Stewart, Gail B. *Terrorists and Terrorists Groups*. Lucent Terrorism Library. Farmington Hills, MI: Thomson Learning, 2002.

Tamara, Thompson. *Emergency Response*. San Diego, CA: Lucent, 2004. Juvenile Audience.

Tan, Andrew T.H. *Politics of Terrorism: A Survey*. London: Routledge, 2006.

Thackrah, John Richard. *Encyclopedia of Terrorism and Political Violence*. New York: Routledge & Kegan Paul, 1987.

Unger, Rhoda Kesler. *Terrorism and Its Consequences*. Malden, MA: Blackwell, 2002.

Vas, E. A. *Terrorism and Insurgency: The Challenge of Modernization*. Dehra Dun: Natraj Publishers, 1984.

Wardlaw, Grant. *Political Terrorism: Theory, Tactics and Counter-Measures*. Rev. and Extended ed. Cambridge, MA: Cambridge University Press, 1989.

Watson, Francis. *Political Terrorism: The Threat and the Response*. Washington, DC: R.B. Luce Co., 1976.

Wilcox, David. *Domestic Preparedness and the WMD Paradigm*. Washington, DC: U.S. Army Command, 1998.

Wilkinson, Paul. *British Perspectives on Terrorism*. London: George Allen & Unwin, 1981.

Wilkinson, Paul. *Contemporary Research on Terrorism*. Aberdeen: Aberdeen University Press, 1987.

Young, Mitch. *The War on Terrorism*. Turning Points in World History. San Diego, CA: Greenhaven Press, 2003.

Zartman, I. William, Editor. *Negotiating With Terrorists*. Leiden, The Netherlands: Nijhoff, 2005.

Zimmerman, Ekkart. *Political Violence, Crises and Revolutions: Theories and Research*. Cambridge, MA: G.K. Hall, 1983.

Zimmermann, Doron. *The Transformation of Terrorism: The 'New Terrorism', Impact Scalability and the Dynamic of Reciprocal Threat Perception*. Zurich: ETH, 2003.

Zinn, Howard. *Terrorism and War*. New York: Seven Stories Press, 2002.

Zimmerman, Ekkart. *Political Violence, Crises and Revolutions: Theories and Research*. Cambridge, MA: G.K. Hall, 1983.

Index